Successful
BUSINESS INTELLIGENCE
Secrets to Making BI a Killer App

Cindi Howson

New York   Chicago   San Francisco   Lisbon
London   Madrid   Mexico City   Milan   New Delhi
San Juan   Seoul   Singapore   Sydney   Toronto

The McGraw·Hill Companies

Library of Congress Cataloging-in-Publication Data

Howson, Cindi.
  Successful business intelligence : secrets to making BI a killer app /
Cindi Howson.
      p. cm.
  Includes bibliographical references and index.
  ISBN-13: 978-0-07-149851-7 (alk. paper)
  ISBN-10: 0-07-149851-6 (alk. paper)
  1. Business intelligence. 2. Business intelligence—Data processing.
3. Management information systems. 4. Information
technology—Management. I. Title.
HD38.7.H696 2008
658.4'72—dc22

                                                    2007046665

McGraw-Hill books are available at special quantity discounts to use as premiums and sales promotions, or for use in corporate training programs. For more information, please write to the Director of Special Sales, Professional Publishing, McGraw-Hill, Two Penn Plaza, New York, NY 10121-2298. Or contact your local bookstore.

Successful Business Intelligence: Secrets to Making BI a Killer App

234567890   DOC DOC   0198

ISBN: 978-0-07-149851-7
MHID: 0-07-149851-6

Sponsoring Editor Lisa McClain	**Researchers** Rosemary LaCoste Brent W. Sefert	**Production Supervisor** Jean Bodeaux
Editorial Supervisor Jody McKenzie	**Graphic Design** Stephen Space, Space Studios	**Composition** International Typesetting and Composition
Project Manager Sam RC, International Typesetting and Composition	**Copy Editor** Jan Jue	**Illustration** ITC
Acquisitions Coordinator Mandy Canales	**Proofreader** Manish Tiwari	**Art Director, Cover** Jeff Weeks
Technical Editor Elizabeth Newbould	**Indexer** Valerie Perry	**Cover Designer** Jeff Weeks

For Norman

About the Author

Cindi Howson is the founder of BIScorecard®, a resource for in-depth BI product reviews, and has 15 years of BI and management reporting experience. She advises clients on BI strategy and tool selections, writes and blogs for *Intelligent Enterprise*, and is an instructor for The Data Warehousing Institute (TDWI). Prior to founding BIScorecard, Cindi was a manager at Deloitte & Touche and a BI standards leader for a Fortune 500 company. She has an MBA from Rice University. Contact Cindi at cindihowson@biscorecard.com.

About the Technical Editor

Elizabeth Newbould is the director of business intelligence at Dataspace, Incorporated (www.dataspace.com), one of the United States' foremost data warehousing consultancies. Elizabeth has more than 15 years of experience working with business intelligence and data warehousing solutions. Her e-mail address is enewbould@dataspace.com.

Contents

Preface

Business intelligence consistently rates at the top of companies' investment priorities. Despite its priority, businesspeople routinely complain about information overload on the one hand and the inability to get to relevant data on the other. BI professionals complain about lack of executive support and business users who don't "get" business intelligence. As a technology, BI usage remains modest, with significant untapped potential.

A couple of "aha" moments led to my writing this book. After I spoke at a business intelligence and performance management user conference, an IT person stopped me to say how inspired he was, that he felt motivated to talk more to the business users and less intimidated by them. In truth, I hadn't thought anything I said was all that inspirational, and it certainly wasn't new. And yet, I had forgotten how big a problem the IT-business disconnect can be, particularly for BI, which lies at the crossroads between business and technology. Shortly after, I read Jim Collins's book, *Good to Great*. In my spare time, I am not normally a reader of business books, but I had heard Collins at another user conference and was curious. In reading this book about what leads some companies to outperform others, it got me thinking about why some companies succeed with business intelligence and others fail. At the same time that I was judging the TDWI Best Practices awards—offering me previews of some who have encountered wild success—I was working with a company who couldn't get their BI initiative off the ground. Neither the business stakeholders nor the systems manager were convinced of its value. The information technology (IT) department was creating customized, inflexible reports directly in the source systems. An IT manager seemed to be the lone voice advocating something better, but he was at a loss to articulate the value of BI. These moments led to an article I wrote last summer for *Intelligent Enterprise*, "The Seven Pillars of BI Success." Initially appearing in the print edition, it became one of the website's most popular articles of the year.

My hope for this book, then, is that it is a resource for both business users and the technical experts that implement BI solutions. In order for businesspeople to exploit the value of BI, they must understand its potential. The customer stories in this book are meant as much to inspire as to offer valuable lessons on both the successes and the pitfalls to avoid. These customers illustrate just how much value BI can bring. When BI is left only for the IT experts to champion, it can provide only limited value. The real success comes when businesspeople take action on the insights BI provides, whether to improve financial performance, provide best-in-class customer service, increase efficiencies, or to make the world a better place.

About Product References

Customers in this book and throughout the industry use a variety of products and technologies in their business intelligence deployments. In describing BI components, I occasionally reference specific vendors and products as a way of providing concrete examples. Such references are not meant to be an exhaustive list of all the products available on the market place or an endorsement of specific solutions.

Recommended Audience

This book is recommended reading for:

- Businesspeople who feel their company is not making the most optimal decisions or who recognize the data their company has amassed is not being exploited to its potential
- Executives who sponsor BI initiatives
- BI program and project managers
- Technology experts who are asked to design and implement any aspect of the BI solution
- Anyone involved with a BI project that is struggling to deliver value

This book is intended to provide practical advice on what is business intelligence, what drives its adoption by leading companies, what are its components, and what are the technical and organizational issues that most affect its success. This book is not a technical reference on how to architect a solution or implement the software. For suggestions on more technical books, see Appendix B.

Chapter 1 defines business intelligence, its history, the business and technical drivers, and the approach to researching this book. Chapters 2 and 3 define the components of a business intelligence solution with the data warehouse on the back-end and the BI tools on the front-end. Chapters 4–13 describe the factors that most contribute to a company's successful use of BI from both a technical and organizational perspective. Chapter 14 offers a glimpse of BI's future with words of wisdom from leading companies. If you are looking to understand ways BI can help your business, Chapter 1, "Business Intelligence from the Business Side," Chapter 5, "The LOFT Effect," and Chapter 9, "Relevance," should be on your must-read list.

I hope this book will turn your business intelligence initiative into a wild success!

—Cindi Howson

Acknowledgments

First and foremost, I want to thank the customers who willingly shared their stories and devoted their time so that others embarking on a business intelligence journey can benefit from their insights and avoid the pitfalls. In particular, thank you to Matt Schwartz, Jonathan Rothman, Anne Marie Reynolds, Jim Hill, Jeff Kennedy, Dag Vidar Olsen, and Rob Vallentine, who also spearheaded the efforts at each of their companies to allow me to talk to the right people. Thank you to each of the vendors who have enabled me to meet so many exceptional customers over the years.

Survey data helped support trends and insights, so I thank everyone who participated in the survey and those who helped promote the survey, in particular Doug Henschen at *Intelligent Enterprise*, Ron Powell at the Business Intelligence Network, and Dave Wells and Steve Cissell at TDWI.

Thank you to Professor Randy Batsell for helping me find Brent Sefert, and thank you to Brent, who ensured I understood each of the case studies' financials. Thank you to Rosemary LaCoste for juggling so many hats, helping me narrow the list of case studies, and researching all my obscure questions.

A number of industry experts have allowed me to include references to their work within this book, all voices who have shaped my thinking and who share a similar goal to help companies make sense of all this stuff: Hugh Watson, Neil Raden, Barb Wixom, Wayne Eckerson, Colin White, and Richard Hackathorn. Thank you as well to Stephen Few for weaning me off my use of pie charts and encouraging me to use advanced visualization software to better analyze the survey. Donna Fedus of Senior Perspectives has my gratitude for helping me delicately explore the role of an aging workforce in BI's adoption.

The journey from concept to book is a long one. To anyone who read my article "Seven Pillars of BI Success," you provided encouragement that the industry needed more insight on how to succeed with BI beyond the technology. Thank you to David Stodder for helping me craft a glimpse of what would become this book. Once you have tech edited one book—a long, thankless task—it is a wonder anyone would want to take this role on again, and yet, I am fortunate that Elizabeth Newbould of Dataspace was once again willing to work with me on this. It was truly a commitment, and I thank her for helping make this book better than I could do on my own! Thank you to my editor, Lisa McClain, for believing in this project when I faltered, to Mandy Canales for keeping all the pieces moving along, Samik Roy Chowdhury and Jody McKenzie for making a finished product, and to Karen Schopp for making sure it reaches more readers! Thank you to Stephen Space, designer extraordinaire, for transforming my stick figures into beautiful artwork and clearer concepts. Thank you to Steve Dine, Al Hughes, and Mark Myers, who helped find the title for this book.

I'm indebted to my friends Jack and Teresa, who kept me from pulling my hair out (almost) and helped me find the LOFT effect. Thank you to Keith for reading early drafts, late drafts, scribbles, and supporting me in so many ways. Thank you, Megan and Sam, for reminding me that, in order to tell people's stories and inspire others, you have to laugh along the way.

Chapter 1

Business Intelligence from the Business Side

Just as the eyes are the windows to the soul, business intelligence is a window to the dynamics of a business. It reveals the performance, operational efficiencies, and untapped opportunities. *Business intelligence* (BI) is a set of technologies and processes that allow people at all levels of an organization to access and analyze data. Without people to interpret the information and act on it, business intelligence achieves nothing. For this reason, business intelligence is less about technology than about creativity, culture, and whether people view information as a critical asset. Technology enables business intelligence, but sometimes, too great a focus on technology can sabotage business intelligence initiatives. It is the people who will most make your BI efforts a wild success or utter failure.

Business Intelligence by Other Names

Business intelligence means different things to different people. To one businessperson, business intelligence means market research, something I would call "competitive intelligence." To another person, "reporting" may be a better term, even though business intelligence goes well beyond accessing a static report. "Reporting" and "analysis" are terms frequently used to describe business intelligence. Others will use terms such as "business analytics" or "decision support," both with varying degrees of appropriateness.

How these terms differ matters very little unless you are trying to compare market shares for different technologies. What matters most is to use the terminology that is most familiar to intended users and that has a positive connotation. No matter which terminology you use, keep the ultimate value of business intelligence in mind:

> Business intelligence allows people at all levels of an organization to access, interact with, and analyze data to manage the business, improve performance, discover opportunities, and operate efficiently.

What Business Intelligence Is Not

A data warehouse may or may not be a component of your business intelligence architecture (see Chapter 2), but a data warehouse is not synonymous with business intelligence. In fact, even if you have a data warehouse, you could only say your company is using business intelligence once you put some tools in the hands of the users to get to the data to make the information useful.

BI

The acronym for business intelligence is BI, and as information technology (IT) people like to use a plethora of acronyms, BI is one more that can sometimes cause confusion. BI as in "business intelligence" is not to be confused with "business investments" (although BI is something the business may invest in), "business insight" (although it is something BI may provide), or "bodily injury" (if you are using BI in the context of insurance). Even within the BI industry, confusion abounds as some people use BI to refer to the whole technical architecture (including the data warehouse, described in Chapter 2) as well as the user front-end tools (described in Chapter 3). Others think of BI as referring only to the front-end tools.

How Business Intelligence Provides Business Value

Business intelligence cuts across all functions and all industries. BI touches everyone in a company and beyond to customers and suppliers. As stated earlier, though, business intelligence can only provide business value when it is used effectively by people. There is a correlation between the *effective* use of business intelligence and company performance.[1]

However, having better *access* to data does not affect company performance[2]; the difference is in what companies *do* with the data.

BI for Management and Control

In its most basic sense, business intelligence provides managers information to know what's going on in the business. Without business intelligence, managers may talk about how they are "flying blind" with no insight until quarterly financial numbers are published. With business intelligence, information is accessible on a more timely and flexible basis to provide a view of:

- How sales are tracking in various regions and by various product lines
- If expenses are on plan or running over budget
- If warehouse capacities are at optimal levels
- If sales pipelines are where they should be

When any particular metric is not where it should be, business intelligence allows users to explore the underlying details to determine why metrics are off target and to take action to improve the situation. In the past, if managers monitored the business via paper-based reports, they had no flexibility to explore *why* the business was operating a certain way. For example, many companies use BI to monitor expenses to ensure costs do not exceed budgets. Rather than waiting until the close of the quarter to discover that excessive expenses have reduced profitability, timely access to expense data allows managers first to identify which business unit is over budget and then to take immediate steps to reduce overtime pay or travel expenses, or to defer purchases.

BI for Improving Business Performance

Used effectively, business intelligence allows organizations to improve performance. Business performance is measured by a number of financial indicators such as revenue, margin, profitability, cost to serve, and so on. In marketing, performance gains may be achieved by improving response rates for particular campaigns by identifying characteristics of more responsive customers. Eliminating ineffective campaigns saves companies millions of dollars each year. Business intelligence allows companies to boost revenues by cross-selling products to existing customers. Accounting personnel may use BI to reduce the aging of accounts receivable by identifying late-paying customers. In manufacturing,

BI facilitates gap analysis to understand why certain plants operate more efficiently than others.

In all these instances, accessing data is a necessary first step. However, improving performance also requires people's interaction to analyze the data and to determine the actions that will bring about improvement. Taking action on findings should not be assumed. People have political, cultural, and intellectual reasons for not taking the next step. To leverage business intelligence to improve performance, you need to consider all these issues. A company may implement a BI solution that provides intuitive access to data. If this data access is not leveraged for decision-making and acted upon, then BI has done nothing to improve business performance. The reverse is also true—when BI is used in a company without a sound business strategy, performance will not improve.

> A key sign of successful business intelligence is the degree to which it impacts business performance.

Measuring the business impact of business intelligence can be difficult as improvements in performance are attributable to factors beyond business intelligence. How to measure business intelligence success is discussed in Chapter 4.

Operational BI

While early business intelligence deployments focused more on strategic decisions and performance, BI increasingly plays a critical role in the daily operations of a company. In this regard, accessing detailed data and reviewing information may be necessary to complete a task. For example, as part of accepting a new order, a customer service representative may first check available inventory. Such an inventory report may be a standard report developed within an order entry system or it may come from a BI solution, whether stand alone or embedded in the order entry application. Other examples of operational BI include the following:

- Travel agents and airlines use operational BI to monitor flight delays so they can proactively re-accommodate passengers with connections.
- Hospitals and emergency rooms will use business intelligence to determine optimum staffing levels during peak periods.

- Restaurants will use BI to estimate the wait time for a table based on the number of current patrons and average length to dine.
- Walt Disney World's Magic Kingdom uses business intelligence for its service that issues park visitors FastPass tickets to avoid standing in long lines for rides.[3] The business intelligence tools monitor waiting times at the most popular rides to balance the number of tickets issued in given periods throughout the day.

Operational business intelligence most differs from BI for management and control purposes in both the level of detail required and in the timeliness of the data. Operational BI may involve accessing a transaction system directly or through a data warehouse (see Chapter 2) that is updated in near real-time multiple times throughout the day. Business intelligence for management and control purposes may also be in near real time but can also be based on weekly or monthly data. The role that operational BI plays in decision making and how successful BI companies are using it is discussed further in the section "Right-time Data" in Chapter 7.

BI for Process Improvement

The operations of a business are made up of dozens of individual processes. BI may support the decisions individuals make in every step of a process. It also may be used to help streamline a process by measuring how long subprocesses take and identifying areas for improvement. For example, manufacturing-to-shipment is one process. In the absence of business intelligence, a company may only realize there is a problem when a customer complains: "My order is late" or "I can get that product faster from your competitor." By analyzing the inputs, the time, and the outputs for each step of the process, BI can help identify the process bottlenecks.

- At Norway Post, for example, postal workers monitor the number of packages and letters sorted by hour. Any changes in these metrics may lead to a process review to see how the workflow can be optimized.
- At an oil and gas company, cash flow was problematic. A review of the process showed that gas was being delivered to customers on time but an invoice was only sent a week later. Reducing the time in the delivery-to-invoice process helped the company solve cash-flow problems. Business intelligence tools allowed the company to identify the problem and then to ensure compliance to a new rule of invoicing within one day of delivery.

BI to Improve Customer Service

The quality of customer service eventually manifests itself in the financials of a company. Business intelligence can help companies provide high customer service levels by providing timely order processing, loan approvals, problem handling, and so on. For example:

- Whirlpool uses business intelligence to monitor its warranty program to understand root causes for warranty problems and improve customer satisfaction with its products.[4]
- Continental Airlines uses business intelligence to monitor how full business class cabins are and to ensure its most valued customers receive complimentary upgrades when space permits.[5]

BI to Make the World Better

Business intelligence for management and control and performance improvement gets a fair amount of media attention. An increasingly important value in business intelligence, though, is in empowering people to improve the world.

- Police departments in Richmond, Virginia,[6] and Humberside, England,[7] for example, have used business intelligence to help police officers respond better to call-outs and to reduce crime rates.
- Opportunity International helps people in some of the most poverty-stricken parts of the world such as Africa, Southeast Asia, and Central America by giving them small business loans. Loan amounts as low as $50 help applicants to start their own businesses.[8] Opportunity International uses business intelligence to track loan amounts, stretch donation dollars, and to compare the impacts in various regions.
- School systems use business intelligence to understand the effects and trends in student grades based on gender, attendance rates, and teaching methods.
- Emergency Medical Associates (EMA) uses business intelligence to analyze patient trends in New York and New Jersey to better predict and prepare for disease outbreaks and to improve emergency room care in area hospitals.

BI for Discovering New Business Opportunities

Business intelligence helps businesses assess and uncover new business opportunities by exploring data and testing theories. For example:

- The Dow Chemical Company uses business intelligence to understand the value proposition of pursuing joint ventures.
- A hospitality company uses business intelligence to explore hotel capacity rates as a way of developing the time-share business.

The Business Intelligence Market

With business intelligence providing significant benefits across so many industries and all business functions, it's not surprising that BI has bubbled to the top of many companies' IT investment priorities. Many analysts firms and surveys cite BI as the number one or number two IT investment priority. From a market perspective, the business intelligence market (which includes the data warehouse platforms discussed in Chapter 2 and the front-end tools discussed in Chapter 3) is a $20 billion market, according to analyst firm IDC.[9] Its growth rate in the past few years has been in the 11% range—impressive, considering unit prices for many business intelligence components have dropped, and in contrast to other information technology markets whose growth has slowed.

As a set of technologies, business intelligence emerged in the early 1990s. Of course, decision-making processes existed long before the information technology to support them. Historically, businesses could rely more on gut-feel decisions because they may have been closer to their customers and the products. The cost to support decisions with facts was high and usually involved gathering data manually. More recently, business and technology forces have converged to make business intelligence mission-critical and an essential part of doing business.

Business Forces Driving BI

The business landscape has changed dramatically in the last 20 years. Many businesses now operate and compete on a global basis with 24/7 operations. The wealth of information at consumers' and businesses' fingertips puts greater pressure on pricing and makes customer churn a constant threat across industries. The pace of change is rapid. Companies compete on time-to-market and product innovations at a frenetic pace. In the United States, an aging workforce and looming pension and healthcare obligations mean costs have to be cut elsewhere.

With the fall of Enron and numerous accounting scandals, shareholders demand still more transparency and accountability. The Sarbanes-Oxley Act of 2002 now makes inaccurate financial reporting a criminal offense.

> Businesses can't afford not to know what's going on, internally and externally, and in levels of detail never before imagined or required.

Shift Within the Workforce

The business environment and BI technology have changed dramatically within the last 20 years, escalating the role of business intelligence as an information technology that gives companies a competitive advantage.

A sizeable portion of senior managers did not grow up with computers. Technology for these people may still be viewed with a wary eye. Giving workers too much access to information may be viewed as a threat to power. Data is something to be hoarded. Contrast that with elementary school children today who learn the value of data analysis early by graphing demographics and sales data in spreadsheets to identify trends. Data analysis and business intelligence is increasingly standard curriculum in many MBA programs. Computer literacy has become a job requirement for anyone entering the workforce.

Companies with such mixed workforces may not readily embrace business intelligence, even though it provides such broad-reaching value. Recognize the role that technical and data literacy plays in the adoption of business intelligence. If you are hoping that tech-savvy Generation Y workers will soon comprise a greater portion of the workforce, they won't.[10] Declining birthrates on the one hand, and later retirements on the other, mean older workers are making up a larger portion of the workforce. People age 40 and older now make up half of the workforce.[11] This means widespread use of computers happened only after half the current workforce graduated college. This is not to say an older workforce won't embrace information technology; it's only that it is not as ingrained as it is for employees who have been using information technology their entire lives.

Some studies have shown that computer usage seems consistent for U.S. workers up until age 50, and then it drops off by 20%. If you are reading this book, you probably embrace information technology as a powerful business tool. Remember, though, that a significant portion of the workforce doesn't. Some don't have cell phones, home computers, or ever use the Internet. The Pew Internet & American Life Project surveyed 4001 Americans about their use and attitudes toward various forms of information technology.[12] They classified people into ten different groups depending on these attitudes. Simplifying the results, the following table shows the percentage split among:

- Those who use and embrace technology
- Those who use technology but find it a burden and hassle to use
- Those who don't use technology or view technology as providing little value

Use and View of Technology	Percentage of U.S. Population	Median Age Range
Embrace	41%	28 to 40
Hassled	10%	46
Wary	49%	46 to 64

Source: The Pew Internet & American Life Project

The difference in median age between the embracers of technology and the wary users of technology is apparent, yet not surprising. I only have to look at my 9-year-old son, who dials a telephone with two thumbs, à la video games, to see the effect of technology on younger generations (my generation dials with the index finger...slowly). The good news, though, is that as technology is easier and more relevant, usage increases. Internet usage among all age groups has increased dramatically in the last few years. Understand the employee demographics in your own company, and be sure to consider these issues as you address BI adoption. As technology usage increases for all ages and as Generation Y (who have used technology all along) comprises a greater portion of the workforce, not only will these workers facilitate greater use of business intelligence, but they will also expect it as a standard business tool.

Technology Changes Enabling BI

Rapid change in technology has been one driver of this frenetic pace of business change; it also has enabled business intelligence for everyone, not just information technology experts, programmers, and power users. Figure 1-1 shows how technology and BI tools have changed over time to extend the reach of business intelligence.

> There is one crucial aspect of extending the reach of business intelligence that has nothing to do with technology and that is Relevance. Understanding what information someone needs to do a job or to complete a task is what makes business intelligence *relevant* to that person. Much of business intelligence thus far has been relevant to power users and senior managers but not to front/line workers, customers, and suppliers.

Data Explosion Contributes to Information Overload   The volume of digital data has exploded. What once was handwritten or typed onto a piece of paper to process an order is now entered into a system with ever more detail. The volume of data that knowledge workers want to

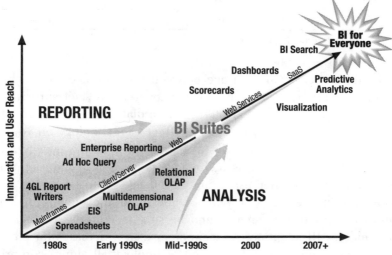

Figure 1-1   Evolution of BI tools.[13]

analyze is projected to grow anywhere from 25% to double in the next year.[14] Add to that details such as clicks on a website to analyze the flow of information and shopping patterns, and you can see how the volume of data has exploded. In the past three years, the amount of digital data in Fortune 1000 companies has grown fivefold and in midsize companies, 50-fold.[15]

The average manager spends two hours a day simply looking for data, and half of the information found is later determined useless.[16]

If you feel like you are drowning in information, it's because you are.

When business intelligence is deployed effectively, all that data becomes a strategic asset to be exploited. The proverbial needle in the haystack may be the single insight about a customer that locks in their loyalty. Or it may be the secret to lowering production costs.

At the Speed of Thought   It might seem that with the explosion of data, accessing more data would get slower. Yet computer processing power and addressable memory have increased to the point that accessing that data can now be done at the speed of thought. Twenty years ago, you might have waited a month for a complex, printed report that ran on a mainframe computer for days. Ten years ago, that same report might have taken hours, a marginal improvement. Today, the same report may run in seconds on a purpose-built business intelligence appliance and be delivered to a BlackBerry mobile device.

Web-Based BI   Web-based business intelligence has allowed tools to be deployed across corporate intranets and extranets to thousands of employees and external customers in a matter of hours. With the client/server computing of the early 1990s, it took days to install and configure PCs for just a handful of users. The Web has simultaneously broadened the reach of BI while allowing IT to lower the cost of ownership of BI.

BI Suites and Toolsets   Business intelligence tools have multiple front-end components, such as business query tools, OLAP, and dash-boards (discussed in Chapter 3). These components are optimized for different users' needs and usage scenarios. Previously, companies had to buy these multiple components from separate vendors. Interoperability was nonexistent and the cost to deploy was high. As a single vendor now offers a full suite or toolset and the components are integrated from a usability and infrastructure point of view, business intelligence can reach more users, based on their unique requirements and again at a lower cost of ownership. Web-based business intelligence and the expanding breadth of BI suites have brought economies of scale to BI, providing more functionality to more users at lower costs than before.

Other Emerging Technologies   Web 2.0 and BI 2.0 technologies are bolstering BI's prevalence and making it more actionable through the following:

- Integration of search with BI gives a Google-like interface to BI and allows users to more easily find relevant information.
- Rich Internet applications that allow users to view a table and dynami-cally sort and filter the data—without being connected to a BI server and without going through an advanced authoring environment.
- Flashier web-based visualizations that both are more appealing and offer rapid insight into trends.
- Integration with mobile devices such that users can receive alerts on BlackBerry devices or access customer reports while visiting the cus-tomer.
- BI gadgets that are mini reports and visualizations immediately acces-sible without having to log into a separate BI application.

- Service Oriented Architecture (SOA) and mash ups allow BI components to be embedded in other applications and within operational processes.

These technologies are discussed in more detail in Chapters 3 and 14.

Battle Scars

Business intelligence is a catalyst for change. Anyone with a vested interest in preserving the status quo may not welcome a business intelligence initiative. Expect some battle scars. One CIO described the company's business intelligence initiative as an emotional process to get through but necessary to execute the business's vision. Those who keep the value of business intelligence and the greater good of the company always in their vision will ultimately succeed.

Some of the BI battle scars include:

- Power struggles between IT and the business when either loses areas of control or disagrees on the scope and approach
- Jobs eliminated when custom report developers were no longer needed
- A marketing manager fired when a company realized just how badly the manager was performing campaign management
- Software and technology that does not always work as expected, and vendors who merge, get acquired, or change strategy in ways that affect your BI deployment

The Research

As a consultant and industry analyst, I did not want my own experiences, opinions, and customers to be the primary influence on defining the secrets to making BI a killer application for businesses. Instead, I wanted these lessons to come from a larger sample of industry leaders and survey respondents. The research for this book then had four main components: a survey, in-depth case studies, a review of literature on award winners, and a peer networking session.

The Successful BI Survey

The Successful BI survey ran for six weeks from April 2007 until mid-May 2007. The full survey is included in Appendix A. Questions that involved ranking of items used a survey feature to randomize the order of the displayed options so that results were not skewed by the order of the possible selections. The survey was promoted through multiple media outlets including:

- Intelligent Enterprise (www.intelligententerprise.com), an online magazine and sister publication of *Information Week* that focuses on business intelligence, content management, and business process management
- The Business Intelligence Network (www.b-eye-network.com), a global resource for business intelligence, data warehousing, customer data integration (CDI), performance management, and information quality
- *Strategic Path,* an Australian-based print publication and website (http://www.strategicpath.com.au) focusing on data management and business intelligence issues
- The Data Warehousing Institute's (TDWI) *BI This Week* newsletter, an opt-in newsletter serving business intelligence and data warehousing professionals
- *BIScorecard* newsletter, an opt-in newsletter serving experts who are actively evaluating business intelligence front-end tools and products

To better analyze the survey results, I decided to challenge myself to practice one of the "secrets" in this book—to use advanced visualization software. Most of the survey charts were produced using Tableau Software. As you'll discover, some of the charts are standard fare and something I could have created directly via the survey software. Others, though, show how visualizing the data in different ways reveals previously undistinguishable patterns.

Survey Demographics   There were 513 qualified responses, from a mixture of large companies (43% of respondents) with annual revenues greater than $1 billion, medium-sized companies (30%), and small businesses (27%) as shown in Figure 1-2.

The majority of survey responses were from the United States (69%), followed by with Europe (12%), Canada, Latin America, Asia, Australia and New Zealand, and South Africa (see Figure 1-3).

In terms of functional area, as shown in Figure 1-4, the largest percentage of survey respondents came from corporate IT, with responses from a mixture of other functional areas. When asked to describe their role within the company, 23% described themselves as a hybrid business/IT person and another 10% were business users.

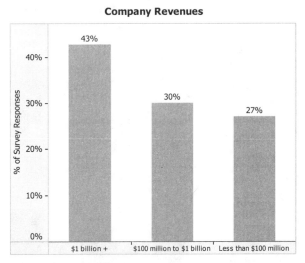

Figure 1-2   Survey demographics by company revenues

Survey respondents come from a mix of industries as shown in Figure 1-5.

The Successful BI Case Studies

Surveys are an ideal method for providing statistical information on trends and insights for explicit questions. However, if the survey fails to pose a question or provide a ranking option as to something that contributed

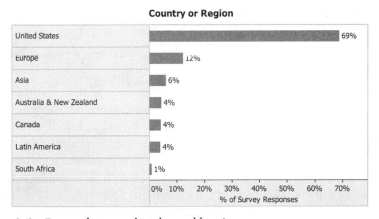

Figure 1-3   Survey demographics by world region

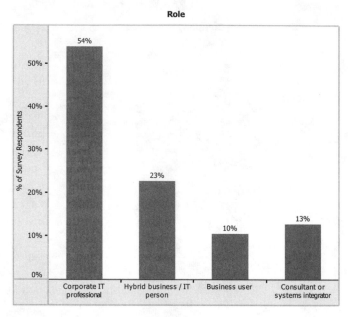

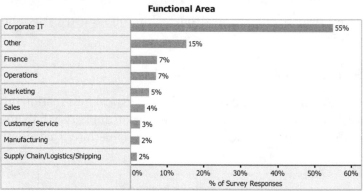

Figure 1-4   Survey demographics by functional expertise and role

to a success or failure, such omissions can mask the true drivers of success. As a way of unearthing these drivers, I scanned the market for companies consistently recognized for their business intelligence initiatives and honored by magazines, industry analysts, and software vendors. Such industry recognition, though, is often a self-selecting process: if a company does not submit an application, analyst firms and magazines are not aware of their achievements. As a way of addressing this limitation,

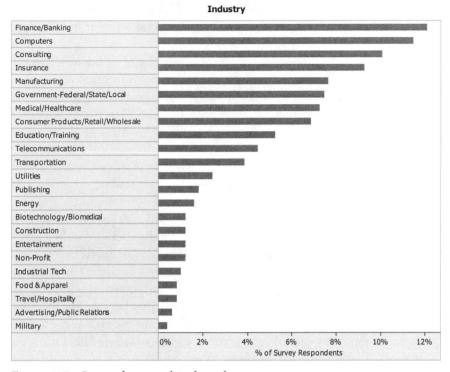

Industry

Industry	% of Survey Respondents
Finance/Banking	
Computers	
Consulting	
Insurance	
Manufacturing	
Government-Federal/State/Local	
Medical/Healthcare	
Consumer Products/Retail/Wholesale	
Education/Training	
Telecommunications	
Transportation	
Utilities	
Publishing	
Energy	
Biotechnology/Biomedical	
Construction	
Entertainment	
Non-Profit	
Industrial Tech	
Food & Apparel	
Travel/Hospitality	
Advertising/Public Relations	
Military	

Figure 1-5   Survey demographics by industry

I looked through years of notes from industry conferences for companies who had wowed me with their stories. I also investigated companies who were recognized for their sustained business value in books and lists such as *Good To Great* and *Fortune*'s fastest-growing companies to understand what role business intelligence played in their company's success.

For in-depth case studies, I pruned the list to a cross section of industries, company sizes, and BI uses. The final list of seven companies highlighted in depth in this book are leaders in business intelligence whose BI initiative has had a significant impact on business performance and who could speak officially about their experiences. Throughout the book, I refer collectively to this final group as the "Successful BI Case Studies." It is a term that some are uncomfortable with; they argue they have not achieved all that is possible. Several, in fact, purposely elect not to apply for any industry awards for this reason. Three of the companies have received multiple industry awards for their BI initiative. A few case studies may not be award winners, but I have included them because of their unique stories and the profound impact BI has had on their companies.

- **FlightStats**   This company is in the early stages of its business intelligence journey. Having demonstrated success with internal customers, they recently released a solution for consumers. Given some of the woes expressed by airline passengers in the last year, I have included FlightStats as a unique company whose entire business model is based on business intelligence.
- **Corporate Express**   I first heard Corporate Express speak at the MicroStrategy World conference in 2006. A number of aspects to their BI deployment are innovative, with an enormous impact on the business performance. During the course of my writing this book, they received the TDWI Best Practices Award for Predictive Analytics.
- **The Dow Chemical Company**   While Dow was honored by Business Objects in 2004 and written about by Cognos in their 1999 annual report, they otherwise are quite humble and quiet about their BI achievements. I began my career in business intelligence at Dow, and while I have been privileged to work with a number of visionary customers throughout my consulting career, I continue to refer back to some of the best practices garnered from Dow's business intelligence project. As I heard through former colleagues at Dow just how wide a net the BI initiative had cast and the role it had on a number of recent mergers and joint ventures, I asked Dow to formally participate in this study.
- **Norway Post**   I was honored to meet Norway Post at Hyperion's 2005 user conference. The story of their transformation from a public entity, with both terrible financial performance and poor customer service, to a private postal service with stellar performance is at times equally painful and inspiring. Just how bad it was and how far it has come serves as a lesson that no matter how conservative a company or the industry in which you operate, having a solid business intelligence platform and performance management culture can lead to incredible success.
- **1-800 CONTACTS**   The company won TDWI's Best Practices Award for BI on a Limited Budget, demonstrating that BI does not have to be expensive. While many companies start with BI in finance and marketing, 1-800 CONTACTS began their BI efforts with front-line workers in their call centers.
- **Continental Airlines**   I admit, I hate to travel. Yet I am one of Continental Airlines' most loyal customers, so I wanted to include them to understand how they can face a resistant traveler, in a difficult industry, and still exceed customer expectations. Continental

received Gartner's BI Excellence Award in 2005. The company's turn-around from bankruptcy to profitability and best in service has been widely written about.

- **Emergency Medical Associates (EMA)** The healthcare industry is perceived as being slow to adopt information technology, and yet EMA is visionary in its use of BI. Having met their BI director at several conferences, I find his excitement at improving patient care and getting even doctors to embrace dashboards contagious.

To gather their stories, I relied on open-ended questions as to how successful they considered their business intelligence initiative, how much it contributed to business performance, and to what they attributed their ultimate success and interim failures. In studying these companies, I asked to speak to the usual suspects—BI program managers, sponsors, users—but in addition, I asked to speak to the skeptics who did not believe in the value of business intelligence or who resisted using the solution internally. What would it take for them to use business intelligence? Finally, while all the companies could cite measurable business benefits from the use of business intelligence, I worked with one of my research assistants, Brent Sefert, a Jones School MBA candidate, to see how and if these business benefits were reflected in the total company performance.

Without the time and insights these companies willingly shared, this book would not have been possible. I, and no doubt, the business intelligence community, thank them for letting us learn from their lessons!

TDWI Peer Networking Session

As the preliminary survey results were in and a number of the case study interviews completed, I hosted a peer networking session at TDWI's Boston conference in May 2007. During this session, we brainstormed causes of and barriers to success, again using open-ended questions. The group's discussion helped crystallize and echoed some of my existing findings. The comments from one participant in particular helped form the acronym in Chapter 5, the LOFT Effect. Participants expressed the greatest frustration that their business stakeholders don't understand the real value of business intelligence. My hope is that this book increases this understanding. Others cited the greatest challenge as being not in the data warehouse or in BI tools, but rather, in the 100+ source systems and the frequency with which source systems change. For those struggling with this issue, I think you will find Dow's story in Chapter 7 illuminating.

Best Practices for Successful Business Intelligence

Based on this research, following are the top ten secrets to successful business intelligence and making BI your company's next killer app. Some of these items are not secrets at all. In fact, they are such well-known drivers of BI success that some practitioners will walk away from projects that do not, for example, have executive-level sponsorship. The secret then is not always in the what, but rather, in the how—how to get executive-level sponsorship.

1. Measure success in multiple ways, using objective measures when available and recognizing the importance of benefits that cannot be readily quantified.
2. Understand the effect of Luck, Opportunity, Frustration, and Threat (LOFT) to catapult your BI initiative from moderate success to wild success.
3. Garner executive support to ensure BI infiltrates all corners of an organization to provide competitive advantage and business value.
4. Start with a solid data foundation and add to it incrementally and continuously to improve the quality, breadth, and timeliness of data.
5. Align the BI strategy with the goals of the business by ensuring IT and business personnel work more as partners and less as adversaries.
6. Find the relevance for BI for every worker in the company, as well as for customers and suppliers.
7. Use agile development processes to deliver BI capabilities and improvements at the pace of change commensurate with the pace of business change.
8. Organize BI teams and experts for success and building a solution with a focus on the enterprise.
9. Choose appropriate BI tools that meet the user and business needs and that work within the technology standards that IT can effectively support.
10. There are several other secrets such as fostering a culture that encourages fact-based decision making and discourages data hoarding, promoting your successes and the applications, and presenting data visually.

Chapter 2

Techno Babble: Components of a Business Intelligence Architecture

Every BI deployment has an underlying architecture. The BI architecture is much like the engine of a car—a necessary component, often powerful, but one that users, like drivers, don't always understand. For some companies new to BI, the BI architecture may primarily be the operational systems and the BI front-end tools. For more mature BI deployments and particularly for enterprise customers, it will involve ETL (extract, transform, and load) tools, a data warehouse, data marts, BI front-end tools, and other such components.

When IT discusses BI with users, we readily fall into technobabble, and senseless acronyms abound. Most car drivers know that cars have a battery, a transmission, a fuel tank—an adequate level of knowledge for having a conversation with a mechanic or salesperson but arguably not so much expertise to begin rebuilding an engine. In this chapter, then, I'll present the major architectural technical components that make up BI and that business users should have at least a high-level understanding of to participate in discussions about building and leveraging a BI solution. If you are a technical expert, you might find this chapter to be overly simplified and it is. If you are looking for a reference on any one of these components, consult the list of resources in Appendix B.

Chapter 3 explores the sleek "chassis" of this BI architecture.

Operational and Source Systems

Operational systems are the starting point for most quantitative data in a company. Operational systems may also be referred to as "transaction processing systems," "source systems," and "enterprise resource planning" (ERP) systems. As Figure 2-1 illustrates:

- **Manufacturing system**   When a product is produced, the production order is entered in the manufacturing system. The quantity of raw material used and the finished product produced are recorded.
- **Sales system**   When a customer places an order, the order details are entered in an order entry system.
- **Supply chain system**   When the product is available, the product is shipped and order fulfillment details are entered.
- **Accounting system**   Accounting then invoices the customer and collects payment. The invoices and payments may be recorded in an operational system that is different from the order entry system.

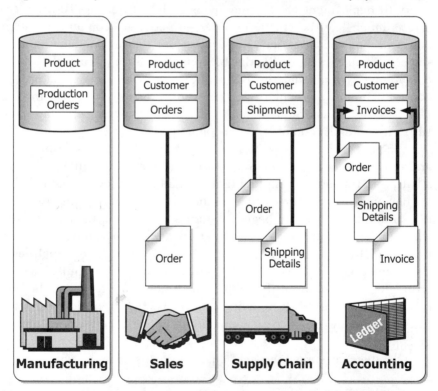

Figure 2-1   Operational systems record data from operational tasks.

In each step in this process, users are creating data that can eventually be used for business intelligence. As well, to complete a task, operational users may need business intelligence. Perhaps in order to accept an order, the product must be available in inventory. As is the case with many online retailers, customers cannot place an order for a product combination (color, size) that is not available; a report immediately appears with a list of alternative sizes or colors.

> When business intelligence is integrated with an operational system or supports an operational task, it is referred to as *operational business intelligence.*

The operational systems shown in Figure 2-1 may be custom-developed transaction systems or a purchased package from companies such as Oracle (Oracle E-business, PeopleSoft, J.D. Edwards), SAP, or Microsoft (Dynamics GP). With custom-developed operational systems or with modules coming from different vendors, data may be manually entered into each system. A better approach is to systematically transfer data between the systems or modules. However, even when data is systematically transferred, the Customer ID entered in the order system may not, for example, be the same Customer ID entered in the accounting system—even though both IDs refer to the same customer!

Ideally, consistent information flows through the process seamlessly, as shown in Figure 2-2. Enterprise resource planning (ERP) systems ensure adherence to standard processes and are broader in scope than custom operational systems of the past. From a data perspective, ERPs reduce duplicate data entry and thus improve data quality (see Chapter 7). With an integrated ERP, a common set of reference tables with consistent customer IDs, product codes, and chart of accounts are shared across the modules or applications.

Within the business intelligence life cycle, the operational systems are the starting point for data you will later want to analyze. If you do not capture the data in the operational system, you can't analyze it. If the operational system contains errors, those errors will only get compounded when you later aggregate and combine it with other data.

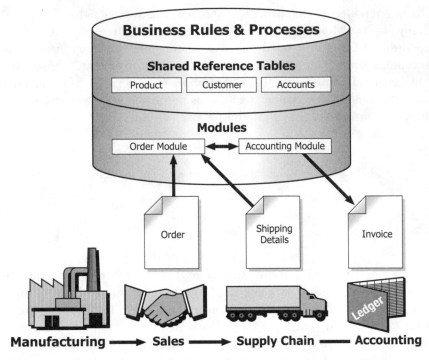

Figure 2-2   ERP systems reduce duplicate data entry and ensure adherence to standard processes.

Additional Source Systems

While much of the data warehouse (described in the next section) is populated by operational systems, data may also come from additional data sources such as:

- Distributors who supply sales and inventory information
- Click-stream data from web logs that show the most frequently viewed products or online shopping cart analysis for partially completed orders
- Market prices from external research firms

Whether this additional data gets loaded into a central data warehouse will depend on how consistently it can be merged with corporate data, how common the requirement is, and politics. If the data is not physically stored in the data warehouse, it may be integrated with corporate data in a specific data mart. Disparate data sources may, in some cases, also be accessed or combined within the BI front-end tool.

Data Transfer: From Operational to Data Warehouse

BI often involves analyzing summary data and combining data from multiple operational systems. To facilitate this, data will be extracted from the operational systems and loaded into a data warehouse, as shown in Figure 2-3.

This process is referred to as *extract, transform, and load* (ETL). More recently, some data warehouse teams have changed the order in which they do certain things and will call it ELT (extract, load, transform).

The "transform" process of ETL is often the most time-consuming, particularly when multiple, disparate systems are involved. Inconsistent codes (product ID, customer ID), handling of incomplete data, changing codes to meaningful terms (1 = not shipped, 2 = shipped) are all part of the transform process.

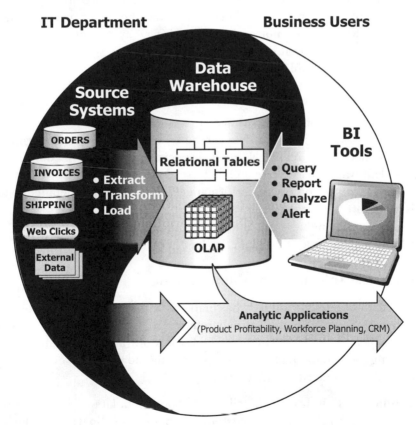

Figure 2-3   Major components in the business intelligence life cycle

Early data warehouse efforts usually relied on custom-coded ETL and many still do. More recently, as packaged ETL solutions have come on the market and become integrated with the BI front-end, customers use purchased ETL solutions. Popular solutions for ETL include Informatica Power Center, IBM Websphere Data Stage, Oracle Data Integrator, Ab Initio, and Microsoft Integration Services (a component of SQL Server).

NOTE Throughout this book, I will mention specific vendor products as a way of providing you with concrete examples. These listings are not exhaustive, and exact product names frequently change amid vendor acquisition and product releases.

Why Not Extract Everything?

In designing a data warehouse, requirements analysts will ask users what they need so that the ETL specialists can figure out what should be extracted from the source systems. Because much of BI is unpredictable in nature and users often don't know what they want until they see it, you might ask "why not extract everything?" in the event that you might one day need that data.

There are a number of reasons why all the data should not be extracted:

- High data replication and storage costs.
- The time window in which data can be ETL'd (extracted, transformed, and loaded) is increasingly small, especially since many companies and data warehouses serve a global user base.
- Negative impact on query performance when too much detailed data is stored in the data warehouse.
- Limited time, money, and human resources force a prioritization of what data to extract to include in the data warehouse.

Enterprise Information Management

As the data warehouse industry has matured and ETL tools have evolved, this market segment is increasingly referred to as *enterprise information management* (EIM). EIM includes ETL tools but also will include data modeling tools, data quality, data profiling, metadata management, and master data management (MDM).

Metadata   IT professionals talk a lot about metadata and go to great pains to make the business understand its importance. So with a chuckle,

I will give you the classic definition: metadata is data about the data. Helpful, isn't it?

Metadata is similar to a card file in a library or book details on Amazon.com. A card file in a library (or the book details on Amazon) tells you which category a book belongs to, when it was published, and so on. Metadata may describe such things as:

- When the data was extracted from the source system
- When the data was loaded into the data warehouse
- From which source system an item originated
- From which physical table and field in the source system it was extracted
- How something was calculated—for example, *revenue = (price × quantity sold) − discounts*
- What the item means in a business context (revenue is based on the amount invoiced and does not include returns or bad debts)

The first few bullets in this list may not be all that interesting to many business users but they are critical in the design and functioning of a data warehouse. These items are also important in knowing how timely the information you are analyzing is. If, for example, the data warehouse did not fully load due to an error, you need to be aware of this and consider this incomplete data in your reports.

As you move down the list, the items become much more important to all business users. A salesperson, for example, may have a different definition of revenue than a finance person would. As more people use BI, metadata is critical in ensuring a common business terminology and in ensuring users really know what the data means.

Master Data Management   David Loshin, president of Knowledge Integrity and a specialist in information quality and master data management (MDM), defines MDM as follows:

Master data management is comprised of the business applications, methods, and tools that implement the policies, procedures, and infrastructure to support the capture, integration, and subsequent shared use of accurate, timely, consistent, and complete master data.[1]

Master data is the code and descriptions for customer, product, charts of accounts, regions, and so on. *Master data management* is what ensures that the product ID from the product table shown in Figure 2-2 preceding is ideally the same ID across all the applications. This product ID is stored and maintained in one common place so that the relevant operational and business intelligence systems can access and share it.

In practice, rarely is there a single product ID for a variety of technical and organizational reasons. In this case, master data will include the mappings of the different product IDs that really are the same product represented in different systems. Master data also includes hierarchies of how individual products, customers, and accounts aggregate and form the dimensions by which you analyze various facts (see the "Data Warehouse Tables" section later). If this all sounds a little boring and unimportant to you, read the story of how pivotal a role master data has played in Dow Chemical's business intelligence success in Chapter 7.

The Data Warehouse

A data warehouse is the collection of data *extracted* from various operational systems, *transformed* to make the data consistent, and *loaded* for analysis. With some business users, "data warehouse" has become a dirty word, associated with "expensive," "monolithic," and of no business value. Other terms, such as *reporting database* and *data mart*, are also used and may sound less monolithic to some business stakeholders. In reality, they both serve similar purposes but might have different scope and technical architecture.

Do I Need a Data Warehouse?

Many ERP implementations were sold on the promise of delivering business insight. They don't. Having a single operational system that ensures consistent business processes and that uses consistent reference data (customer, product codes) will make business analysis significantly easier. But there are a number of fundamental differences between operational systems and data warehouses, highlighted in Table 2-1.

It is because of these myriad differences that I would argue all companies need a data warehouse, regardless of the size of the company. The technical architecture of the data warehouse may vary, but its necessity does not. I have worked with customers with fewer than 20 employees and less than $1 million in revenues who needed a "reporting database," and I have worked with customers with greater than $20 billion in revenues who needed a "data warehouse."

Why Bother with a Data Warehouse at All?

Many customers new to BI want to skip the data warehouse and deploy a BI tool directly against the operational system. This may seem like

Difference	Operational System	Data Warehouse/Data Mart
Purpose	Primary function is to process orders, post journal entries, complete an operational task	Primary purpose is to provide access to information to manage the business by providing insight that leads to improved revenues, reduced costs, quality customer service, and alignment of strategic goals.
History	Current information with very little history	Larger amounts of history allow multiyear trend analysis, this year versus last year comparisons.
Timeliness	Real-time information	Information extracted on a periodic basis (hourly, daily, weekly). More recently, operational data warehouses may extract information in real-time or several times throughout the day.
Level of detail	Detailed data down to the line item or level of data entry	Aggregated data with varying degrees of granularity.
Response time	Fast inputs, but slow queries	Read-only; tuned for fast queries.
Table structure	Normalized tables in thousands	Parts of the data warehouse may be normalized but the parts business users query are normally denormalized star or snowflake schemas. The data warehouse will have fewer tables than the source systems have.
Dimensions	Rarely hierarchical groupings	Hierarchical groups give level of time, chart of accounts, product groupings, customer groups, and so on.
Reporting and analysis	Fixed reports by one detailed dimension (cost center, plant, order number)	Fixed or ad hoc reporting and analysis by multiple dimensions across all business functions.

Table 2-1   Comparison of Operational Systems with Data Warehouses

a faster approach to business intelligence. In some instances, it may be an acceptable way to start with BI, and this approach addresses operational BI needs. However, for most companies, you will want a data warehouse when:

- You need to perform cross-subject or cross-functional analysis, such as products ordered versus inventory on hand. Such information may exist in two different systems or different modules within an ERP system and are thus combined into the data warehouse.
- You want to perform analysis on summary information, aggregated by time (month, quarter) or by some other hierarchy (product groupings). These hierarchies often don't exist in transaction systems, and even when they do, running such voluminous queries within a transaction system can slow it to the point of interfering with data entry.
- You need consistently fast reporting and analysis times. Because of their different purposes and design, data warehouses allow for faster queries than operational systems.

Data Marts

A data mart is a subset of the data coming from a central data warehouse. A data mart also may be used to feed a central data warehouse. Whereas a data warehouse is designed to serve the needs of the enterprise, a data mart may serve the needs of a particular business unit, function, process, or application. Because a data mart is aligned with a particular business requirement, some businesses may want to skip the data warehouse and build an independent data mart. According to industry research, fewer companies now do this[2] as independent data marts have been met with limited success and over time have a higher implementation cost.

Data Warehouse Tables

Within the data warehouse, data is physically stored in individual *tables* within a relational database. Your company may use the same relational database software for your ERP system as for your data warehouse (for example, Oracle, Microsoft SQL Server, IBM DB2) or a relational database specifically designed for business intelligence (Teradata, SAS Intelligence Storage).

Experts will deploy a number of different table design approaches to support the diverse business needs, performance requirements, and storage constraints. Most data warehouses have two types of tables: (1) a *fact table* that contains keys into the dimension tables and numeric information to analyze, such as sales, inventory, or calls. Such facts are often referred to as *measures*; and (2) *dimension tables* that allow analysis of measures from different perspectives such as product, time, or geography.

A fact table can have millions of detailed rows of data, commonly referred to as having a "finer granularity," or can be significantly smaller, containing mainly summary numbers. To improve the performance of queries, database designers may choose to create *aggregate or summary tables* around a fact table such that there may be a DAILY_SALES_FACT table, MONTHLY_SALES_FACT table, and YEARLY_SALES_FACT table. One fact table together with its associated dimension tables is referred to as a *star schema,* as shown in Figure 2-4.

Dimension tables are also referred to as *lookup tables* or *reference tables.* The dimension tables can be broken into more than one table; for example, detailed material IDs may reside in a MATERIAL_ID table. The groupings and product hierarchy for the material IDs may reside in a separate table such as PRODUCT_GROUPING. This type of structure is referred to as a *snowflake design* and is used in data warehouses that have extremely large dimensions. You can think of dimensions as the ways by which you want to analyze facts, for example, sales *by geography* or sales *by product.*

In a transaction system, data is stored in a way that allows for fast data entry with minimal amounts of data duplicated across the physical tables. Data is said to be stored in *normalized* tables in a transaction system when a minimal amount of data is replicated in each table and a data element needs to be updated in only one place. For example, the same customer

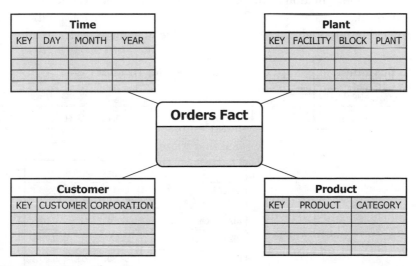

Figure 2-4   Star schema

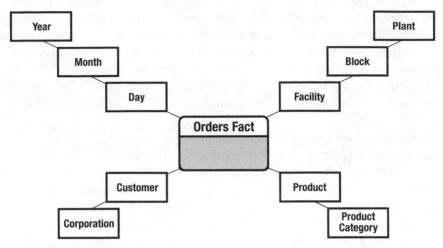

Figure 2-5   Snowflake design

name does not appear in multiple rows in a table. In a data warehouse or data mart, the emphasis is on storing data in ways that facilitate analysis and that speed query performance. Data redundancy is less of a concern, and as the data warehouse is a read-only environment, there is less concern about having to change multiple instances of the same value in thousands of tables and rows. Normalization in an operational system means the facts and the dimensions will be spread across many tables. For example, order information may exist in both an ORDER_HEADER table and an ORDER_LINES table as shown next. Trying to report on which customers bought which products means joining multiple tables and aggregating information from multiple tables, which will produce incorrect query results. Earlier, in the Figure 2-4, all of the order information was extracted into a single ORDERS_FACT table, making it easier to query.

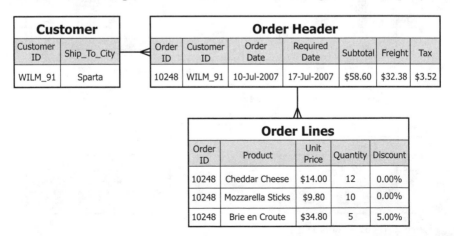

Dimensions and hierarchies often do not exist in the transaction system. For example, the transaction system may store a plant ID for the individual facility that produces a product, but it may not contain information about where the plants are located and to which business units they belong. This hierarchical information is often only stored in a data warehouse or in a separate master data management system.

In some respects, business users may not care about how the data is physically stored, whether in the data warehouse or in the transaction system. A business view in the BI tool (see Chapter 3, the section "A Business View of the Data") will often hide such technical issues. However, the better that business users can define requirements in advance, the better that data modelers might be able to store data in a way that facilitates the analysis. For example, if a user wants to analyze something like staffing levels versus sales performance and these two subjects exist in different fact tables and data marts, such analysis can be a challenge with certain BI tools. If users want to routinely analyze these two different subject areas together, then the data modeler may ultimately decide to store them in one common fact table.

The Data Warehouse Technology Platform

To drive a car, you need roads, highways, and a transportation infrastructure, just as in a BI environment a number of servers and networks may be involved:

- The server(s) on which the relational database management system (RDBMS) is running
- The server(s) that run the ETL software and processes
- The web server(s) that provide the entry point into the BI environment
- The BI server(s) that process queries, dashboards, and reports (see Chapter 3)

As part of this technical infrastructure, multiple servers may mirror each other for performance, load balancing, failover support, and so on. The network between the servers and the end users (whether internal business users or external customers) are also critical pinch points in the BI environment. Much of the time, this infrastructure gets taken for granted unless there are performance or reliability issues.

For smaller businesses, targetted BI deployments, or those with scalability issues, two emerging technologies are worth noting: appliances and Software as a Service (SaaS).

Appliances

Data warehouse appliances combine the server, the database, and the data storage into one system.[3] *Business intelligence* appliances that also include BI capabilities are even newer. Leading data warehouse appliance vendors include Netezza and DATAAllegro. Hardware vendors such as IBM and HP also increasingly offer data warehouse appliances. Cognos Now! is a new business intelligence appliance. The promise of an appliance is a complete, optimized solution that delivers better performance at a lower cost of ownership than if a company were to purchase and install these individual components.

Software as a Service

In a SaaS model, BI deployment gets even simpler as customers simply subscribe to a solution. A third-party vendor hosts the technical infrastructure that customers then access via the Web. Customer relationship management (CRM) vendor salesforce.com uses a SaaS model. Business intelligence solutions available as a SaaS include Business Objects CrystalReports.com, SeaTab's Pivot Link, and LucidEra.

Best Practices for Successful Business Intelligence

The BI architecture consists of the ETL tools and processes, the data warehouse, the technical infrastructure, and the BI user tools. The operational systems provide the basic data that feed the data warehouse either in real-time or on a periodic basis. The underlying foundation of a BI architecture is complex. The implementation can either facilitate business intelligence or become so monolithic and inflexible that it becomes a technical, data wasteland. To ensure the BI architecture meets the business requirements:

- Business users should have a working understanding of the technical issues, components, and terminology that affect their requirements and ability to access data.
- IT personnel should minimize technobabble and avoid overemphasizing the technical architecture for technology's sake.

The Business
Intelligence Front-End

If the business intelligence *architecture* is like the engine of the car, then the BI *front-end tools* are like the body: sporty, sleek, fast, and where the razzle-dazzle of color, handling, and chrome finish all matter. You can have a perfectly architected data warehouse, and yet if you don't have the right BI front-end tools, you won't achieve business intelligence success. Technical capabilities matter here but so do subtle differences such as look-and-feel and ease of use. Conversely, while you can have a powerful, intuitive BI front-end, if you have not paid attention to the underlying technical components discussed in the last chapter, your initiative will fail and users will blame the tool for any underlying problems. You need to get both aspects right, even if it's only the tools that are visible.

This chapter describes the various BI front-end tools that are highly visible to business users. Chapter 12 discusses the importance of matching the tools with the right user segment and the role such tools have played in successful companies. As discussed in Chapter 1 (the section "Technology Changes Enabling BI"), vendors offer an increasing breadth of capabilities within one BI suite. Throughout this chapter, I will mention specific vendor modules to provide concrete examples. This list is not exhaustive and as vendors acquire each other and/or introduce new modules, specific names may change. For updated product names and modules, consult the BIScorecard web site.

Business Query and Reporting

Business query and reporting tools are often referred to as "ad hoc query tools." This terminology is a little misleading, as in fact the queries are not always ad hoc (as in spontaneously crafted) but rather are often fixed reports. The difference is that a business user, usually a power user, may have built the report, rather than an information technology (IT) person. The business environment changes at a rapid pace, and unable to wait weeks or months for IT to develop a new report, business users often demand the ability to create queries and reports themselves. Business query and reporting tools allow for this and are most often used for decision-making and management purposes. The business query and reporting tool is a key module to provide users with self-service information access.

In some cases, a report is truly ad hoc; it's a one-off business question that will never be posed again. Ad hoc queries may be exploratory in nature as users try to find the root cause of a problem, test a theory, or consider changing a business model. Table 3-1 lists some sample fixed reports that may lead to an ad hoc query. As users explore the data, what started as an ad hoc query or one-time question may later become a fixed report. It's important to recognize the iterative nature of business intelligence and to ensure you have flexible business intelligence tools.

Getting to the data is just one capability of business query tools; the other aspect is presenting and formatting the data in a meaningful way, loosely referred to as *reporting*. The terms "query" and "reporting" are sometimes used interchangeably because a business query and reporting tool will have both capabilities—getting to the data and formatting it to create a report.

Fixed Report	Purpose	Related Ad Hoc Query
Inventory by Product	To determine if an order can be fulfilled today by the primary warehouse	If I'm short at my main warehouse, can I supply the product from elsewhere?
Top 10 Customers By Quarter and Product	To understand which customers generate the most revenue	Who fell off this quarter's list? Are there certain products we can cross-sell?
Raw Material Receipts and Delivery Times	To determine how long it takes to acquire raw materials and which supplier can fulfill purchase orders fastest	Are there other suppliers who can respond faster?
Patients Per Hour	To understand busy periods and wait times	Do staffing levels correspond to busy times?

Table 3-1   Sample Fixed and Ad Hoc Reports

Business query and reporting tools vary widely in their formatting capabilities. The most basic of formatting capabilities allow for changing the font of column headings and making them bold and centered. Conditional formatting will, for example, display numeric values red when negative or below target and green when positive or above target. Simple report styles include displaying information in a cross-tab report, a chart, or a master-detail report with groupings and subtotals. Tools may provide a set of templates to create nicely formatted reports that use a consistent corporate look and feel. More complex formatting capabilities include the ability to present multiple charts on a page, perhaps coming from different data sources.

Examples of business query tools include BusinessObjects Web Intelligence, Cognos 8 Query Studio, and SAS Web Report Studio.

A Business View of the Data

Business query tools allow business users to access a data source via business terms without having to write any SQL. The data source could be a data warehouse as described in Chapter 2, or it might be direct access to an operational system. A key feature of a business query tool is that it has a business view or metadata layer that hides the complexity of the physical database structure from the business user by:

- Using business terminology rather than physical field names. For example, a user may select a dimension such as Customer Name rather than a cryptic field such as CUST.L33_NAME (the physical table and field name in the Relational Database Management System [RDBMS]).
- Automatically connecting related tables via joins.
- Providing metrics that may calculate and aggregate facts such as revenue, number of customers, number of orders, number of incidents, and average selling price.

Figure 3-1 shows an example of building a query with the BusinessObjects universe, one of the first products to introduce the concept of a business view.

This business view is the most important piece of your BI front-end tools and one in which the business and IT must work together to model. For integrated BI platforms, the business view is common to all the BI tool modules: business query, reporting, analysis, and dashboards. When the business view looks too much like the data warehouse

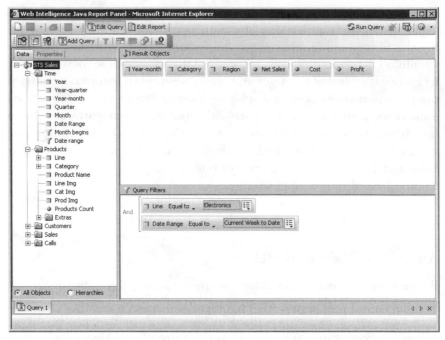

Figure 3-1   The BusinessObjects universe presents users with a business view of the data. (Reprinted with permission.)

What Is Structured Query Language (SQL)

SQL, pronounced "sequel," is a computer language used to communicate with a relational database.[1] SQL is a common language regardless if you use a database from Oracle, IBM, Microsoft, or Teradata. Querying a database with SQL can be fairly complicated. Business query tools will generate the SQL behind the scenes so business users don't need to learn how to write SQL code. While there is a common set of SQL commands, such as SELECT and SUM, each database vendor may have its own SQL extensions or dialect. RANK, for example, is a popular SQL expression among business users but it is an expression that not all relational databases support. Sometimes when trying to develop a complex business query, you may run into limitations inherent in the SQL language. For example, a query about sales for this quarter would generate simple SQL. Asking a query about which products were cross-sold to the same customers this year versus last year would require very complex SQL and may be better answered in an OLAP database.

or source system with confusing table and field names, business users are overwhelmed and can too easily build incorrect queries. Poor business view design also forces users to put too much logic and too many calculations inside individual reports and dashboards. For these reasons, in some organizations, the power users within a business unit, function, or department, are responsible for building the business view or metadata layer; in others, it is the central BI group or data warehouse team that will build and maintain the business view.

Production Reporting

Whereas business query and reporting tools allow for basic report formatting, production reporting tools have much more sophisticated formatting and design capabilities. Some people may refer to this category of tools as pixel perfect, operational, or enterprise reporting. Again, the terminology can be misleading as some business query and reporting tools can create pixel perfect reports, be embedded in operational systems, and are used across an enterprise. For lack of a better term, I will refer to this module as "production" reporting. Examples of production reporting tools include Actuate e.Report, BusinessObjects Crystal Reports, Microsoft Reporting Services, Oracle Publisher (which supersedes Oracle Reports), and Information Builders WebFOCUS.

A production reporting tool may access a transaction system directly to create a document such as an invoice, a bank statement, a check, or a list of open orders. When the reporting is not against the transaction system, it may be against an operational data store or detailed data within a data warehouse. IT usually develops these reports for the following reasons:

- The data source is an operational system in which you can't take the risk that "untrained" users may launch resource intensive and runaway queries with a business query tool.
- Reports are often accessed through and embedded within the transaction system.
- The information requirements are common to all users and departments and are static, such as for regulatory reports.

Because professional IT developers are often the users of production reporting tools, IT may also use these tools to develop management style reports, particularly when a company does not have a business query tool.

Characteristic	Production Reporting	Business Query and Reporting
Primary author	IT developer	Power user or business user
Primary purpose	Document preparation	Decision making, management
Report delivery	Paper or e-bill, embedded in application	Portal, spreadsheet, e-mail
Print quality	Pixel perfect	Presentation quality
User base	Tens of thousands	Hundreds or thousands
Data source	Operational transaction system	Data warehouse or mart, occasionally transaction system
Level of data detail	Granular	Aggregated
Scope	Operational	Tactical, strategic
Usage	Often embedded within an application	Most often BI as separate application

Table 3-2   Differences Between Production Reporting Tools and Business Query Tools (Source: BIScorecard.com)

Table 3-2 highlights some key differences between business query tools and production reporting tools. None of these differences is an absolute, except that they serve the needs to distinct user groups and in many cases, distinct applications.

Online Analytical Processing (OLAP)

Online Analytical Processing (OLAP) is a capability that focuses on *analyzing* and *exploring* data, whereas query and reporting tools put greater emphasis on accessing data for *monitoring* purposes. OLAP moves the focus from "what" is happening, to exploring "why" something is happening. To uncover the "why," users may not know precisely what information they are looking for and instead will navigate and drill within a data set to uncover particular details and patterns.

OLAP provides interactive analysis by different dimensions (i.e., geography, product, time) and different levels of detail (year, quarter, month). For many users, OLAP has become synonymous with "drill-down" and "pivot" capabilities. Many BI products, though, will now provide drill-down and pivot capabilities without a full-blown OLAP engine or OLAP database on the back-end.

As the technology and users have evolved and matured, the distinctions between OLAP and reporting have increasingly blurred.

OLAP users want highly formatted reports that are based on multidimensional data; report users immediately want to drill when they see a problem with a particular metric in a report. They don't want to be forced to launch a separate tool as they move from reporting into analysis and exploration.

The following characteristics continue to distinguish OLAP tools from business query and reporting tools:

- **Multidimensional** Users analyze numerical values from different dimensions such as product, time, and geography. A report, on the other hand, may be one-dimensional, such as list of product prices at one point in time.
- **Consistently fast** As users navigate different dimensions and levels within a dimension, OLAP means fast—the speed of thought. If a user double-clicks to drill-down from Year to Quarter, waiting 24 hours, 24 minutes, or even 24 seconds for an answer is not acceptable. Report users, of course, do not want slow reports either, but some reports take this long to run and must be scheduled.
- **Highly interactive** Drilling is one way users interact with OLAP data. *Pivoting* gives users the ability to view information from different perspectives such as by geography or by product. *Slicing* allows users to filter the data within these dimensions such as sales for New York only and then for New Jersey only, or crime statistics for Leeds only and then Manchester only. This kind of interactivity within a non-OLAP report ranges from nonexistent to only recently possible.
- **Varying levels of aggregation** To ensure predictable query times, OLAP products pre-aggregate data in different ways. Reporting, to the contrary, can be at the lowest level of detail: rather than sales by product, you might have individual line items for a particular order number.
- **Cross-dimensional calculations** With multiple dimensions come more complex calculations. In OLAP, you might want to analyze percentage contribution or market share. These analyses require subtotaling sales for a particular state and then calculating percentage contribution for the total region, country, or world. Users may analyze this percentage market share by a number of other dimensions, such as actual versus budget, this year versus last year, or for a particular group of products. These calculations often must be performed in a particular order and involve input numbers that users might never see. Detailed reports, however, often rely on simple subtotals or calculations of values that are displayed on the report itself.

In understanding OLAP requirements, it's important to distinguish between OLAP platform issues and OLAP user interface issues.

OLAP Platforms

The OLAP platform is about how the data is stored to allow for multidimensional analysis. The cube shown in Figure 2-3, in Chapter 2, represents the OLAP database. On the one hand, business users should not have to care at all about how the data is stored, replicated, and cached, and yet the OLAP architecture greatly affects what you can analyze and how. The OLAP architecture also influences what OLAP front-end you can use.

There are four primary OLAP architectures as described in Table 3-3. Relational OLAP (ROLAP) platforms store data in a relational database so data is not necessarily replicated into a separate storage for analysis. Multidimensional OLAP (MOLAP) platforms replicate data into a purpose-built storage that ensures fast analysis. Hybrid OLAP (HOLAP) uses a combination of storage techniques. Dynamic OLAP (DOLAP) will automatically generate a small multidimensional cache when users run a query.

With each OLAP architecture, there are trade-offs in performance, types of multidimensional calculations, amount of data that can be analyzed, timeliness of data updates, and interfaces through which the data can be accessed.

Architecture	Primary Difference	Vendor
ROLAP	Calculations done in a relational database, large data volumes, less predictable drill times.	Oracle BI EE, SAP Netweaver BI, MicroStrategy, Cognos 8, BusinessObjects Web Intelligence
MOLAP	Calculations performed in a server-based multidimensional database. Cubes provide write access for inputting budget data or performing what-if analysis.	Oracle's Hyperion Essbase, Microsoft Analysis Services, TM1, SAS OLAP, Cognos PowerCubes
HOLAP	Aggregations in a cache but with seamless drill-through to relational.	Microsoft Analysis Services, SAS OLAP, Oracle's Hyperion Essbase
DOLAP	Mini cache is built at query run time.	BusinessObjects Web Intelligence, Oracle's Hyperion Interactive Reporting (formerly Brio)

Table 3-3   OLAP Architectures

Historically, many OLAP products used a MOLAP storage, which led to inflexible cube databases, management of more replicated data, and limitations on the data volumes and level of detail that can be analyzed. All of this has sometimes scared IT away from OLAP.

> I would argue that every BI deployment needs an OLAP component; not only is it necessary to facilitate analysis, but also it can significantly reduce the number of reports either IT developers or business users have to create.

With OLAP, a report is just a starting view, say, Sales for 2007 by Country—a summarized starting point. As users click, drill, and pivot, the end result might be Sales, Unit Price, Volume for one quarter, for two products, in a particular city—a detailed, focused end-point. In a strictly relational reporting world, the starting view and end result would be two entirely separate reports, with dozens of iterations in between.

OLAP Viewers

Microsoft Excel is one of the most popular interfaces to OLAP data. In fact, for three of the leading OLAP products (Oracle's Hyperion Essbase, Microsoft Analysis Services, SAP Business Explorer), the spreadsheet was initially the *only* interface. Users would open a spreadsheet and could immediately begin drilling within cells and Excel Pivot Tables to retrieve and explorer their data.

Today, Excel continues to be an important OLAP interface, but in addition, users can explore data via OLAP viewers. These OLAP viewers may be web-based (whereas Excel is desktop-based) and will have advanced charting and navigation capabilities. In addition, business query tools and production reporting tools may also be able to

---

What Are Multidimensional Expressions (MDX)?

MDX is a query language similar to SQL but used to manipulate data within an OLAP database. Microsoft created MDX as a language to work with its original OLAP server, now referred to as SQL Server Analysis Services. As MDX gained industry acceptance, a number of other OLAP databases added support for MDX such that today OLAP viewers will generate MDX to access and analyze data in a number of different OLAP databases.

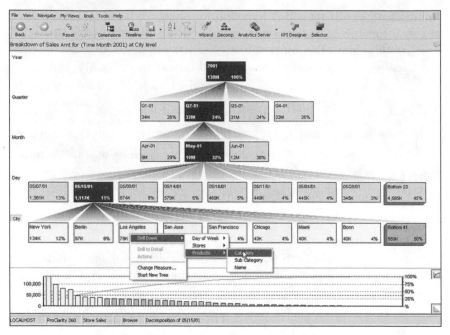

Figure 3-2   Microsoft ProClarity's decomposition tree helps users navigate multidimensional data. (Reprinted with permission.)

access OLAP data sources and allow users to drill around with a report. Figure 3-2 shows an example of a decomposition tree via Microsoft ProClarity, a relatively unique way of visually navigating through hierarchical information.

Just as business query and reporting tools allow users to retrieve data from relational databases without knowing SQL, OLAP viewers allow users to access data in an OLAP database without knowing multidimensional expressions (MDX). Many of the leading BI suite vendors offer OLAP viewers to third-party OLAP data sources, sometimes via the business query and reporting tool, or via a production reporting tool, or via a special OLAP viewer. Examples of specialty OLAP viewers include Microsoft ProClarity (acquired by Microsoft in 2006) and Panorama NovaView.

Microsoft Office

It's often said that Microsoft Excel is unofficially the leading BI tool. Business intelligence teams have tried to ignore it and sometimes disable it, because it can wreak havoc on the one thing a data warehouse is supposed to provide: a single version of truth. Yet users are passionate about spreadsheet integration, and it is the preferred interface for power users. The issue for BI teams and businesses, then, is how to facilitate the integration while managing its use. In the past, Excel "integration" was often limited to a one-time export of data from the BI tool to a disconnected spreadsheet. More recently, BI vendors have taken new approaches to spreadsheet integration in ways that allow Excel and the BI environment to work better together, perhaps even extending BI's reach. Duet, a product jointly developed by SAP and Microsoft, for example, uses the familiar Office interface for accessing reports from the SAP transaction system and from the data warehouse. The theory is that anyone comfortable with e-mail can access and interact with a report. This is an example of how Office integration has moved beyond just the Excel spreadsheet to include other Microsoft Office applications such as PowerPoint, Word, and Outlook. In addition to solutions from BI suite vendors, XLCubed is a niche BI vendor and product that uses an Excel add-in as a way of accessing data in Microsoft Analysis Services and TM1 OLAP.

Dashboards

Stephen Few, president of Perceptual Edge and a visualization expert, provides the best definition of a dashboard:

> A dashboard is a visual display of the most important information needed to achieve one or more objectives; consolidated and arranged on a single screen so the information can be monitored at a glance.[2]

BI dashboards are similar to car dashboards—they provide multiple indicators or reports in a highly visual way. A dashboard may be comprised of:

- A map that color-codes where sales are performing well or poorly
- A trend line that tracks stock outs
- A cross tab of top-selling products
- A key performance indicator with an arrow to show if sales are according to plan

Figure 3-3 shows an example of a customer support dashboard created with MicroStrategy Enterprise Dashboard. The dashboard includes advanced visualization such as spark lines (the open cases trend) and a bullet graph (closed cases versus target) to pack more information in a smaller display. (Advanced visualization is discussed further in Chapter 14.)

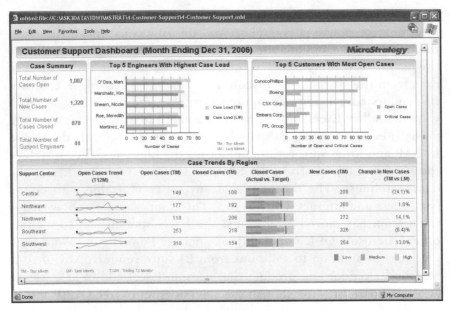

Figure 3-3   MicroStrategy Enterprise Dashboards allows users to view multiple indicators at a glance. (Reprinted with permission.)

Ideally, users want to assemble their own dashboards with the information relevant to their job. Not all tools allow this, though, and may force IT to build dashboards in advance.

A key characteristic of dashboards is that they present information from multiple data sources. Exactly how they do this and what constraints there are in the accessibility and number of data sources vary widely from product to product.

The concept of dashboards is nothing new. Early Executive Information Systems (EIS) of the late 1980s tried to deliver similar capabilities. What has changed is the technology. EISs were often custom-coded, inflexible dashboards based on quarterly data. New dashboards are user-built, flexible, and sometimes updated in real time. As shown in Figure 3-3, they also increasingly leverage advanced visualization capabilities that facilitate greater insights and conveying more information in less space. If your company had an early EIS failure, don't let that dissuade you from delivering dashboards as part of your total BI solution.

Scorecards

The terms "dashboards" and "scorecards" are often used interchangeably, although they are indeed different things. A major difference between them is that a *scorecard* focuses on a given metric and compares it to a

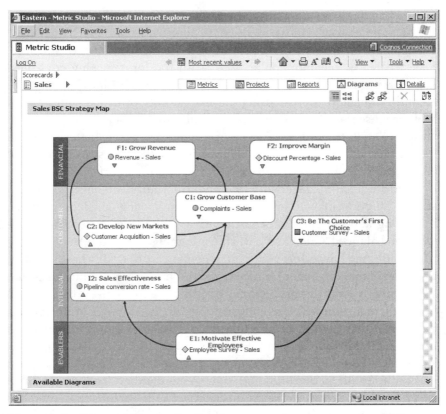

Figure 3-4   Cognos 8 Metrics Studio allows executives to manage key performance indicators. (Reprinted with permission.)

forecast or target, whereas a *dashboard* will present multiple numbers in different ways. Some dashboards may additionally display metrics and targets with visual traffic lighting to show the performance of that metric, but you should not assume that all dashboard tools support this capability.

Strategic scorecards contain metrics from the four key areas that drive the success of a business (people, customers, financial, operations) and will include strategy maps to show how the metrics relate to one another. Such scorecard products are often certified by the Balanced Scorecard Collaborative. Figure 3-4 shows an example of a strategy map created with Cognos 8 Metrics Studio.

Although there are a number of powerful scorecard products on the market, the biggest challenge in deploying scorecards is in getting the business to agree on common objectives, drivers, targets, and accountability. Configuring the software requires significantly less effort.

Performance Management

Performance management and business intelligence historically have been treated as separate applications, with the former being controlled primarily by finance and the latter by IT or individual business units. More recently, a single vendor will offer both BI and performance management tools because the information needs and purposes of both sets of tools are closely related. In rudimentary deployments, BI provides better access to data. In more focused initiatives, BI provides better access to data *so that an individual or an entire company can improve their performance.*

Performance management tools help optimize, manage, and measure that performance by providing the following key components: budgeting and planning capabilities, financial consolidation, and strategic or balanced scorecards. Business intelligence often provides the underpinnings for performance management in that (1) these applications need access to data for planning and measurement purposes and (2) what may start out as a simple BI initiative for "better data access" becomes more purpose driven when put in the context of optimizing performance according to the goals of the business. Balancing the often diverse priorities of different business units and users is also easier when these requirements are evaluated against those goals.

Craig Schiff, a performance management expert and president of BPM Partners, describes the connection between performance management and BI as follows:

> Performance management is really about the business processes (supported by technology) that enable a business to set strategic goals and measure how successfully it is executing on those goals and objectives. The technology that supports these processes includes BPM packaged applications such as budgeting, planning and consolidation, as well as BI tools such as extract, transform and load (ETL), report and query, and OLAP multidimensional cubes. BI is an essential part of BPM; but, while BPM is helping accelerate adoption of BI, BI can exist without BPM.[3]

While I have not seen indication that performance management has helped accelerate BI adoption or vice versa, it is clear that the two are interrelated. 2007 has seen a number of vendor acquisitions as the BI and performance management markets converge.

NOTE   While performance management may have its roots in finance, it is by no means limited to financial plans. Performance management may relate to workforce planning, supply chain optimization, capacity planning, and so on.

Alphabet Soup: BPM, CPM, EPM, PM

Here come those acronyms again! Industry analysts, media, and vendors will refer to performance management with any number of acronyms: business performance management (BPM), corporate performance management (CPM), enterprise performance management (EPM), and performance management (PM). They all refer to the same things. The one major point of confusion is when "BPM" is used to refer to business *process* management, a completely different field. It is a shame that this acronym has become confusing because the BPM Standards Group, whose charter was to define standards and concepts pertaining to *performance* management, uses it as its name.

Planning

Many companies have manual planning processes compiled through thousands of disconnected spreadsheets. Planning tools help automate and control the process. Part of the planning process is reviewing historical actuals for a basis of comparison. These actuals most likely come from the data warehouse or a data mart (either OLAP or relational). An initial plan may be based on business rules such as percentage change from one year to another. Plans may be prepared either "bottom up," in which individual managers provide their plans to roll into a company-wide plan, or they may be "top down," in which plans are made at the highest level and individual units provide details on how that plan can be achieved.

Once a plan has been finalized, managers want to monitor adherence to and progress toward the plan. Such monitoring can be part of a dashboard or a scorecard.

Financial Consolidation

As individual business units aggregate into a total company, financial consolidation tools help ensure things such as intercompany eliminations, currency conversion, and Sarbanes-Oxley compliance. While all OLAP data sources will have multiple dimensions and multiple hierarchies, a financial consolidation tool must have a chart of accounts (specific dimension that defines for example, how assets such as cash, inventory, and accounts receivable aggregate on a balance sheet). Financial consolidation may be provided by the ERP system or by a dedicated tool.

Financial consolidation tools differ from other aspects of a performance management or BI system in that their primary purpose is to produce the financial reports of a company, whereas much of the other information is for management reporting and analysis.

Analytic Applications

Henry Morris of International Data Corporation (IDC) first coined the term *analytic application* in 1997.[4] According to IDC, for software to be considered an analytic application, it must have the following characteristics:

- Function independently of the transaction or source systems.
- Extract, transform, and integrate data from multiple sources and allow for time-based analysis.
- Automate a group of tasks related to optimizing particular business processes.

Business query tools, OLAP, and dashboards may all be components of an analytic application, but it is this last bullet item that most sets an analytic application apart from other BI modules.

There are different types of analytic applications including customer, financial, supply chain, production, and human resources applications. You can either buy or build an analytic application. When you "buy" an analytic application, you buy a range of prebuilt functionality such as the ETL routines, the physical data model, the OLAP database model, and prebuilt reports with functional metrics. When you "build" an analytic application, you determine how and whether to calculate "average sale per store visit" and in which reports you want this metric to appear. With a prebuilt analytic application, this and other metrics are provided for you. With "build" analytic applications, the development environment may provide templates and engines that allow you to assemble applications. A BI platform vendor may provide analytic applications, and numerous niche vendors also provide analytic applications for specific industries or functional areas.

Emerging BI Modules

The modules discussed in this chapter have relatively wide usage and product maturity. Business query and reporting tools, production reporting, and OLAP have evolved over nearly two decades. Dashboard and scorecard software are more recent, with more limited usage, but are mature software products. There are also some modules that are still considered niche solutions or emerging technologies. These include predictive analytics, BI search, advanced visualization, mash-ups, and rich Internet applications, to name a few. Successful BI survey results on the importance of these modules and ways in which case study companies are leveraging them are discussed in Chapter 14.

Best Practices for Successful Business Intelligence

The BI front-end consists of the tools and interfaces that business people use to access the data and monitor trends. These tools include business query and reporting, production reporting, OLAP, Excel, dashboards, and scorecards. Performance management tools are used in conjunction with BI tools and the BI architecture to improve planning, produce financial reports, and measure performance against the objectives and goals of the company. Because the BI tools provide the face for the business intelligence architecture and processes, it's easy for the tool to get an inordinate amount of attention. They are, however, only one aspect of a business intelligence solution, albeit an important one. As you work to exploit the full value of business intelligence:

- Never underestimate the importance of these tools in engaging users to leverage data for competitive advantage.
- Understand that the business tools must work in conjunction with the underlying technical architecture; an intuitive tool is only as reliable and useful as the data that it accesses.
- Ensure the business and IT jointly develop a business-focused metadata layer or business view upon which a number of the front-end tools rely.
- Consider the distinct capabilities of the different tool segments and offer the appropriate tool to the appropriate user group (discussed more in Chapter 12).
- Stay abreast of emerging technologies that will provide the best user interface for as-yet underserved BI users.

Chapter 4

Measures of Success

There is not a clear yardstick for *successful* business intelligence. One deployment deemed a success may be viewed a failure by another person, and vice versa. While the industry would like to give a single, objective measure—such as return on investment (ROI)—the reality is that ROI is derived from imprecise inputs upon which few stakeholders agree. Interestingly, the most successful business intelligence deployments don't use ROI as a measure of success. Instead, there are multiple measures of success, with varying degree of importance and accuracy.

> "Success is measured by end user perception. They must participate actively and have a sense of ownership to the project."
> —Kelli McIntosh, integration specialist, BDP International

Success and Business Impact

In the Successful BI survey, I asked respondents to rate their BI deployment as either very successful, moderately successful, or mostly a failure. As Figure 4-1 shows, the majority (68%) rated their deployments in the middle of the road as *moderately* successful. Only 24% considered their deployments as *very* successful. The good news is that only a very small percentage (8%) rated their deployment as mostly a failure. Some vendors (usually newer entrants), consultants, and media outlets claim the BI failure rate is significantly higher, even 50%.[1] They have a built-in incentive to make you think that BI has been a disaster so that you will buy more tools and services to fix these failures.

Some cynics would argue that only the people relatively happy with their BI deployment responded to the survey, so failures might theoretically be underrepresented. Perhaps. However, some believe that dissatisfied

53

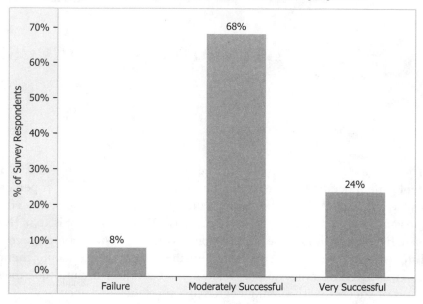

Figure 4-1   Assessment of BI success or failure

people are more likely to complain than those who are satisfied. As well, this general assessment of the BI industry also mirrored responses from a 2006 BIScorecard/*Intelligent Enterprise* survey.[2] Regardless, mediocrity is not something to strive for, and while the failure rate is not catastrophic, the percentage of very successful deployments could and should be significantly higher.

One measure of BI success is how much business intelligence contributes to a company's performance, and as shown later in Figure 4-4, this is the preferred measure of BI success. Here, the results are slightly better, as shown in Figure 4-2. Thirty-two percent of respondents said their BI solution contributes *significantly* to company performance. That this is 8% higher than those who describe their solution as "very successful" shows an interesting dichotomy. Table 4-1 shows the correlations between how a respondent rates their BI deployment and the perceived business impact.

Business performance can be evaluated based on a number of different aspects. Which aspects are most important depends on the specific industry and whether you are a publicly held company, nonprofit, or government agency. Revenue, profitability, cost-to-serve, growth, efficiencies,

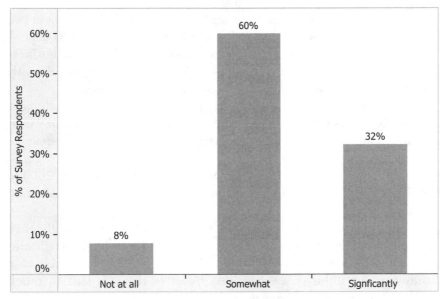

How Much Has BI Contributed to Your Company's Performance?

Figure 4-2   Degree to which BI contributes to company performance

and stock price are all ways to measure business performance. The survey question did not specify which aspect of business performance was most impacted by business intelligence.

	Significantly Contributes to Company Performance	Somewhat Contributes to Company Performance	Does Not Contribute at All	Successful BI Deployment Totals
Very successful BI deployment	18%	6%	0%	**24%**
Moderately successful	14%	50%	4%	**68%**
Mostly a failure	0%	4%	4%	**8%**
Contribution to company performance totals	**32%**	**60%**	**8%**	**100%**

Table 4-1   Relationship Between Successful BI Deployment and Contribution to Company Performance

Why the Disconnect?

In analyzing the survey results, my initial expectation was that these two questions would be much more tightly correlated—that if your BI deployment were wildly successful, it would contribute significantly to business performance. Or conversely, if the BI solution is contributing significantly to the business, it would of course be viewed as very successful.

The disconnect seems to be from the knowledge of how much more is possible versus what little has been achieved. Norway Post, for example, has achieved significant business value from its BI and performance management initiatives: revenues increased 73% from 2000 to 2006, profitability went from −655 million NOK (Norwegian krone) in 2000 to +853 million NOK in 2006, while employee and customer satisfaction improved (see Figure 4-3).[3]

Dag Vidar Olsen, manager of Norway Post's Business Intelligence Competency Center, is hesitant to describe their business intelligence deployment as successful, and in fact, won't submit their case study for any industry awards (yet) because there is still so much to do.[4] "We haven't solved every area of the business. In finance, it's been very successful. The production and operational reporting is excellent, yet we lack these capabilities in human resources and marketing."

While Norway Post's improvement in company performance has been exceedingly positive, Olsen is hesitant to attribute this to business intelligence. "Business intelligence is of course an enabler. Could we have done this without BI? It would have taken a longer time, more hard work, and we wouldn't have had the truth of where we stand. BI managed to show each manager their status *right now.* It changed the culture to one

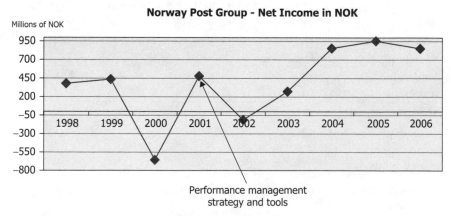

Figure 4-3   Norway Post's net income turnaround (Source: Annual Reports)

About Norway Post

Norway Post is one of the country's biggest employers, with over 23,000 employees and revenues of 23 billion NOK (~$3.79 billion). The company privatized in 2002 but continues to be government owned. With privatization, Norway Post converted into a stock company and has implemented all the same steering and reporting standards as a publicly held stock company. It provides traditional mail and parcel delivery throughout the Nordic region along with express delivery, banking services, logistics, and electronic services. To provide some perspective, the distance from northern Norway to the southern part is similar in distance from New York City to Miami, Florida, in the United States, and yet 87% of the letters are delivered within one day. With changing laws of the European Union and changing consumer requirements, Norway Post's business model faces competitive and market pressures. Norway Post's vision is "to become the world's most future-oriented post and logistics group."

About BI at Norway Post

- **Start of BI efforts:** 1995, refocused in 2001
- **Executive level sponsors:** CFO and CIO
- **Business Intelligence Competency Center (BICC):** Yes, new in 2007
- **Number of users:** 2,880 or 15% of all employees
- **Number of source systems feeding the data warehouse:** 7 custom general ledger systems
- **ETL/EIM tools:** SAS Data Integration and custom extracts
- **Data warehouse platform:** SAS SPD
- **Data warehouse size:** 4TB, with portions updated 9 times throughout the day
- **BI tools:** Hyperion System 9, SAS BI and SAS Enterprise Guide

of accountability: you have poor profitability—what are you going to do about that?"

Olsen mirrors an interesting perceptual difference of business intelligence's impact on the business: information technology (IT) professionals view the impact as being lower than that of how the business professionals view the impact. The percentage of business users seeing the business impact as significant is 15% higher than the percentage of IT professionals saying the impact on company performance has been significant. This difference in perception was echoed by a number of people from successful BI case studies. A small percentage of survey respondents (6%) consider the BI deployment as being very successful yet as not having significant business impact. In this regard, it seems that it is possible to build a perfectly architected BI solution that has no impact on the business or on the way users leverage information.

How to Measure Success

There are a number of ways to measure the success of your BI deployment, some qualitative and some more quantitative and objective. Figure 4-4 illustrates the various measures of success (and failure), with improved business performance and better access to data being the most frequently cited forms of measurement. The challenge here is that qualitative benefits such as "better access to data" are rarely a way of garnering executive level support and funding for BI investments.

While measures such as ROI, cost savings, and number or percentage of active users are more objective measures, they appear to be used less frequently as a measure of successful BI.

Measures of BI Success or Failure

Measure	Percentage
Improved business performance	70%
Better access to data	68%
Support of key stakeholders	53%
User perception that it is mission critical	50%
Return on investment	43%
Percentage of active users	31%
Cost savings	31%
Number of defined users	17%

Figure 4-4   BI success is measured more by a perception of improved business performance and qualitative measures than by quantitative measures.

Return on Investment

The projected ROI is often required to fund a BI project, but it is a measure that few companies calculate once BI capabilities have been provided or enhanced. One reason companies rarely calculate this is that while it is fairly easy to determine the cost or investment portion of a BI implementation, it is not easy to determine the return, a common challenge for many IT investments.

As Norway Post demonstrated, it's debatable how much of a revenue increase or improvement can be attributed to BI versus other factors. Identifying cost savings is easier when you eliminate specific reporting systems or reduce head count. However, even with cost savings, head count may not be reduced, but instead held constant while the business grows. In other words, there has been cost *avoidance* by providing a BI solution. How much cost has been avoided is yet another debatable number, ultimately making ROI a precise number derived from imprecise inputs.

There have been several industry studies to determine the average ROI for BI projects. International Data Corporation (IDC) first published a study on the ROI for data warehouses in 1996. IDC determined the average 3-year ROI was 401% for the 62 projects measured. The Data Warehousing Institute (TDWI) published a study in 2000 showing an ROI of 300%. While 47 companies participated in the study, less than a quarter measured ROI. In December 2002, IDC released another ROI study focusing on the value of business analytics, the applications that reside on top of a data warehouse. The average ROI was 431%, and the median was 112%, with less than a year payback period.[5] Some companies had returns of more than 2000%, and IDC reported that the most successful projects were when the business analytics implementation corresponded with business process improvements.

As an example, Continental Airlines has invested $30 million in real-time data warehousing.[6] Based on over $500 million in cost savings and revenue improvement, this is an ROI of over 1000%. Yet Data Warehouse Manager Anne Marie Reynolds says they really don't measure their BI success according to ROI. "When we need to get an upgrade, it's helpful to identify one key success but we don't estimate the total ROI. It's hard to get people to commit to the numbers. If a certain project has measurable ROI, we will document that. But now BI is just the cost of doing business and part of the infrastructure. A better measure of success is in the growth in the number of uses for the data and the number of users who are successful in getting their business questions answered."[7]

Reynolds' comments highlight an important challenge with business intelligence: often, an organization's BI efforts will stall, because they can't articulate the expected ROI. When something has become the "cost of doing business," then trying to document costs savings, efficiencies gained, and revenue contribution can be painful, if not impossible. Imagine if someone asked you to provide the ROI for having an office telephone! Documenting the ROI of a business intelligence project is meant to ensure the project will provide measurable business value. If you are struggling to estimate the ROI, you are probably trying to quantify too precisely imprecise benefits, or you haven't given enough thought for how business intelligence will support your company's key business drivers.

Calculating ROI

Despite the limitations of using ROI as a measure of success, it is a number that provides a basis for comparison to other BI implementations and IT initiatives. It also is a measure well understood by business users who have to buy into the value of business intelligence. In this respect,

---

About Continental Airlines

Continental Airlines is the world's fifth-largest airline, with 3,100 daily departures throughout the Americas, Europe, and Asia. Having once had one of the poorest reputations in the industry in the early 1990s, the airline now has one of the best and is one of the few that have avoided bankruptcy following the September 11th terrorist attacks. *Fortune* magazine has repeatedly named Continental the number one Most Admired Global Airline on its list of Most Admired Global Companies.

About BI at Continental

- **Start of BI efforts:** 1998
- **Executive level sponsor:** CIO
- **Business Intelligence Competency Center:** Yes, since 1998
- **Number of BI users:** 1,400 data warehouse users counted with an estimated additional 24,000 through custom BI applications, or 57% of employees
- **Number of source systems used for BI:** 27
- **ETL/EIM tools:** Custom
- **Data warehouse platform:** Teradata
- **Data warehouse size:** 8TB, with portions updated in real time
- **Number of subject areas:** 24
- **BI tools:** Hyperion, SPSS, custom applications

even "guesstimating" your actual ROI can be helpful for internal promotion purposes. It's also interesting to note that while most survey respondents used multiple measures of success, a higher percentage of companies who said their BI had a significant impact on business performance also used ROI as a measure. This in no way suggests *cause*, but it might be an indication of the degree to which a company prioritizes technology investments and in which a measurable benefit must be demonstrated.

> Use ROI as an objective measure of success, even if it's only a back-of-the-envelope calculation and not all stakeholders agree on the cost savings and revenue contribution from business intelligence.

The basic formula for calculating ROI over a 3-year period is

$$ROI = [(NPV\ Cost\ Reduction + Revenue\ Contribution)/Initial\ Investment] \times 100$$

Net present value (NPV) considers the time value of money. In simplistic terms, if you have $1 million to deposit in a bank today, next year, assuming 5% interest, it would be worth $1,050,000. The formula to calculate NPV of a 3-year cost or revenue is

$$NPV = F/(1 + r) + F/(1 + r)^2 + F/(1 + r)^3$$

F is the future cash flow from the cost reductions and revenue contributions. R is the discount rate for your company. Five percent may be the interest a bank is willing to pay, but companies will have a different rate that takes into account the expected return for other investments and opportunity costs from investing in business intelligence versus other capital projects. In estimating the revenue improvement, take the amount revenue has actually increased and then assign a percentage of that for which BI has been a key enabler.

Number of Users

While business impact may be in the eye of the beholder, you would think that the number of BI users is a much more objective measure of success. Yet here too, there is room for debate and fudging of definitions. In the "Successful BI Peer Networking Session" (see the Chapter 1 section on research), someone asked "if a user receives a print out or static PDF (Adobe Portable Document Format) from a BI tool, should they be counted as a BI user?" This is a really tricky question. Some vendors would count this person as a user who would have to pay for a BI recipient license. If you use the concept I put forth in Chapter 1, that business intelligence is "a set of technologies and processes that allow people of all levels of an organization to access, interact with, and analyze data…and is about creativity, culture, and whether people view information as a critical asset," then technically, yes, that person should be counted as a user.

I would, however, like you to reach a little higher when you think of who is a BI user, and as confirmed in the peer networking, survey, and case study interviews, most people do not count static recipients as BI users. Recipients of *static* information cannot readily interact with and analyze the data. They may not have a live connection to the BI system to control either what information they receive or when. So while such recipients may benefit from BI, I would not count them as BI users.

BI Users as a Percentage of Employees

So let's assume there is direct access to the BI system or to the data warehouse. Here too, companies may undercount users based on different definitions and ways in which BI is used. When I discussed number of users with Continental Airlines, for example, they initially told me they had 1400 data warehouse users.[8] With over 44,000 employees, that is less than 3% of a BI user base, well behind the industry average. At first blush, it didn't sound like BI had permeated all ranks at Continental. In fact, it has, but it depends on what you count.

The 1400 users are only users who have a direct logon to the data warehouse. If a user hits the data warehouse through an application, that user is not counted in the 1400. As an example, within the operations control centers at each airport, dispatchers view daily on-time performance and flight status for all planes. These various performance indicators are projected on a large wall within the center for all the dispatchers to see. While the information is coming from the data warehouse, because the display is from a custom application, the data warehouse team does not count these dispatchers as among the 1400 users. As well, whenever a passenger checks in at the airport, gate agents immediately see a color-coded display to indicate the OnePass (Continental's frequent flyer program) elite level of the passenger.[9] The gate agents access the data warehouse through a custom application, so they also are not counted as BI users because the data warehouse only sees the application as one user. Indeed, BI usage is high throughout Continental Airlines and yet it is not a way they measure BI success and is a metric that is undercounted.

Despite the discrepancies in what to count, there is a major difference between the case studies in this book and the industry as a whole, and that is in the degree of BI penetration. In a survey I coauthored for TDWI in 2005, the estimated percentage of *potential users* with a BI license was 41% and the percentage of users who routinely logged into the BI application was only 18%.[10] The problem with the way we posed this survey question is that we left the definition for the denominator or the "potential" BI users up to the survey respondent. Many in the BI industry still consider information workers as the only potential BI users, and yet, case after case in this book shows that information workers are only a portion of the total BI potential.

In the Successful BI survey, then, I specifically asked about the percentage of total *employees* (versus potential BI users) that have access to a BI tool; the average is 25%. As the following chart illustrates, companies who describe their BI deployment as very successful have an 8% higher percentage of BI users than those of moderate success. Indicating that the industry has not yet fully realized how wide a net BI can cast, when asked if the BI deployment were wildly successful and budget were not an issue, what percentage of employees *should* have access to a BI tool, respondents said they thought only 53% to 55% of employees *should* have access to a BI tool.

Percentage of Employees Who Use BI

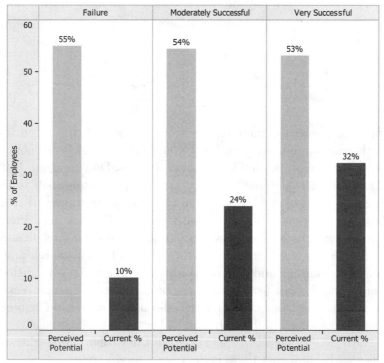

> To be successful with business intelligence, you need to be thinking about deploying BI to a 100% of your employees as well as beyond organizational boundaries to customers and suppliers.

Business intelligence as a set of technologies and processes is still relatively young at less than 20 years old. A number of technical innovations as well as improving data literacy and technical proficiencies in the workforce will allow BI penetration to be 100% of employees. Think about it: does everyone in your company have a cell phone? Did they 20 years ago? And yet, portable phones (more the size of briefcases), existed in the late 1980s. Such "portable" phones had little adoption due to usability and cost reasons. Nowadays a cell phone is a must-have business tool; it is a purchase that does not have to be justified with ROI. It is considered a required item that is part of the "cost of doing business." BI eventually will be viewed in the same way. If you think this sounds too technocratic or too futuristic, consider how absurd these quotes appear with the clarity of hindsight:

"There's no reason anyone would want a computer in their home."
—Ken Olson, founder of Digital Equipment Corporation (DEC), 1977

"I think there is a world market for maybe 5 computers."
—Thomas Watson, chairman of IBM, 1943[11]

Some argue that certain users will never need BI. Indeed, this may be partly true, but currently we just haven't made BI relevant enough for all users, particularly beyond information workers. Don't imagine 100% of employees using traditional business query and reporting tools. Instead, picture all employees having access to information to support their daily decisions and actions, with tools that work in ways they need them to. For some users, that's a business query tool, for others it's a spreadsheet, and for others it's a widget of information. When BI is made relevant and accessible to frontline and field workers as well as externally to customers and suppliers, then BI usage will reach beyond 100% of employees. The concept and importance of relevance is discussed further in Chapter 9.

No matter what you think the total BI potential is—100% of employees or only 55% of employees as shown in the earlier chart—the survey results clearly show that there is huge untapped potential.

BI for Everyone or for Only Certain User Segments?

When analyzing the percentage of BI users according to different user segments, the information workers or business and financial analysts have the highest penetration at 52% of the total as shown in Figure 4-5. Executives and managers are the next highest segments.

The successful BI case study companies have a greater penetration rate across almost all these user segments, and in particular, for professional workers. The Dow Chemical Company has approximately 12,000 worldwide internal BI users, which accounts for 83% of its professional workers.[12] Corporate Express has 3000 U.S.-based BI users, which accounts for almost 100% of its professional workforce. This is a drastic improvement over its original user base of 500 just 3 years ago.

External users such as customers and suppliers show the lowest deployment rates at 11% and 8% respectively. There are some technical issues when BI reaches beyond company boundaries, but some of the larger barriers are organizational and a matter of being aware of the benefits.

In working with a manufacturing company, it was critical for them to include information from distributors in their BI platform so they could better see how product was selling in various retail outlets. The data

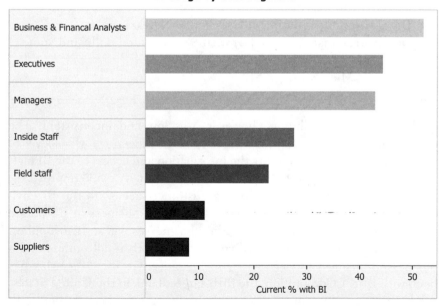

BI Usage by User Segment

Figure 4-5   Of the percentage of total employees by user segment, information workers show the highest BI penetration.

About Corporate Express

Corporate Express US, Inc., a subsidiary of Corporate Express NV (NYSE: CXP) is one of the world's largest business-to-business suppliers of office and computer products and services, with 2006 sales of approximately $4.9 billion in North America. The company operates in more than 17 countries and is reportedly the only business-to-business (B2B) office products company with a true one-company global capability. It delivers an average of $16 million in office and computer products every business day in North America, servicing approximately 90% of the Fortune 500 companies. In addition to commercial brands, Corporate Express also has its own private label of office products, a line of business that has grown rapidly in the last three years, empowered by business intelligence.

About BI at Corporate Express

- **Start of BI efforts:** Initially 2000, revamped in 2004
- **Executive level sponsor:** CFO
- **Business Intelligence Competency Center:** Yes
- **Number of BI users:** 3,000 internal or 34% of employees, plus 10,000 customers
- **Number of source systems used for BI:** 7
- **ETL/EIM tools:** Ab Initio
- **Data warehouse platform:** Oracle and Netezza
- **Data warehouse size:** 10TB, with 98% updated daily and some updates every 10 minutes
- **BI tools:** MicroStrategy, SPSS

quality from the distributors, however, was low and inconsistent. The distributors could not readily see this and had no incentive whatsoever to improve it. By giving distributors the information and access to the BI platform, they also derived value from the data and quality could improve.

For Corporate Express, providing customers access to the BI environment has become a necessary part of doing business.[13] Corporate Express focuses exclusively on providing businesses with office supplies, whereas competitors such as OfficeMax have both retail outlets and a business-to-business model. A recent customer win for OfficeMax has been with BB&T Corporation, the fifth-largest bank in the United States. A key reason for this win is OfficeMax's ability to provide customers with online reporting to better manage the procurement process and the cost of office supplies.[14] Corporate Express expects its new customer reporting and analysis capabilities to be a significant competitive differentiator in terms of breadth of data, speed of analysis, and level of detail. The solution will be provided to Corporate Express' top 1000 customers and over 10,000 external users at those customers.

Percentage of Active Users

I was pleasantly surprised by the survey results that the percentage of *active* users is a more often cited measure of success than the number of *defined* users. The reason for my surprise has nothing to do with this measure's importance, but rather, how difficult it is to determine. Then again, fewer than a third of companies do measure this!

Historically, business intelligence tools have been implemented primarily on a departmental basis, where greater emphasis is on using the BI platform and less on monitoring the system. As deployments scale to the enterprise and become more mission critical, monitoring system performance and usage is key to scaling to increased analytic requirements and numbers of users. The ability to monitor activity for the entire BI platform (from data warehouse to BI front-end tools—see Figure 2-3 in Chapter 2) has been somewhat lacking in the industry. Specific solutions from vendors such as Teleran and AppFluent provide these capabilities, but these are tools that an individual business unit department would rarely purchase. For BI tool vendors, MicroStrategy, BusinessObjects, and Information Builders are examples of a few that have a longer history of providing built-in capabilities to determine usage.

User activeness is another measure of success that Corporate Express monitors on a regular basis. Three years ago, the percentage of users who used BI on a daily basis was less than 10% of the registered BI users. Daily usage has since grown 14-fold and is about 23% of the 3000 registered users.[15]

Other Measures of Success

Other ways to measure the success of your BI initiative include the following:

- **Number of business intelligence applications** This includes dashboards, business views, and custom applications such as BI content embedded in an operational system.

- **Number of new requests**   An interesting theme among case studies in this book is that the demand for new applications, data sources, enhancements, and so on, significantly outpaces the BI team's ability to deliver the improvements. Business users want more, faster, as they are constantly coming up with new ways to exploit their BI capabilities. This is not the same measure as a "report backlog." Instead, it is a measure of requests that the BI team should fulfill rather than requests for capabilities business users should be able to do themselves.
- **Number of standard and ad hoc reports**   While this is an interesting number, be careful, as more is not always better. If one standard report with greater interactivity and better prompting can serve the needs of 100s of users (versus having 100 different reports for 100 users), then a single report is better. It is extremely difficult if not impossible to assess the number of truly useful versus redundant reports. Having a lower number of reports that are more useful provides a lower cost of ownership and an easier ability for information consumers to know where to find relevant information. Usage monitoring capabilities within a BI solution allow system administrators to track how often particular reports are accessed.
- **Elimination of *independent* spreadsheets**   "Independent" is a key word here as delivering BI via spreadsheets may be an enabler to user adoption, as long as a live link is maintained back to the BI platform.
- **Increased employee satisfaction**   This is achieved by empowering employees to get the information they need to do their jobs well.
- **Increased customer service**   This has an impact on revenues, so here too, assign a percentage for how much BI contributed to improved customer service.
- **Time reduced in any process**   BI can help reduce the time to complete a number of processes whether product time to market, order fulfillment, application approval, and so on.

Best Practices for Successful Business Intelligence

The success of a BI deployment can be measured by both intangible criteria such as better access to data and by objective criteria such as revenue improvement, number of users, and return on investment. The impact on the business performance should be the ultimate criteria of BI success, keeping in mind that how that performance is measured depends on the specific industry and whether you are a publicly held company, nonprofit, or government agency. In evaluating the success of your business intelligence deployment:

- Use ROI as an objective measure of success, even if this is only calculated on the back of an envelope.
- Don't underestimate the value of intangible, nonquantifiable benefits such as better access to data and positive user perception. Do try to assign a dollar value to these softer benefits and state the value in terms of how they align with the strategic goals of the business.
- Use multiple measures of success.
- When initially embarking on your project, agree to and build into the program or project plan the measures of success. Ensure that the sponsors, stakeholders, and project team all agree to the measures.

Chapter 5

The LOFT Effect

As I analyzed trends from the successful BI companies, a consistent theme emerged. Many had been plugging along at business intelligence to varying degrees for years. What catapulted them from BI mediocrity to success were multiple aspects. A few people described the change as "an aligning of the stars" or a "perfect storm." When I look closely at the factors that led to the change from mediocre business intelligence to greater success, there were varying degrees of Luck, Opportunity, Frustration, and Threat: LOFT.

The Role of Luck

The funny thing about luck is that you never really know if a positive outcome truly arises from luck or if it is from fortuitous timing and exceptional insight. While working at Dow Chemical, there were times I felt luck played a big role in our BI efforts, but in hindsight, perhaps it wasn't luck at all. Perhaps it was the effect of some very smart people working toward a common goal.

> "Luck is what happens when preparation meets opportunity."
>
> —Elmer G Letterman[1]

When Dow first began its BI initiative in 1993, it was an IT-driven project designed to reduce the costs associated with multiple, custom reporting systems. There were three aspects to Dow's information management strategy then, all of which played major roles in business intelligence:

- Dow Diamond Systems, which involved implementing SAP globally as its primary ERP system, replacing numerous custom applications.

The breadth of the implementation was enormous, and it encompassed all of Dow's major work processes including supply chain logistics, customer service, manufacturing, inventory management, accounting, and finance.[2] Not only was this a systems implementation, but also was a work process redesign and optimization effort. Diamond Systems allowed Dow to reduce its systems by 80% and cut its sales and general administration costs by 50%.[3]

- Dow Workstation, which involved standardizing all desktop computers and operating systems globally. Up until this point, if a business felt like buying from IBM, HP, Gateway, Dell, or any mom-and-pop build-it-yourself computer outlet, they could. Without a standard workstation, implementing a global, client/server BI solution would have had even more technical barriers to overcome than those brought by the newness of data warehousing and business intelligence.

- The Global Reporting Project, whose charter was to build a global data warehouse with standard access tools to replace multiple, regional, custom reporting, and decision support systems. Initially, Dow thought reporting and analysis would come directly from SAP. However, as sites came online, the regional decision support systems that had previously served the businesses so well began to degrade, and IT could not keep pace with the demand for custom-built reports within SAP.

When I first began working on the Global Reporting Project in 1993, I had never even heard the term "data warehouse." My indoctrination into the project was a gift from my boss: a just published book by Bill Inmon, *Building the Data Warehouse*. Management reporting was not new to me, but up until this point my work—and most everyone's in information systems—was regionally focused. Located in Horgen, Switzerland, I did what my individual business unit (hydrocarbons) in Europe wanted to do. I was unaware of and pretty much ignored what my counterparts in the same business unit in Texas were doing.

Meanwhile, the Global Reporting Project was not in the least bit regionalized. It was our business to know what all the regions and business units were doing in terms of reporting and analysis. Team leaders came from the United States, locations throughout Europe, and later Hong Kong. This global focus was a major organizational and cultural shift from a work perspective. Indeed, we also had cultural, "national" barriers to overcome—the Europeans laughed at some of the U.S. counterparts who canceled meetings abroad at the last minute for lack

About the Dow Chemical Company

Dow Chemical is one of the world's largest chemical companies, with $49 billion in annual sales and operations in 175 locations around the world. Its products are used in a wide range of goods, including toys, tools, textiles, pharmaceuticals, personal care items, and water purification technologies. In 2001, Dow merged with Union Carbide, consolidating its position in the chemical industry. With the rise in feedstock costs and increasing world demand, the company must continually look for more efficient ways to operate to ensure profitability and preserve availability of natural resources. All shared services (finance, supply chain, customer services, purchasing) and the commercial divisions rely on business intelligence for strategic, tactical, and operational decisions.

About BI at Dow

- **Start of BI efforts:** 1993
- **Executive level sponsor:** CIO
- **Business Intelligence Competency Center:** Yes
- **Number of BI users:** 12,000 or 28% of employees, plus an additional 10,000 customers
- **Number of source systems used for BI:** 5
- **ETL/EIM tools:** Currently custom, beginning to use IBM DataStage
- **Data warehouse platform:** Oracle
- **Data warehouse size:** 7 TB with 70% updated daily
- **BI tools:** BusinessObjects, Cognos PowerPlay, SAS JMP

of having a passport. Despite these profound changes and logistical hiccups, we quickly adapted and took advantage of an almost 24-hour work window. Whatever work I started in the morning, a counterpart in the United States added to in his time zone, and yet another continued in Hong Kong. The Dow Workstation and global area network allowed us to share files easily and seamlessly.

While the Global Reporting Project seemed like a good idea at the time, what none of us fully realized was that the regional businesses didn't want what we were building.

SUCCESS: An Idea from Frankfurt, Germany

Prior to the SAP implementation, Dow Europe had a relatively exceptional reporting system it called simply decision support system (DSS). It
was mainframe-based and might be deemed archaic with today's Web and
rich Windows interfaces, but at the time, it had all the key elements sales
and marketing wanted: good data with easy drill down. As the contrast
to newer tools such as Microsoft Excel revealed the DSS' limitations, the
Frankfurt, Germany, sales office came up with its own reporting solution.
It was a custom-built client/server application, optimized for field sellers,
with personalized data, and intuitive, graphical interface. Jens Garby,
global director Commercial IT and eBusiness, then the sales director
for Germany, showed it to the European polyethylene director, Romeo
Kreinberg (who later became the global vice president of performance
plastics). Even 15 years ago, Kreinberg was an executive who saw the
potential of information technology. He had power and influence, where
the information systems department had none. Kreinberg decided to
make the Frankfurt initiative bigger, better, and broader. His new reporting application was boldly named SUCCESS.

While the SUCCESS team rapidly delivered a slick interface, with
flashy charts and fast drill-down times, the Global Reporting Project
floundered amid data quality issues and queries that ran for hours.
"Global" was not all it was cracked up to be. We held a meeting with
European executives and their business analysts to give a status update.
For lunch, we served "spaghetti" to convey the theme of how messy it
was to merge information globally.

Dow Globalizes

About 18 months into the project, we got lucky. Very lucky! Under the
leadership of a newly appointed CEO, Bill Stavropoulos, Dow globalized
its 15 business units. As the global reporting team learned the news in
the cafeteria, many echoed a similar thought, "wow, did we get lucky!"
No longer would businesses be run on a regional basis, but rather, on a
truly global basis. Overnight, the global data warehouse became the *only*
source of information for managers to run their businesses. Regional
DSSs became useless overnight. The original SUCCESS project? It
served the needs of field sellers for a while but data quality declined as
regional transaction systems were phased out, and maintenance for the
application was problematic when the original programmer left the company. The experience with the SUCCESS initiative, however, provided
critical lessons to everyone on the Global Reporting Project that continue
to hold true today for anyone in the BI industry:

(1) Business intelligence has to be easy to use—with personalized data—and be fast, and (2) great ideas often come from the prototypes built within departments and individual business units who are more agile, focused on the needs of a smaller constituency.

Rather than viewing these initiatives as a threat or dismissing them as only point solutions, they should be considered for inspiration and a way to understand the business requirements.

The truly global aspect of the Global Reporting Project was one step ahead of Dow's regional businesses that subsequently globalized 18 months into the BI project. With the clarity of hindsight, perhaps this globalization had little to do with luck. Perhaps it had everything to do with the forward thinking of the IT leaders and having a visionary project manager—Dave Kepler, the original Global Reporting project manager, went on to become CIO just a few years after he started the Global Reporting Project. At the time, it certainly felt like luck!

Opportunity

FlightStats' foray into business intelligence has been evolutionary. The company, Conducive Technology, started out as an interactive multimedia company. It designed a dial-up travel booking system for American Airlines rewards members in the mid-1990s.[4] As that business was acquired by a competitor and spun off, the company changed focus from multimedia to air freight forwarding. In its effort to determine which were the best flights to put freight on, the company began acquiring statistical information on flight performance. Much of the publicly available data is too old and limited to be useful for booking purposes. For example, the Department of Transportation (DOT) provides information for a limited number of airlines but only three months after the flight.[5] In 2004, as Conducive Technology was improving its database for its freight customers, the company realized that nobody was collecting and mining real-time flight data for external use.[6]

CEO Jeff Kennedy saw an opportunity to exploit this data. What started as a database to optimize air freight logistics has morphed into FlightStats, a platform and set of services to "transform information into travel intelligence."[7] FlightStats collects worldwide data from multiple data sources including airlines, the Federal Aviation Administration (FAA), global distribution systems (such as Sabre, Amadeus, Galileo),

---

About FlightStats

Conducive Technology Corporation is a privately held company and the leading provider of worldwide flight performance information to the global travel and transportation industries. The FlightStats platform delivers real-time and historical flight information that lowers travel-related costs and improves the travel experience. The company's roots go back to the early 1990s, when they developed a dial-up booking system for American Airlines. The company later moved into air freight forwarding. In its effort to determine which were the best flights for freight, the company began acquiring statistical information on flight performance. FlightStats has provided this information to airlines, airports, and travel agents since 2003. The consumer-facing solution was launched in May of 2006.

About BI at FlightStats

- **Start of BI efforts:** 2001
- **Executive level sponsor:** CEO
- **Number of BI users:** 15 internal users, with more than 1 million consumers per month
- **Number of source systems used for BI:** Dozens of real-time, flight sources, external to FlightStats
- **ETL/EIM tools:** Pentaho's Kettle
- **Data warehouse platform:** PostgreSQL
- **Data warehouse size:** 520 GB with millions of new records a day updated in real-time
- **Number of subject areas:** 2
- **BI tools:** JasperReports with OpenReports

---

and airports. Data is updated in real time, and a historical reporting and analysis data mart is updated daily.

With on-time performance at its lowest level in seven years[8] and with the industry under increased pressure to provide a passenger bill of rights, FlightStats has a unique opportunity to help solve passenger woes by providing travel agents and consumers access to near real-time flight performance information.

As an example, Figure 5-1 shows flight performance for the Newark, New Jersey, to Fort Lauderdale, Florida, route during the two-month period of February 15, 2007, to April 15, 2007. Notice along the left side of the figure a five-point scoring system. The scores consider not only how many flights were late, but also the magnitude of the lateness.

Performance	Rating	Carrier	# Flights Operated	# Flights Codeshare	Ontime %	Max Avg	Max Max	Cancelled Flights		Diverted Flights	
Poor	★★★★★ (1.5)	U5 USA 3000 Airlines	33	0	57%	26	114	0	0%	0	0%
	★★★★★ (1.4)	CO Continental Airlines	638	0	64%	33	443	17	2%	2	0%
	★★★★★ (1.4)	NW Northwest Airlines	0	637	64%	33	443	17	2%	2	0%
	★★★★★ (1.0)	KL KLM	0	57	61%	41	146	1	1%	1	1%
Very Poor	★★★★★ (0.5)	B6 JetBlue Airways	251	0	47%	69	328	8	3%	0	0%

Figure 5-1 FlightStats performance ratings show JetBlue's poor performance out of Newark, winter 2007.

To be fair, this route is one of the worst in winter as New York area snowbirds head south for the winter. It's a busy route subject to extreme weather conditions. February 15, 2007, includes the Valentine's Day ice storm that plagued the Northeast, leaving some JetBlue passengers stranded on the tarmac for up to 11 hours. A Nor'easter April 15th wreaked additional havoc for all airlines. None of the airlines appears to have had a glowing performance during this period, but the differences are noteworthy. Continental Airlines, the next biggest operator for the same route, had a 64% on-time performance with an average delay of 33 minutes, compared with JetBlue's 47% on-time performance and average delay of 69 minutes. The following Route Performance Summary shows how Continental's performance is better than the overall route, while JetBlue's is worse.

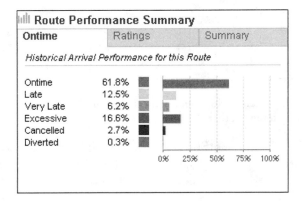

The level of detail that FlightStats provides makes the information actionable. Following the travel fiasco in February, JetBlue's CEO David Neeleman publicly apologized to its passengers, declaring it the "the worst operational week in JetBlue's seven year history."[9] While it's true that the weather events made travel a nightmare for everyone during that period, performance on this Newark route for March 15 to May 15 again shows JetBlue at the bottom and below the route average. Travelers armed with this information do have a choice then: tolerate the delays, fly another airline, or fly an alternate route. Figure 5-2 shows FlightStats'

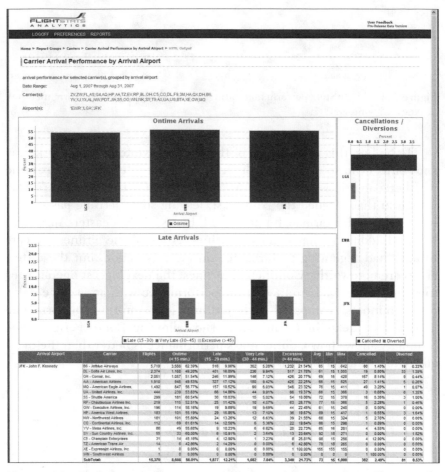

FLIGHTSTATS ANALYTICS

User Feedback / Pre-Release Beta Version

LOGOFF   PREFERENCES   REPORTS

Home ► Report Groups ► Carriers ► Carrier Arrival Performance by Arrival Airport ► HTML Output

Carrier Arrival Performance by Arrival Airport

arrival performance for selected carrier(s), grouped by arrival airport

Date Range: Aug 1, 2007 through Aug 31, 2007

Carrier(s): ZV,ZW,FL,AS,G4,AQ,HP,AA,TZ,EV,RP,9L,OH,C5,CO,DL,F9,3M,HA,QX,DH,B6, YV,YJ,YX,AL,NW,PDT,JIA,S5,OO,WN,NK,SY,TR,AX,UA,US,BTA,XE,OW,MQ

Airport(s): 'EWR';'LGA';'JFK'

Arrival Airport	Carrier	Flights	Ontime (< 15 min.)		Late (15-29 min.)		Very Late (30-44 min.)		Excessive (> 44 min.)		Avg	Min	Max	Cancelled		Diverted	
JFK - John F. Kennedy	B6 - JetBlue Airways	5,719	3,568	62.39%	518	9.06%	302	5.28%	1,232	21.54%	85	15	642	80	1.40%	19	0.33%
	DL - Delta Air Lines, Inc.	2,374	1,168	49.20%	401	16.89%	236	9.94%	517	21.78%	61	15	1,000	19	0.80%	33	1.39%
	OH - Comair, Inc.	2,051	1,057	51.54%	246	11.99%	146	7.12%	426	20.77%	69	15	428	167	8.14%	9	0.44%
	AA - American Airlines	1,916	946	49.53%	327	17.12%	180	9.42%	426	22.25%	66	15	825	27	1.41%	5	0.26%
	MQ - American Eagle Airlines	1,492	847	56.77%	157	10.52%	90	6.03%	348	23.32%	76	15	411	49	3.28%	1	0.07%
	UA - United Airlines, Inc.	444	239	53.83%	66	14.86%	44	9.91%	86	19.37%	66	15	366	3	0.68%	6	1.35%
	S5 - Shuttle America	299	181	60.54%	30	10.03%	15	5.02%	54	18.06%	72	15	378	16	5.35%	3	1.00%
	RP - Chautauqua Airlines Inc	219	115	52.51%	25	11.42%	10	4.57%	63	28.77%	77	15	366	5	2.28%	1	0.46%
	OW - Executive Airlines, Inc	196	114	58.16%	19	9.69%	19	9.69%	44	22.45%	61	15	240	0	0.00%	0	0.00%
	HP - America West Airlines	183	101	55.19%	29	15.85%	13	7.10%	36	19.67%	89	15	417	1	0.55%	3	1.64%
	NW - Northwest Airlines	181	101	55.80%	24	13.26%	12	6.63%	39	21.55%	68	15	324	5	2.76%	0	0.00%
	CO - Continental Airlines, Inc.	112	69	61.61%	14	12.50%	6	5.36%	22	19.64%	66	15	296	1	0.89%	0	0.00%
	YV - Mesa Airlines, Inc.	88	49	55.68%	9	10.23%	6	6.82%	20	22.73%	76	16	291	4	4.55%	0	0.00%
	SY - Sun Country Airlines, Inc.	55	33	60.00%	6	10.91%	2	3.64%	13	23.64%	92	18	271	0	0.00%	1	1.82%
	C5 - Champlain Enterprises	31	14	45.16%	4	12.90%	1	3.23%	8	25.81%	98	15	256	4	12.90%	0	0.00%
	TZ - American Trans Air	14	6	42.86%	2	14.29%	0	0.00%	6	42.86%	75	18	265	0	0.00%	0	0.00%
	XE - Expressjet Airlines, Inc	1	0	0.00%	0	0.00%	0	0.00%	1	100.00%	156	155	155	0	0.00%	0	0.00%
	WN - Southwest Airlines	1	0	0.00%	0	0.00%	0	0.00%	0	0.00%	0	0	0	1	100.00%	0	0.00%
	SubTotal:	15,370	8,608	56.01%	1,877	12.21%	1,082	7.04%	3,340	21.73%	73	15	1,000	382	2.49%	81	0.53%

Figure 5-2 FlightStats performance ratings show it's better to fly JetBlue out of John F. Kennedy airport rather than Newark.

newest BI interface, FlightStats Analytics, with information for the three New York–area airports in August. Less than 55% of flights into any of the three New York-area airports arrived on-time. At John F. Kennedy airport, however, JetBlue flights arrived on-time 62% of the time, the best performance of any of the airlines and above the airport's average.

For FlightStats, successful business intelligence comes with recognizing a unique opportunity in the data they've amassed and enhanced. Initially, such data was only available to freight customers, then to travel agencies and airlines, and as of late 2006, to consumers. As this book goes to print and as the airline industry finishes one of its worst summers for on-time performance, FlightStats is introducing FlightStats Analytics to offer airports, airlines, and the travel industry greater analytic abilities to this unique data.

Opportunity at Emergency Medical Associates

Emergency Medical Associates (EMA) echoed a similar theme of opportunity as FlightStats. The healthcare industry is not known for being leaders in business intelligence or information technology, and yet, Emergency Medical Associates is. Ten years ago, EMA differentiated itself based on a unique electronic patient management system that few emergency rooms had.[10] Through this system, EMA amassed data related to emergency room diagnosis and operations that nobody had yet mined. One of EMA's senior physicians had a vision of using this data for the patients' good. He saw an opportunity to leverage the unique data EMA had amassed. Jonathan Rothman, director of data management, explains, "EMA is fortunate in its ability to take data and turn it into actionable information. By improving emergency room operations, our patients benefit, the physicians benefit, and our whole organization benefits."[11]

Opportunity at Dow

Whether it was luck or foresight that gave Dow's global data warehouse more acceptance is debatable. However, the degree to which Dow exploited this asset and realized its importance only came with the merger of Union Carbide in 2001 that made the Dow Chemical Company the largest chemical company in the world. The merger promised a number of synergies, and when the deal finally closed, the expected synergies were even greater than originally anticipated. Dow employees who had taken their information systems somewhat for granted up until this point, now realized just how good they had had it compared with Union Carbide's antiquated systems. Dow quickly updated its estimated merger savings to double that of the original estimates.[12] The opportunities for synergy were there; could Dow exploit them?

Dow's CIO Dave Kepler explains that the operational systems and global data warehouse were key requirements to drive the synergies from the merger with Union Carbide. "We had to improve the way people worked, made decisions, and interacted with customers."[13]

Do Business Requirements Always Map to Opportunities?

Often with business intelligence projects, business users first must define their requirements and IT then builds a solution. FlightStats, EMA, and Dow Chemical all illustrate a different paradigm, though.

About Emergency Medical Associates

Emergency Medical Associates (EMA) is a group of 250 emergency physicians who are contracted to manage and staff emergency departments at 18 hospitals throughout New Jersey and New York. They treat more than 700,000 patients per year. The data warehouse contains information on over 8 million ER visits, making it one of the largest sources of ER data in the world. EMA uses business intelligence to improve the quality of patient care in the ER, predict disease outbreaks, and make ER operations more efficient.

About BI at EMA

- **Start of BI efforts:** 1999
- **Executive level sponsor:** Chief technology officer
- **Business Intelligence Competency Center:** Yes
- **Number of BI users:** 220 users which include 40% of the company's employees as well as external hospital staff
- **Number of source systems used for BI:** 11
- **ETL/EIM tools:** Custom
- **Data warehouse platform:** Oracle
- **Data warehouse size:** 100 GB, updated daily
- **Number of subject areas:** 3
- **BI tools:** BusinessObjects XI

Whenever a new opportunity presents itself, the requirements may not be well known. The business users may first have to test new processes and business models as part of pursuing the opportunity. IT must learn to expect that precise requirements will change on a daily basis, but always within the framework of the broader vision. This can be a frustrating process for IT staff who need to know exactly which fields to extract from a source system and how to transform them onto a dashboard or a report. The reality is, the business users may only

Successful BI companies start with a vision—whether it's to improve air travel, improve patient care, or drive synergies. The business sees an opportunity to exploit the data to fulfill a broader vision. The detail requirements are not precisely known. Creativity and exploration are necessary ingredients to unlock these business opportunities and fulfill those visions.

know detailed requirements once they've been able to experiment with different tools and explore information to determine what most supports their vision. For example, EMA knew their patient data presented a unique business opportunity to improve care and emergency room operations. It was only after exploring the data and prototyping different reports and dashboards that the team arrived at the final metrics that provided the best insights and benefits.

Frustration

When companies first embark on business intelligence, a frequent starting point is to address the biggest pains. Sometimes the degree of frustration has to reach a boiling point before business intelligence becomes a priority. Frustration can come in many forms, whether it's the inability to answer simple questions, being held accountable for things without the right tools to do a job well, or, as many managers describe, the frustration at managing blindly without facts to support their decisions.

At Continental Airlines, the data warehouse began in 1998 driven by two key initiatives: revenue management and customer relationship management. Continental had only recently emerged from its second bankruptcy. Part of the airline's turnaround strategy was a *Go Forward Plan* that promised to transform the customer's flying experience and to appeal to more business travelers.[15] Mike Gorman, senior director of customer relationship management, recalls trying to understand one thing about a single customer. "We couldn't. We had 45 different databases with customer information."[16] It took a few years to get to a single view of the customer but now, detailed customer information is available within seconds of an event.

Frustration was a similar theme at 1-800 CONTACTS. 1-800 CONTACTS has been selling contact lenses via mail order, phone, and the Internet for 11 years.[17] It has a unique challenge, though, in that its customers must go to a competitor—eye doctors—to receive a prescription.[18] A key differentiator for 1-800 CONTACTS is customer service. The company first released its data warehouse in early 2005 as a way of addressing growing frustration among its customer service representatives. "All the agents were clamoring for information. We hire competitive people. The biggest dissatisfaction in their job was to have to wait until the next morning to look at a piece of paper taped to the wall to see how they were performing," recalls Dave Walker, vice president of operations. Employee turnover was high, and on exit interviews, agents complained

---

About 1-800 CONTACTS

1-800 CONTACTS is the world largest supplier of contact lenses, with inventories over 20 million. Orders are placed by phone or via the Web (1800contacts.com). On any given day, the company sells as many contact lenses as 2,500 retail optical shops combined. 1-800 CONTACTS was founded in 1995 by two entrepreneurs, and within the ten years since the company was founded, they've grown from $4 million in annual sales to $249 million in 2006.

About BI at 1-800 CONTACTS

- **Start of BI efforts:** 2004
- **Executive level sponsor:** CFO
- **Business Intelligence Competency Center:** Yes
- **Number of BI users:** 400 or 60% of employees
- **Number of source systems used for BI:** 3
- **ETL/EIM tools:** Microsoft Integration Services
- **Data warehouse platform:** Microsoft SQL Server
- **Data warehouse size:** 125GB with 80% updated every 15 minutes
- **Number of subject areas:** 3
- **BI tools:** Microsoft BI

---

most about being held accountable for things they couldn't control without access to information to improve their performance.

In many companies, a common complaint is having multiple versions of the truth. Executive meetings start with a debate about how numbers are compiled and whose are correct rather than with a discussion of the insights such numbers provide. Corporate Express had been using business intelligence tools for seven years when the CEO grew increasingly frustrated that nobody was using the same numbers. There were 31 different BI experts creating similar reports and all coming up with different numbers.[19] Frustration at the executive level cleared the way for the BI platform and team to be revamped, reorganized, and eventually declared a success.

Threat

After going through two bankruptcies, there is nothing like the threat of another bankruptcy to spur a business into profound change. Up until 1995, Continental had not been profitable since 1978, when the airline industry was still regulated by the federal government. It ranked last out of ten major airlines for on-time arrival, baggage handling, customer complaints, and denied boardings from overbooking of flights.[20] The jobs of 40,000 employees were at stake, particularly with a cash crisis looming. CEO Gordon Bethune and COO Greg Brenneman developed the Go Forward Plan, consisting of the following goals, to turn the airline around:

- *Fly to Win* by changing the mix of customers from mostly leisure travelers to more business travelers and focusing on routes that were profitable.
- *Fund the Future* by tracking cash, managing the balance sheet, and investing in the fleet.
- *Make Reliability a Reality* by moving from tenth place on customer service metrics to the top 50% and improving the fleet.
- *Working Together* by giving employees incentives aligned with the airline's turnaround strategy, improving communication, and establishing a results-oriented culture.

The Go Forward Plan had an immediate effect on the airline, returning it to profitability in 1995. Business intelligence supported the Go Forward Plan in a number of ways, including providing people access to data to optimize revenues, reduce costs, and improve service, as well as communicating and monitoring achievement of key performance indicators. From 1995 to 2001, Continental reported consistent profits, but like many airlines, has struggled to return to consistent profitability after the September 11, 2001, terrorist attacks and rising fuel costs. Figure 5-3 shows the ratio

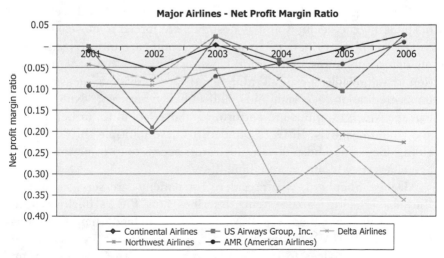

Figure 5-3   Net Profit Margin Ratios for Major U.S. Airlines (source: 10Ks)

of net income to revenues for five of the major U.S. airlines. Information for United Airlines is not included here as significant losses in 2005 and subsequent restructuring skew the chart display. The figure shows the extreme pressures under which all the airlines are currently operating. It's noteworthy that Continental was profitable in 2006 while some of its chief competitors operated under bankruptcy protection and posted losses. For the last five years, its average net profit margin ratio is better than any of the other major airlines. In addition to improved financial performance, whereas Continental once ranked tenth out of ten in customer service measures, it now routinely is recognized for its customer service with awards from J.D. Power and Associates, *Fortune*, and the *Official Airline Guide* (OAG). Continental faces threats on many fronts in terms of competitors, airline safety, and rising costs. Business intelligence is pivotal in Continental's ability to respond to these threats.

Threats that propel a company to more successfully leverage business intelligence often come from forces beyond the company's control. Rising healthcare costs have reached crisis levels in the United States. The state of New Jersey, where EMA operates a number of emergency rooms, has a Charity Care Law (NJ) that requires hospitals to treat patients regardless of their ability to pay.[21] Under this law, the state will reimburse these hospitals, but the formula for reimbursement has changed significantly in the past several years such that hospitals on average are reimbursed only a third of the $1.6 billion spent annually.[22] Reimbursements under Medicare and Medicaid have also not kept pace with hospital costs or inflation, paying only 89 cents and 73 cents, respectively, for every dollar spent. The rise of managed care has further challenged hospitals. Under these threats, patient care is threatened as hospital income declines and as hospitals are forced to close.

In addition to financial threats, the healthcare industry also faces regulatory pressures. The Joint Commission is a national organization that provides hospitals and healthcare providers measurements for accreditation, accountability, and public reporting.[23] Now patients can see which hospitals are performing above, equal to, or below other accredited hospitals. EMA responded to these multiple threats by providing doctors and hospital administrators access to information to manage emergency rooms more efficiently.

Denise Shepherd, vice president for patient care services at Saint Barnabas Health Care System, describes how EMA's business intelligence solution called WEBEMARS™ has helped their emergency room. "WEBEMARS™ has and continues to provide invaluable data management services to the Saint Barnabas Health Care System and our Emergency Departments. Information provided by WEBEMARS™ is used at each Saint Barnabas Health Care System hospital and across the system to drive performance improvement and ensure the highest quality of care for our Emergency Department patients."[24]

The Role of Time

With some of the successful BI companies, it seems that time has played a role in their success, that BI had to be failing or mediocre for a period before these companies learned how to use business intelligence more effectively. However, time is not a prerequisite for success. 1-800 CONTACTS, for example, only began their data warehouse project in the fall 2004 with the first application available in spring 2005. Their success and impact on the call center was immediate.

Figure 5-4 shows the relationship between the length of a BI deployment and the perceived success. The survey responses show that being very successful is indeed possible within the first year of deployment. Twelve percent of first-year BI deployments rate their projects as being

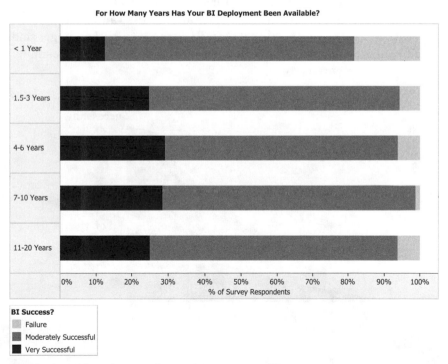

Figure 5-4   Time does not have a big impact on BI success.

very successful. However, this is the largest proportion of failures, at 20% of first-year projects. Beyond the first year, though, the rate of very successful projects stays about the same at 24% to 28%, with no significant change if the deployment has been available for two years or ten.

If There Is No LOFT Effect, Is Successful BI Still Possible?

As a business intelligence consultant, I was bothered by the concept of the LOFT effect: I didn't like the idea that a BI team could do everything else right—executive sponsorship, alignment with the business, solid data architecture—and the BI initiative might only be moderately successful. At this point, there is not enough data to say that the LOFT effect is a *prerequisite* for wild success. It is, however, a common characteristic among the more successful companies. It's also clear that the degree to which BI best practices are followed has an impact on the degree of success, so even if there is a LOFT effect present, don't expect success unless you are applying other best practices. As shown in Figure 5-5, the LOFT effect intensifies the benefits of following BI best practices, allowing for greater success and business value.

Discussing the role of "threats" on BI success, one BI manager said, "well, when people are fat and happy, you don't have to be as smart."

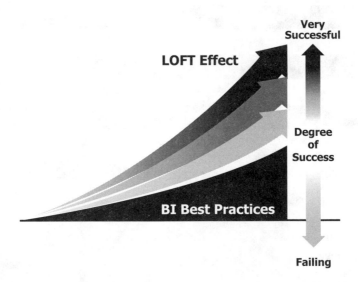

Figure 5-5   The LOFT effect (Luck, Opportunity, Frustration, Threat)

Supporting his point, one of the cultural aspects that most differentiates successful BI companies from the moderates and failures was the degree to which the survey respondents perceive their companies as being lean and operating efficiently (see Figure 13-2 in Chapter 13). There is not enough data to determine if business intelligence *enabled* this efficiency or if efficiency happened first, and thus better BI use *followed*.

Also, it's important to note that not all the successful BI case studies showed *all* aspects of the LOFT effect, but they did show more than one element. BI teams can use the LOFT effect as a way of communicating with the business to see how business intelligence can be used more effectively. Most business units and companies routinely perform a SWOT analysis—strengths, weaknesses, opportunities, and threats. BI teams can study the opportunities and threats portions to understand where BI can help the business pursue opportunities and address threats.

Best Practices for Successful Business Intelligence

The degree to which a company is successful with business intelligence is influenced by forces beyond the direct control of the BI team, whether luck, opportunity, frustration, or threat (LOFT). In the most successful BI companies, a LOFT effect has moved them from being moderately successful with business intelligence to extremely successful and having a profound impact on the business.

To move your BI efforts from one of moderate success to wild success:

- Understand the LOFT effect and proactively look for these elements that affect your company or business unit. The business and BI teams should explore the role that business intelligence can play in exploiting business opportunities, addressing frustration or pain, and squashing the threats.
- Don't use time (measured in years) as an excuse for lack of success. Successful BI is possible within a short time frame.
- Do continue to follow all the other BI best practices described in this book, recognizing that the LOFT effect is only an *intensifying* effect.

Chapter 6

Executive Support

If you ask people what the number one enabler for a successful BI deployment is, most will respond "executive support." It's an easy answer as executive support is key to the success for almost any companywide initiative—change in business strategy, new product launch, or reorganization. However, getting that executive support may not be easy, particularly if senior executives don't believe in or understand the value of business intelligence.

> "Our BI initiative is not successful or fully utilized because of the lack of vision, sponsorship, and leadership from the executive level."
>
> —Hybrid business/IT professional, transportation industry

Executive Support and Success

When survey respondents were asked to rate the importance of various cultural and organizational aspects that affect the success of a BI project, executive support consistently ranked at the top of the list, along with IT and business partnership (see Figure 6-1). 53% of survey respondents ranked executive support as essential. There was little difference in this ranking regardless of the company size, duration of the BI project, or if a respondent's BI project was deemed very successful or a complete failure.

Consistent with the survey results, the successful BI case studies often cited—unprompted—executive support as one of the reasons they have been so successful.

Despite the relative importance of this, not all BI initiatives have executive level sponsorship. The majority of BI deployments (74%) do have executive sponsorship, but 26% do not. As shown in Figure 6-2,

Importance of Organizational Aspects to BI Success

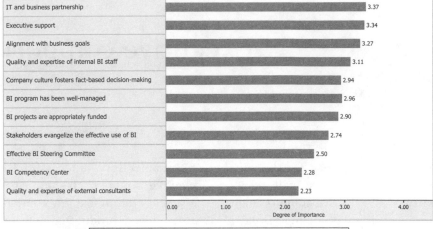

	Degree of Importance
IT and business partnership	3.37
Executive support	3.34
Alignment with business goals	3.27
Quality and expertise of internal BI staff	3.11
Company culture fosters fact-based decision-making	2.94
BI program has been well-managed	2.96
BI projects are appropriately funded	2.90
Stakeholders evangelize the effective use of BI	2.74
Effective BI Steering Committee	2.50
BI Competency Center	2.28
Quality and expertise of external consultants	2.23

4-Essential   3-Very important   2-Important   1-Not very important

Figure 6-1   Executive support is one of the most important aspects to successful BI.

Executive Sponsorship and Degree of BI Success

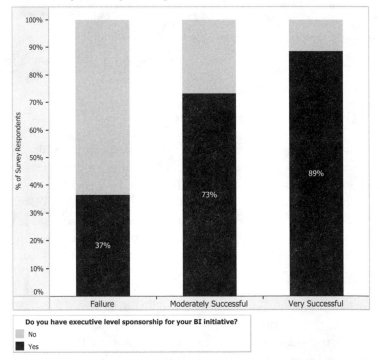

Failure — 37%
Moderately Successful — 73%
Very Successful — 89%

Do you have executive level sponsorship for your BI initiative?
No
Yes

Figure 6-2   A greater percentage of very successful BI projects have a higher rate of executive sponsorship.

the impact on a project's success is noticeable: of the companies who describe their BI projects as being very successful, 89% have executive sponsorship, whereas in the projects described as a failure only 37% had executive sponsorship.

Which Executive Is the Best Sponsor?

Business intelligence projects can be sponsored by any executive: the chief executive officer (CEO), the chief operating officer (COO), chief financial officer (CFO), chief information officer (CIO) or IT manager, VP of marketing, or another line of business leader. The CIO is most often (in 35% of projects) the sponsor of a BI initiative, followed by the CEO (20%).

While the CIO may often be the sponsor for business intelligence, this executive does not appear to be the most effective sponsor on average. Figure 6-3 shows the relationship between the sponsoring executive and

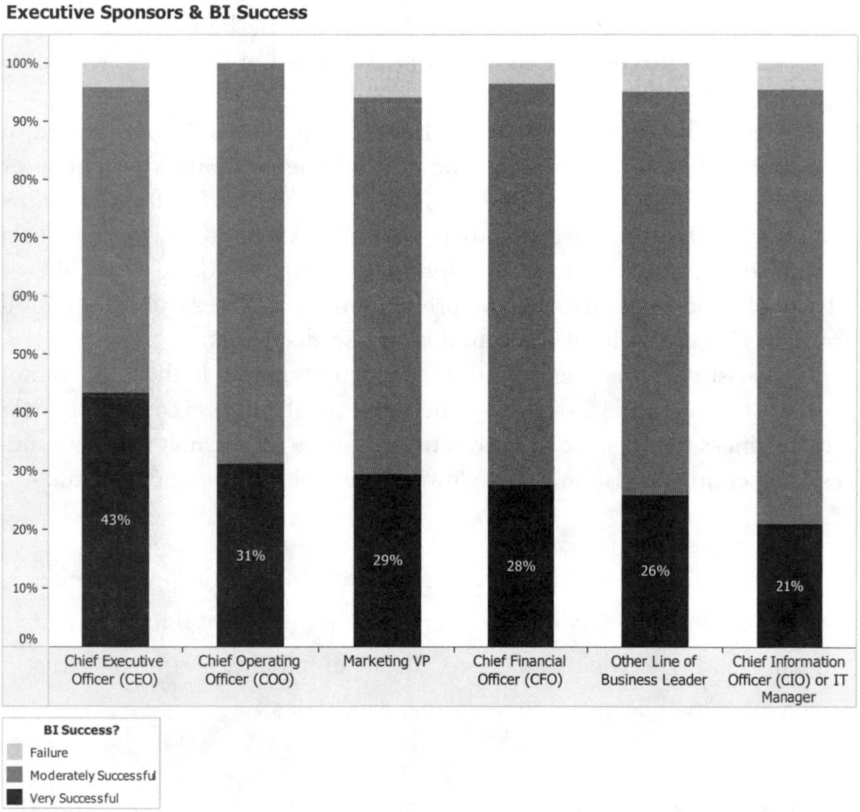

Executive Sponsors & BI Success

BI Success?
Failure
Moderately Successful
Very Successful

Figure 6-3   The CEO as the BI sponsor has the highest rate of BI success.

how successful a company rates their BI initiative. The portion of companies who have the CEO as their sponsor and classify their project as being very successful is 43%. This is higher than the average rate of success at 24% of survey respondents. Contrast this with the portion of companies who have the CIO as the sponsor and describe the project as very successful at only 21%, slightly lower than the average.

If you are a CIO reading this book, don't panic (yet). While it's not good news that the CIO is not necessarily an ideal sponsor, the problem is not with the individual executive per se but rather with the degree of influence the CIO wields with the business. If the CIO is viewed as a technocrat rather than a core member of the business team, then this lack of business alignment will get reflected in lower BI success rates and lower overall effective use of technology.

Public relations firm Burson Marsteller has been tracking the role of CIOs on boards of directors and executive committees for several years. They have found that in global Fortune 500 companies in which the CIO is a member of the board of directors, companies showed 9.2% higher annual returns than relevant indices.[1] The bad news is that in their study, a paltry 8% are members of the board of directors, with only a slight increase from 2003 to 2004.

There is, however, a difference between membership on a board of directors and in being an active member of the company's executive or operating committee. In the Successful BI survey, 67% of respondents say their CIOs are active members of the business team or operating committee. A 2007 eSurvey by *Optimize Magazine* found that 34% of CIOs were actively involved in driving major business decisions and another 45% are at least consulted on these decisions.[2]

These survey findings reveal an important point: if the CIO is not involved in the strategy of the business and is also the executive sponsor for a business intelligence initiative, the initiative will be met with less success; the company also may have lower financial performance overall.

Ultimately, the most effective sponsor for a business intelligence initiative is the individual who understands the full value of business intelligence and who wields influence, instills credibility, and fosters trust with all of the business and functional executives.

At Corporate Express, for example, the executive sponsor for the BI initiative is the CFO, Robert VanHees. Both the BI team and the

The Changing Role of the CIO

The role of the CIO is undergoing a transformation in many companies. This change can be attributed to the greater role technology plays in business. In the past, CIOs may have been viewed only as the technology keepers and data center managers. This is still the case in companies and industries in which technology is viewed as an operational necessity, not as an enabler or as a provider of competitive advantage. If the CIO's role is largely left to overseeing maintenance of systems, this type of CIO is not an ideal sponsor for a business intelligence initiative, as BI is less about technology and more about business. In *Managing IT as a Business*, author Mark Lutchen explains that some CIOs may stay in the predominantly technology role for personality reasons on the part of both the CIO and the CEO: if the CIO lacks interpersonal skills or an understanding of the business, that CIO will not become an integral part of the business committee. Conversely, if the CEO does not value or understand information technology, the CEO may not want someone on the business team who can make him or her feel stupid. Lutchen explains, "...most CIOs have not done a very good job of communication in ways that make CEOs comfortable. Thus, a CEO who is already less than conversant in technology, does not want to demonstrate further public weakness (or possibly be humiliated) concerning IT should he or she fail to understand what the CIO is talking about (even though that may be entirely the CIO's fault)."[3]

individual business units that use BI feel strongly that the CFO was the right sponsor. When the IT department had greater ownership of business intelligence, BI usage was low, numbers were inconsistently reported, and there was no measurable impact on business performance. Getting to greater BI success took a change of leadership, technology, and a personnel reorganization. Swapping out tools, reducing head count, and changing reporting lines would not have been possible without that executive level sponsorship. That the CFO—rather than other functional or line of business VPs—supported the changes ensured that competition between the functions didn't interfere with progress. No individual function or business unit could take a "not invented here" attitude.[4]

Employees describe VanHees as having the second highest influence in the company, after the president and CEO. Although he was not the original sponsor of Corporate Express' BI revitalization, he quickly saw the value of the initiative and is now a champion for the effort. When VanHees was the CFO for Corporate Express in Europe in 2005, everyone struggled with basic data access involving 12 different ERP systems. A European data warehouse was only just being implemented. VanHees returned to the United States in September 2006 (almost two years after the company began its BI revitalization) as CFO for Corporate Express North America. He found business intelligence in the United States to be years ahead of what the company had in Europe. In talking about the impact the CFO has had on the BI project, Matt Schwartz, director of business analysis, says, "You might be successful in isolation, but if you don't have that executive apostle going around, no doors get open, and there is no budget."

Expect Changes in Sponsorship

The executive sponsor for a BI initiative may change throughout the BI life cycle. As Table 6-1 shows, a number of the successful BI case studies all experienced a change in executive level sponsorship. In some cases, the change was pivotal in moving BI from mediocrity to success. Consistent with industry research, the CIO sponsors wield a significant degree of influence and are active members of executive committees. For all the case study companies, while there is one designated sponsor, there is widespread support for business intelligence at the executive level.

Successful BI Company	Initial Sponsor	Sponsor when BI Very Successful
1-800 CONTACTS	CFO	(same)
Continental Airlines	CIO (who is a corporate officer)	(same)
Corporate Express	IT initiative without C-level sponsorship	CFO
The Dow Chemical Company	IT management	CIO who serves on the executive committee.
Emergency Medical Associates	CTO and vision from CEO	(same)
FlightStats	CEO	(same)
Norway Post	IT initiative	CFO

Table 6-1   Executive level sponsors at Successful BI Case Studies

Getting Executive Buy-In

While most recognize the importance of executive level support for BI, getting that support can be difficult. In some companies, "data warehouse" is a dirty word, and business intelligence is synonymous with expensive, never-ending projects. Business intelligence *is* a never-ending initiative, but that doesn't mean working endlessly without delivering business value.

A BI analyst at a telecommunications firm expressed his frustration: "the political issues are show stoppers without CXO edicts. Another issue is getting all levels of management to 'get it' as they tend to lack the big picture. It seems that they do not lead but instead are reacting to their environment." At this company, the BI team tried the "guerilla marketing as long as we could, but without executive level support, we got nowhere." Like most good people who get frustrated at lack of progress and vision, this particular analyst eventually moved to a company who saw the value of BI.

Some have it easier than others. The arrival of a technically savvy executive who has encountered BI success elsewhere may make life easier for the BI team. In many cases, however, executive support has to be earned, even re-earned. Some specific things the BI team can do to earn executive level support:

- Demonstrate small successes and communicate the business benefits.
- Manage expectations.
- Exploit frustration.

Demonstrate Small Successes

When you have completed a successful project—however small you must start—you will earn the trust and support of whichever executive benefits from that first project. This executive will quickly become your BI champion and advocate for promoting BI to other departments, functions, business units (absent political power struggles and assuming they are strategically aligned).

As an example, ENECO Energie is one of the top three gas and electricity suppliers in the Netherlands. ENECO executives initially frowned upon BI. According to Ton van den Dungen, manager, Business Intelligence Center of Excellence, the attitude was "There is not one successful BI project. It's too expensive." So in 2003, with an entrepreneurial approach, ENECO's initial BI project consisted of manual extracts from source systems and Microsoft Excel Pivot Tables. Accounts receivable was the only subject area with the goals of better understanding why receivables were high and identifying opportunities to reduce them. The pilot cost only 350,000 euros (EUR) and helped ENECO save 4 million EUR ($5 million). Following the pilot's success, the BI team could get support and funding for a full BI architecture that included a data warehouse and suite of BI tools.

ENECO's initiative demonstrates a key secret to success: successful BI companies start their BI initiative with or without executive sponsorship. They demonstrate success early and ramp up only once they've garnered that executive buy-in. Success at this early stage has to be measured in hard business benefits. ENECO could cite a specific value saved in millions of euros.

> Use the measurable business benefits that leading companies describe throughout this book—improved patient care, faster synergies following a merger, increased customer satisfaction, immediate sales lift, cost reductions in advertising campaigns—to inspire conversations with your executives on how your company can exploit business intelligence.

Manage Expectations

Managing expectations is paramount in earning and retaining executive support. Never overpromise and underdeliver. Particularly if you are starting out without executive support, position your efforts as only a prototype or point solution. Communicate clearly that the BI deployment will not be scaled up or out without an executive champion. This can be a difficult balancing act, particularly when vendors undermine your efforts. A BI project manager for a medical center expressed frustration:

> All the BI vendors come in and show these executives a bunch of eye-candy and make it sound easy, when it's not. So we had no funding, no resources for our project. The BI vendors set us up for failure. An executive will have a team of 10 analysts that he can ask a question of. The executive has no idea how their staff gets the numbers, the manual processes, the data manipulation. So the comparison is that it takes their staff an hour to give an answer versus a BI project that takes six months. Nobody has a handle on what it costs to do manually and how vulnerable they are.

Exploit Frustration   Recall the discussion of the LOFT effect in Chapter 5. If you currently lack executive level sponsorship, ask the sought-for sponsor: "How much time do you spend in meetings arguing about the numbers?" Find out the degree of pain and frustration.

At Corporate Express, executives throughout the company were increasingly frustrated at the multiple versions of the truth. People argued about the numbers, and nobody agreed on the reality. If an individual's performance seemed weak, the numbers could always be blamed. "After we implemented MicroStrategy, we didn't argue about the numbers, and there was just support for what is the performance and then identifying the business opportunities. If everyone comes to the table and knows the data is consistent, we can sooner address the pressing business issues," explains Walter Scott, vice president of marketing.

How you frame the frustration is important. Executives don't want to hear about what a mess the data is or how tightly locked it is in the operational system. The focus has to be on the degree of frustration and that business intelligence—done well—can relieve that frustration and provide measurable business value. You have to be able to fill in the blank:

> The _frustration_ is killing us, and business intelligence can provide _benefit_ .

For example: "The *time we spend debating numbers* (frustration) is a problem, and business intelligence can provide a *single set of numbers and allow us to focus more on innovation* (benefits)." Or "We are *losing market share*, and business intelligence can help us *increase sales by 5%*."

The Role of an Executive Sponsor

Executive sponsors support the BI effort in the following ways:

- Articulate commitment to the initiative and to the impact it will have on the organization.
- State the business intelligence vision in the context of the company's strategy. They may help craft this vision.
- Approve budget.
- Clear political barriers.
- Act as the go-to person for ultimate resolution of issues that can not be resolved by the BI team or the BI Steering Committee (see Chapter 11). Such issues are rarely technical in nature and more often involve prioritization, organizational issues, and project scope.

Executive sponsors are seldom involved in the day-to-day tasks and issues of the BI team.

Best Practices for Successful Business Intelligence

Executive support is one of the most important secrets to successful BI and the degree to which BI contributes to business performance. Fail to garner executive level support and your project will be met with only moderate success, perhaps in isolated deployments. Executive support is not guaranteed and is something that must be earned.

- Recognize that the best executive sponsor is one who has credibility and influence with all the business units and functions, not just with IT or just with finance.
- The sponsoring executive may change throughout the BI life cycle.
- Until you can prove the value of BI, some executives will skeptically think that BI is just another IT drain on investment dollars.

If you have been diligently following all the other best practices in this book and still don't have executive level support, face the harsh reality that your company may never fully appreciate the value of business intelligence without exogenous change.

Chapter 7

D Is for *Data*

Data is the fundamental building block for a business intelligence application.

Successful business intelligence is influenced by both technical aspects and organizational aspects. In general, companies rate organizational aspects (such as executive level sponsorship) as having a higher impact on success than technical aspects. And yet, even if you do everything right from an organizational perspective, if you don't have high quality, relevant data, your BI initiative will fail.

Figure 7-1 shows how the data architecture provides the pillars for BI front-end tools and applications. Each pillar within the data architecture is important, with data quality being the most important.

Data Quality

Figure 7-2 shows that data quality is rated as the most important technical aspect for successful business intelligence according to the Successful BI Survey respondents. Forty-six percent of survey respondents rated this item as essential to a successful BI deployment. This rating remained the same regardless of whether the respondent was an IT professional or a business user. IT professionals should find this rating encouraging as there is a widely held belief that business users do not consider data quality to be as important as sexy BI tools, query performance, and other, more visible aspects of business intelligence.

Data quality is such an important issue, and yet one that is not well understood or that excites business users. It's often perceived as being a problem for IT to handle when it's not: it's for the business to own and correct. Because IT can often bandage data quality problems during the extract, transform, and load process (see Figure 2-3, Chapter 2), businesspeople don't take accountability for data quality.

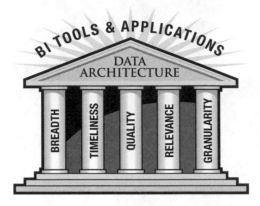

Figure 7-1   The data architecture is the foundation for successful business intelligence.

> Achieving a high level of data quality is hard and is affected significantly by organizational and ownership issues. In the short term, bandaging problems rather than addressing the root causes is often the path of least resistance.

Larry English is one of the leading experts on information quality, and he ranks information quality as the second biggest threat to humankind, after global warming.[1] Initially, I thought his comments were hyperbole, framed to garner readership interest. Yet he cites compelling statistics to support his dire claim. As an example, he notes that 96,000

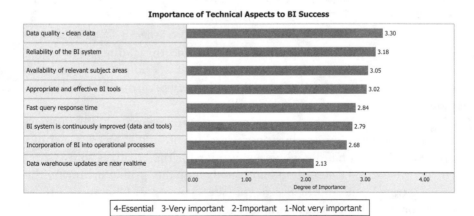

Figure 7-2   Data quality is the most important technical criterion for BI success.

hospital patients die each year from errors arising out of poor data quality. He estimates that the cost of process failure and rework from poor data quality in the United States alone is $1.5 trillion or more.[2] Analyst firm Gartner estimates that 25% of *critical* data in Fortune 1000 companies is wrong.[3] In a TDWI survey, more than half of respondents said their company has suffered losses, problems, and costs due to poor-quality data.[4]

I don't know where data quality rates in terms of threats to humankind, but it is a big problem and one that rates highest in terms of successful business intelligence. As business user Eric Bachenheimer, director of client account management at Emergency Medical Associates (EMA) describes, "If you don't have trust or faith in your data, you're dead in the water. It will take you a long time to get that faith back." Early in EMA's business intelligence deployment, there was little data governance. The BI application manager got dragged into data validation in the source systems simply because the data appeared to be incorrect in the business intelligence reports. Ultimately, the cause of the data quality problems was not because of the ETL process, or the way data was modeled in the data warehouse or represented in the reports: it was because two hospitals submitted data in the source system differently. However, because it was the reports that displayed the bad data, the BI administrator was forced to develop a stopgap solution. Getting businesspeople to understand the issues that affect data integrity can be a slow process. EMA started their BI efforts in 1999, and implementing a data stewardship program has been one of the top priorities for 2007. Jonathan Rothman, director of data management, describes, "I'm trying to get the business to take ownership over data validation as well as taking ownership over providing the data warehouse quality, error free data."

Data Problems Start at the Source

Data quality problems frequently start in the source systems. A client in the oil and gas industry had significant data quality problems following the merger of multiple companies. While all the companies used SAP as the ERP (enterprise resource planning) system, they had deployed SAP in slightly different ways with company-specific data-capture rules. When business users wanted to report information by bill of lading—a fairly important and routine way of tracking materials—they couldn't. Bill of lading was not mandatory in the source systems! If it were captured, it could appear in any one of a number of fields: bill of lading (an obvious choice but an input field not always used), document reference, delivery note, or comments. Getting anyone to be held accountable for making bill of lading mandatory and entered in a consistent place required executive level support and organizational change, neither of which was possible at the time. People refused to use the data warehouse because it was wrong. The data warehouse team refused to change the ETL process because it violated their principle of correcting data quality issues in the source systems. Stalemate.

Learn from this company's lesson: You can only report on what is captured—and captured consistently and accurately.

Eventually, the data warehouse team made an exception, then another, then another. BI usage increased as users slowly gained confidence in the integrity of the data warehouse. Contrast the experience of this oil and gas company with that of Dow Chemical.

When Dow first began its business intelligence effort 14 years ago in 1993, SAP was a newly implemented ERP system that forced many of the work processes to change. Some of the work processes reengineered well and others did not. Using Six Sigma as a way of measuring data quality, Dow at the time was a 1.5 sigma level.[5] There were a number of hiccups from the reengineering efforts and bad data in the system as each business entered data into SAP slightly differently, based on their distinct requirements. Four years ago, Mike Costa, then a senior director in information systems and the main owner for business intelligence, had what he describes as an aha moment. "When we design work processes, we don't design governance around the work processes, and yet it impacts information management and delivery in the data warehouse. Managing all the stuff to the left of the architecture [see Figure 2-3, Chapter 2]—the process design, governance, security—if you miss any one, it impacts quality and the integrity of the data warehouse." As a result, the CEO and CIO promoted Costa to corporate director of quality process & architecture, continuing to give him control over the data warehouse, but in addition, giving him authority to change the operational processes that affect the full business intelligence life cycle.

"You can spend millions building the data warehouse, but if you don't have the back office under control, you are wasting money."

—Mike Costa, former corporate director of quality process & architecture, The Dow Chemical Company

His role was separate from any individual function, work process, or business unit. Today, data quality in the back office is a 5.9 to 6.0 sigma level, and in the data warehouse it is a 5.9.

After leading the BI effort at Dow for the past decade, Costa recently retired from Dow and now serves on the board of directors for Central

---

About Six Sigma

Six Sigma is a management strategy that focuses on product and service quality. Whereas many management strategies focus on quality by monitoring the number of defects after the fact, Six Sigma focuses on the processes that lead to the defects. "It provides specific methods to re-create the process so that defects and errors never arise in the first place."[6] The higher the sigma level, the less likely the process will lead to defects. For example, airlines in terms of safety operate at a sigma level higher than 6, whereas baggage handling is in the 3.5 to 4 range.[7] So for every million bags handled, between 6,000 and 23,000 are mishandled (or 7.92 per 1,000 as of June 2007[8]). Most companies operate at a 3.5 to 4 sigma level.

The Six Sigma proponents tie the sigma level or quality level directly to improved profitability, arguing that a large portion of higher product and service costs can be attributed to poor quality.

	The Cost of Quality	
Sigma Level	Defects per Million Opportunities	Cost of Quality
2	308,537 (Noncompetitive companies)	Not applicable
3	66,807	25 40% of sales
4	6,210 (Industry average)	15–25% of sales
5	233	5–15% of sales
6	3.4 (World class)	<1% of sales

Each sigma shift provides a 10% net income improvement.

Source: Harry, Mikel, Schroeder, Richard, *Six Sigma: The Breakthrough Management Strategy Revolutionizing the World's Top Corporations*, Doubleday: 2000, page 17.

Six Sigma has been a key strategy at Dow Chemical for the last decade. As the preceding table illustrates, the move in data quality in the data warehouse from a 1.5 sigma level to 5.9 is significant. Not only is the level of data quality noteworthy, but also, that the company measures it!

Michigan University Research Corporation. He advises Fortune 10 companies on ways to improve data quality and operational processes.

When Data Is Everywhere

Combining data from multiple, disparate source systems also contributes to data quality problems. Norway Post, for example, has seven different general ledger systems.[9] Figure 7-3 shows how hard it was for users to get to any meaningful data from multiple systems. Prior to implementing a common data warehouse, users would do manual extracts into over 6,000 different Excel spreadsheets. If you struggle to discern the data access model in Figure 7-3, it is because it was *that* convoluted, a common situation for companies without an enterprise information architecture.

Seven years ago, as part of its performance management initiative, Norway Post phased out the manual, multiple extracts and made the common data warehouse the point of access for reports, plans, and statistical analysis (see Figure 7-4).[10] To further simplify the information

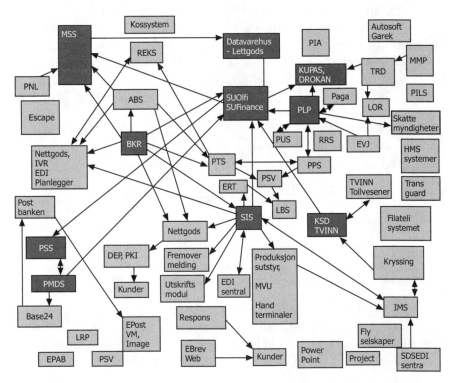

Figure 7-3   Norway Post's disparate data sources (reprinted with permission)

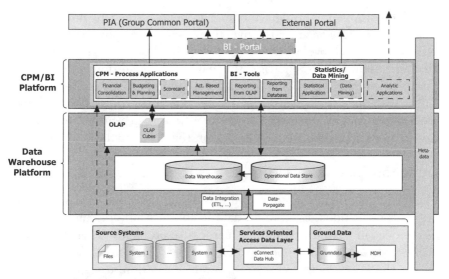

Figure 7-4 Norway Post's Integrated Performance Management System (reprinted with permission)

architecture, the company has begun the process of phasing out multiple, custom general-ledger systems to replace them with Oracle business applications.

Not everyone has the luxury of standardizing on a packaged ERP system, particularly companies whose business model is based on external data, as is the case with FlightStats. FlightStats collects data from multiple data sources: government sources such as the Federal Aviation Administration (FAA), airports, and global distribution systems such as Sabre, Apollo, and Amadeus. Each data source provides flight information in a different format and often contains different information. For example, some data sources report aircraft positional information while others report gate data or runway data. The data must be interpreted and normalized into a unified flight record that contains all information from all sources and then integrated to form a common flight history record. So, for example, if you are flying from New York to Australia, there may be two flight records: one that comes from Continental Airlines for the New York to Los Angeles route and a second one that comes from Qantas for the Los Angeles to Melbourne leg. Additionally, the FAA provides positional and runway information. FlightStats will merge the information on these events that come from multiple, disparate data sources into a single flight history record for each leg. Every event has distinct nuances. For example, if a flight is delayed and crosses over the end of day, there are now two records for the same day, airline, and flight number. The data model has been refined to handle these types of events. It's been an iterative, three-year process to understand the data nuances, achieve a high level of data quality, and apply consistent business definitions. Following the capture of real-time information, this detailed data is periodically extracted, transformed, and loaded into a data warehouse designed for historical reporting and statistical analysis. Customers can access both the real-time data warehouse and the historical data warehouse, depending on their information needs.

Common Business Definitions

FlightStats highlights another aspect to data quality and that is common business definitions. Even when data is correctly entered and accurate, differences in business definitions can cause problems. Whenever users access data and assume one business definition is being followed when in fact the BI platform follows a different definition, users will assume data in the BI platform is wrong. Instead, it's simply a matter of definition. A major U.S.-based telecommunication company said one of their barriers to success was different business definitions. They had more than 33 different definitions for "customer churn." Clearly, the rationalization of business definitions is a problem the business has to tackle. IT can only *implement* those business definitions.

Successful Data Architectures

Beyond data quality, how best to store and model the data in the data warehouse is a theory of frequent debate. There are two predominant philosophies advocated by data warehouse visionaries, sometimes referred to as the fathers of data warehousing, Bill Inmon and Ralph Kimball. Their philosophies are similar in many respects, but where they differ most is in how to store the data. In simple terms, Inmon advocates storing the data in granular, normalized form once, with relevant data marts (whether a subset or aggregate of the detailed data) modeled off the normalized data model. Inmon's approach is often referred to as the "Corporate Information Factory" or "hub and spoke" approach. Kimball, meanwhile, advocates using star schemas as a business presentation layer, referred to as the "data mart bus architecture." This star schema may or may not be built with extracts directly from the source systems or from data stored in a stage area. Research from professors Thilini Ariyachandra (University of Cincinnati) and Hugh Watson (University of Georgia) is one of the few studies that have looked at the degree to which approach is more successful.[11] According to their survey, 39% predominantly follow Inmon's Corporate Information Factory or hub-and-spoke architecture, while 26% follow Kimball's data mart bus architecture. Both deployment approaches showed equal degrees of success. The only architecture that showed notably lower success rates was independent data marts.

The survey did not, however, look at who uses a combination of either approach, something that Dan Linstedt, chief technology officer for Myers-Holum, most often encounters. He advocates the Inmon, third-normal-form approach when there are multiple, disparate data sources.[12] He will use the Kimball dimensional approach when there is a single source system and for the presentation layer. Storing the data in third-normal form is one of the keys to success that Continental Airlines cites (see Chapter 2 for an explanation of normalization). The commitment to staging the data this way has allowed Continental to ensure consistency and reusability, while also providing flexibility for all the departments and business applications that access the data warehouse.

With the exception of Continental Airlines, the use of a particular data model approach is not something other successful BI case studies or survey respondents spoke about. In practice, I can attest that a poorly designed data model, particularly one that business users access, can prevent users from asking and answering their business questions with any degree of ease, and sometimes, not at all. Conversely, a data model optimized for business reporting and analysis facilitates insight and improves user adoption.

Master Data Management (MDM)

Master data management seems to be the latest buzz in the BI industry (see Chapter 2 for an explanation of MDM). Some of this buzz is fueled by vendor acquisition and innovation, and some by the hope that master data management will help improve data quality.

There are different types of master data: product, customer, region, facility location, and chart of accounts, to name a few. In Chapter 2, Figure 2-1, master data existed in multiple transaction systems. The order entry system used a different set of customer codes from the invoice system. Ideally, these codes would be the same regardless of the transaction system, and yet, that is rarely the case. Often, custom transaction systems will devise their own codes. ERP systems (shown in Chapter 2, Figure 2-2) will often share code tables across multiple modules, reducing the number of different codes for the same element. Note: With an integrated ERP system, the number of distinct codes is reduced only by the degree to which disparate code tables have been eliminated. Data entry errors will continue to exist. In other words, you may still have multiple records for the same customer ("Howson" and "Howsin," for example), but those records are stored in one system.

As a fictitious example, assume customer "Preferred Purchasing" places an order. The customer number, 123, from the order entry system is used. When the product is shipped, the customer is invoiced. The customer number in the invoice system (I456) is different from that in the order system and includes an alphabetical character. This difference in codes can cause enormous data quality problems when information from the two different systems is combined. In the absence of common code files or a master data management system, the data warehouse team is left to define its own coding system (see Figure 7-5). Without doing this, business users cannot create even the simplest reports such as customer order quantity and invoice amount.

In Figure 7-5, a common customer code—989—for Preferred Purchasing is implemented as part of the extract, transform, and load process, to allow users to analyze data by customer regardless of which transaction system the data originated in. The next issue, though, is when data needs to be aggregated. Preferred Purchasing may have hundreds of locations around the world. For each location and sometimes

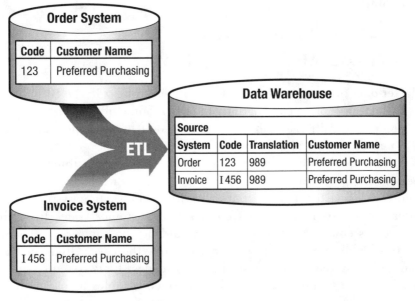

Figure 7-5   Customer master data

each contact person, there may be a unique customer code. If a user wants to understand global purchases by all the locations around the world, then these regional and global rollups must be maintained.

At question in the industry is if these codes and hierarchies should be maintained in the ERP system, the data warehouse, or in a separate master data management system. Increasingly, MDM experts advocate storing master data management separately and allowing both the transaction systems and data warehouse to access it. This has been Dow's philosophy since the late 1980s, when it began implementing its own global code system, Infrastructure for Code Administration (INCA). As shown in Figure 7-6, master data is created in INCA. INCA then distributes data to SAP (the ERP system), Siebel (the CRM system), the Human Resources (HR) system, the Product Lifecycle Management (PLM), and other source systems, which can append application-specific data as needed. Information is then extracted into the data warehouse.

Dow's global codes and approach to master data management were clearly ahead of the industry and continue to be so today. Dow recognizes its global codes as an ingredient to its successful use of business intelligence, particularly on a global basis. Despite MDM's importance at Dow, even Costa recognizes the challenges of organizing for MDM and securing funding. "It is a lost child that nobody wants. Whenever resources get cut, MDM is sunset. It's so behind the scenes that nobody understands the value." While MDM today may garner little business attention, one market research firm described 2006 as an "inflection point" with data governance driving market growth which leapt to thirty percent in 2006[14].

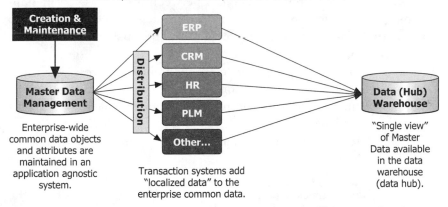

Figure 7-6   The Dow Chemical Company's MDM strategy[13] (reprinted with permission)

Right-Time Data

In business intelligence's infancy, data warehouses were updated on a monthly, sometimes weekly, basis. As BI extends into operational applications, these data warehouses are increasingly updated in near realtime. The update to the data warehouse may be seconds behind transaction system updates, or minutes or hours, whatever best serves the business requirements. Industry expert Colin White, president of BI Research, refers to this as *right-time business intelligence*.[15]

While much of right-time business intelligence is about supporting operational decision-making, the timeliness of updates also increasingly allows decision makers to take swift action on strategic and tactical decisions. If, for example, a new product launch (strategy) is not performing as expected, it doesn't do executives much good to find this out three months into the launch based on monthly data warehouse updates. More timely updates allow for more timely insight and corrective action. 1-800 CONTACTS, for example, released its first data warehouse in spring 2005 with nightly loads from the source system.[16] It wasn't until six months later when the data warehouse moved to updates every 15 minutes that senior executives embraced the system. While the call center may use the dashboard for operational purposes, the dashboard provides executives with a snapshot of how the business is doing in near realtime. Spikes in the number of inbound calls to the call center act as an early warning system for an upcoming increased load in the distribution center.

Dr. Richard Hackathorn, founder of Bolder Technology, talks about three components of data latency that affect decision making:[17]

- *Capture latency* is the time it takes between a business event happening and a piece of data being captured in a source system to when that data has been extracted into the business intelligence architecture.
- *Analysis latency* is the time it takes to disseminate, access, view, and analyze the updated information. Such dissemination and analysis may be in the form of a dashboard update, an alert, or a report refresh.
- *Decision latency* is the time to make a decision and take action based on the analysis.

Hackathorn suggests that reducing this data latency reduces the time to action. The reduced time to action has a corresponding business value as shown in Figure 7-7. Measuring that business value is important in determining how much it costs to reduce data latency. If the cost to update the data warehouse in near realtime exceeds the business value gained, then it should not be done.

As an example, some of the data that FlightStats acquires is publicly available from the Department of Transportation. However, it is based on data and events two months prior and includes only a subset of routes and carriers. Perhaps it is timely enough for corporations to negotiate preferred airlines or to support Congress's debate on the need for a Passenger Bill of Rights, but it is not timely enough for individual consumers or travel agents to act upon. FlightStats, meanwhile, updates its flight performance information in real time. Travel agents who subscribe to FlightStats data will receive an alert for a delayed or canceled flight so that passengers with connecting flights can be rebooked proactively while still mid-air on the delayed flight. The business value to the agent in providing this degree of service is a competitive differentiator and key in retaining customers. Therefore, FlightStats can charge for the access to the real-time flight information as there is business value in reducing decision latency. As CEO Jeff Kennedy declares, "building a smart, scalable, real-time data acquisition system has been key to our success."[18]

In the Successful BI Survey, near real-time updates to the data warehouse were rated only important on average (below essential or very important in Figure 7-2). However, it is a characteristic that many successful BI case studies share (see Table 7-1) and that 14% of survey respondents describe as essential.

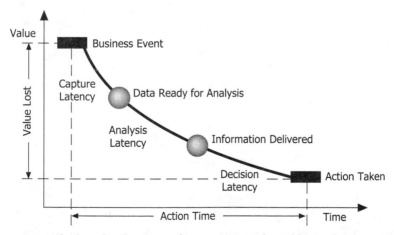

Figure 7-7   The benefit of reducing latency (Copyright Bolder Technology, Inc. Reprinted with permission)

Successful BI Company	Most Frequent Update
1-800 CONTACTS	Every 15 minutes
Continental Airlines	Real time
Corporate Express	Mostly daily, with some data every 10 minutes
The Dow Chemical Company	Daily
Emergency Medical Associates	Daily
FlightStats	Real time
Norway Post	9 times a day

Table 7-1   Successful BI Case Studies Have Near Real-Time BI

Not all BI applications require real time, and the frequency of the data warehouse updates is something to evaluate for each data source and application. Mike Pekala, a finance director and power user at Dow, cautions, "having even daily data at times is a burden versus a benefit. If a customer only orders twice a month, management panics when we get to the 14th of the month and daily sales velocity is looking bad because the customer has not placed their second, large order. There are times when real-time data causes issues because people do not understand the underlying details. They are just looking at a highly summarized report."

Data Quality's Chicken and Egg

Given just how difficult it is to achieve data quality and how far the industry is from addressing the root causes of data quality, it begs the question: what do you do first?

Fix the data and then strive for business intelligence?
or
Deliver business intelligence tools on top of messy data and later fix the data as you go?

This would sound like a no-brainer. Of course nobody in their right mind would embark on a business intelligence initiative with bad data! In reality, many do, because they have little choice. The business sponsors don't understand why the data quality is so bad and may not be in a position to address the root causes. Meanwhile, the BI team has to be responsive to deliver on the business's request to deliver BI capabilities. It would seem that the BI team is being set up for failure. In some respects they are rather doomed. At issue is, when is the data good enough? A second issue is that until the consequences of multiple, disparate systems with messy codes, inconsistent business definitions, and incorrect data entry are exposed to the business via BI tools, there is little incentive to address the root causes. Given this chicken-and-egg situation, my recommendation is that if you have severe data quality issues, continue with the BI project but with clear expectations and a limited scope.

> Communicate loudly and widely where there are data quality problems and the associated risks with deploying BI tools on top of bad data. Also advise the different stakeholders on what can be done to address data quality problems—systematically and organizationally. Complaining without providing recommendations fixes nothing.

All too often, the BI team complains about bad data but provides no recommendations on how to improve data quality. Use Figure 7-8 as a way of determining where your company is on the continuum of best practices for data quality.

Depending on the extent of the data quality issues, be careful about where you deploy BI. Without a reasonable degree of confidence in the data quality, BI should be kept in the hands of knowledge workers and not extended to frontline workers and certainly not to customers and suppliers. Deploy BI in this limited fashion as data quality issues are gradually exposed, understood, and ultimately, addressed. Don't wait

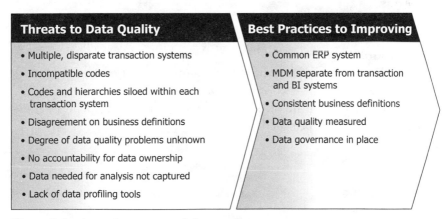

Figure 7-8   A continuum toward data quality

for every last data quality issue to be resolved; if you do, you will never deliver any BI capabilities, business users will never see the problem, and quality will never improve.

Best Practices for Successful Business Intelligence

The data architecture is the most important technical aspect of your business intelligence initiative. Fail to build an information architecture that is flexible, with consistent, timely, quality data, and your BI initiative will fail. Business users will not trust the information, no matter how powerful and pretty the BI tools. However, sometimes it takes displaying that messy data to get business users to understand the importance of data quality and to take ownership of a problem that extends beyond business intelligence, to the source systems and to the organizational structures that govern a company's data.

- Assess the degree to which your source systems and BI applications have data quality problems, and recognize the role it plays in business intelligence success.
- Ensure the source systems capture what you want to report and analyze.
- Understand the role of operational processes in ensuring data quality and the degree to which disparate transaction systems challenge data quality.
- Separate master data from transactional and business intelligence systems.
- Agree on consistent business definitions.
- Review organizational structures to determine who owns the data and can ensure its integrity.
- Make continuous improvement in data quality part of a companywide initiative.
- Evaluate increasing the timeliness of data warehouse updates against the business value provided.

Chapter 8

The Business-IT
Partnership

Business and information technology (IT) professionals can become equally exasperated with one another as they are often such opposites. However, the degree to which the business and IT can partner together is the single most important organizational aspect to successful business intelligence (see Chapter 6, Figure 6-1). According to the successful BI survey, 55% identified the business-IT partnership as essential for success, followed closely by executive level support (53%). For the sake of successful business intelligence, then, opposites better attract!

Voices of Frustration

In the successful BI survey, respondents from both the business side and IT side expressed frustration with one another, regardless if their BI deployment was a failure or a success.

"Business and IT have a great deal of difficulty communicating, clearly because of different language and different mind-sets."

> —*A hybrid business-IT person from a major insurance company*

"IT is the main reason why our BI effort failed."

> —*A business user from a utility company*

"The company wanted answers but did not want to understand how they were facilitated. 'It's an Information Systems problem. You solve it. Just give me the answer. Now!'"

> —*An IT professional with a New Zealand transportation company*

"Lack of partnership between IT and the business hurts us at times. There is no realization on the part of the business as to how they affect timelines and implementations."

—An IT professional with a large U.S. retailer who describes their BI deployment as very successful

"The partnership and trust between the Information Systems BI team and the business is essential. Information Systems must understand the business and be involved in what they are trying to achieve."

—Margie Lekien, a BI Leader with Landstar System, Inc., who describes their BI project as very successful

The frustration and divide between the business and IT has ramifications far beyond business intelligence. Yet given the distinct aspect of this technology, lack of partnership has a more profound effect in BI's success. As both sides blame one another, a key secret to reducing blame and increasing understanding is to recognize how these two sides are different.

The Business-IT Yin-Yang

The concept of yin and yang originated in ancient Chinese philosophy.[1] The yang—the white portion of the symbol—represents movement, initiative, heat, and fire. The yin—the black portion of the symbol—represents passiveness, cold, and water. The yin-yang is a good symbol for the business-IT relationship because while it does reflect opposites, it is said the yin-yang also conveys "balance" and "a duality that can not exist without both parts."[2] Within the white yang portion of the symbol, there is also a small black circle (and the black yin portion has a small white circle) to show each side has elements of the other and is stronger when they interact. The differences are not absolute.

Yin
(IT)

Yang
(Business)

The following table compares characteristics of businesspeople and IT people. They are archetypes, and as with any archetype there are exceptions, but I would suspect that if each group of professionals were given a personality test, consistent traits would emerge. As an example, when an archetypal businessperson wants to address a problem, he or she will schedule a face-to-face meeting so differences, opinions, and ideas can be shared. An IT person, on the other hand, would prefer to fire off an e-mail, avoiding direct interaction (and providing documentation on the disagreement). A businessperson would comfortably skip documenting and testing a system, and happily just slam in a new version of software. The prospect of doing this might cause heart palpitations for an IT professional—the risks and lack of a systematic approach are overwhelming. Okay, perhaps both archetypes would like to skip documenting the system, but it illustrates the extreme differences in work styles.

Business Person Archetype	IT Professional Archetype
Extrovert	Introvert
Sociable	Solitary
Freewheeling	Methodical, systematic, disciplined
Risk taking	Risk averse
Prefers face-to-face meetings	Minimal face-to-face communication. E-mail and instant messaging is fine.

In reviewing drafts of this chapter, I and my technical editor were concerned that my proposed archetypes would offend some readers. While she agreed with my observations, we wanted to support these archetypes with hard data. So I turned to one of the most widely used personality tests: Myers-Briggs Type Indicator (MBTI). MBTI breaks personalities into four aspects[3]:

- Energy: Extroverts (E) draw their energy from being with other people whereas introverts (I) draw their energy from themselves and solitary activities.
- Perception: Sensing types (S) prefer to deal with reality whereas intuitive (I) types are more imaginative and future-focused
- Judgement: Thinkers (T) are more objective and logical in assessing a situation whereas feelers (F) are people who will judge a situation more by how people are affected
- World Orientation: Judging (J) personality types like structure in their world whereas perceiving (P) types are more spontaneous, flexible, and thrive on change.

In considering the business archetypes described in the earlier table, the business person shows a personality type that is extroverted, feeling, and perceiving or EFP. The IT archetype is more introverted, thinking, and judging or an ITJ personality type. Now, don't let some of the Myers-Brigg terminology lose you here – everyone is a "thinker", but from a personality point of view, a T-type suggests an approach to decisions from a more logical, almost clinical point of view whereas F-types consider more the people impact of their decisions. I don't think the personality extremes for perception (sensing or S and intuitive or I) are distinguishing characteristics in the business and IT archetypes.

The Center for Applications of Psychological Type (CAPT) analyzed more than 60,000 MBTI test results that determine a person's personality type with a selected career. Sure enough, ITJ types (which corresponds to my IT archetype) more often choose technical careers; and a career as a computer operator or systems analyst appears at the top of the list for this personality type.[4] Meanwhile, EFP types most often choose careers that have more people interaction, breadth of skills; careers as marketing and management professionals moved to the top of the list for this type.[5]

This is not to say that you won't find an EFP type in IT, or an ITJ type as a business user; it simply means that the distinct personality types are indeed more prevalent in each role (think the larger black area of the yin-yang versus the small black circle). It's not a baseless stereotype.

Despite the MBTI research, some may still dismiss these differences in work styles and personalities as stereotypes. However, one difference that cannot be so easily dismissed is that of incentives. In many companies, the business is motivated and rewarded for behavior that increases revenue. Increasing revenue may involve designing new products and testing new market segments, all with a lot of risk. IT meanwhile is often rewarded for cutting costs and providing a stable IT environment, where risk is discouraged. To a degree, this dichotomy is necessary. You can't swap out systems on a regular basis and expect the company to continue to operate. As with most things, the solution to closing this incentive gap lies in the middle.

IT people should be rewarded for being responsive to business requests that improve business performance. Providing a stable, low-cost computing environment should be only a *portion* of their total variable compensation and performance evaluation.

Meet the Hybrid Business-IT Person

One way in which business and IT people are bridging the gap is by cultivating hybrid business-IT people. These hybrids are typically businesspeople by training or career who gain technology skills. They may not be programmers or system engineers, but they speak enough of the IT language to translate business needs, opportunities, and requirements in ways that IT traditionalists understand. They also look for ways in which information technology is a business enabler. As described in the Chapter 1 section on the Successful BI survey, 23% of the survey respondents describe themselves as hybrid business-IT persons.

> A hybrid business-IT person can act as a powerful bridge between the different business intelligence stakeholders: the business who derives the value and IT who enables the systems. Hybrid business-IT persons understand the business and how to leverage technology to improve the business. Conversely, they understand enough of the technology to identify opportunities to apply new technology to solve business problems.

I would also describe myself as one of these hybrids. I stumbled into the field of IT in the 1980s. While I excelled at math, computer science at the time was not the place for women, so I pursued my other passion: writing. Being a lousy typist (then and now), I developed a knack for this new thing: word processing. When the university network kept crashing, I had to find innovative ways to recover corrupted files (what—retype an entire paper?!?!?) and discovered the world of personal computers and local area networks. Fortunately, for me, training in those days meant vendor-specific certification and given how newfangled some of this technology was, nobody laughed at my Bachelor's degree in English, but I entered the workforce already in the middle of two disciplines.

Dow Chemical was my second job out of college, and in an unusual twist, I was hired directly by a business unit (not the information systems department) to fill a newly created role as a business systems specialist. So here is an easy way to ensure business-IT partnership: make sure IT personnel are directly on your payroll and not a chargeback or overhead cost. (I only later learned all the political consequences of this unusual reporting line.) The business unit I worked for, hydrocarbons, gave me only broad guidelines to work within, and I answered only to this business unit. When we wanted a local area network, I defined the requirements, bought the system, and installed it. I *might* compare requirements with the central information systems group (out of diplomacy or curiosity), but I didn't have to follow any of their standards. The hydrocarbons business even went so far as to buy our own meeting scheduler (pre–Microsoft Outlook) and to build an integrated transaction system (pre-SAP). As much of what the hydrocarbons business did was ahead of what the European information systems department was offering other business units at the time, there was an enormous amount of friction between the two. Describing the dynamics as an "us versus them" mentality was an understatement.

My business users were happy and the hydrocarbons unit was using information technology in ways that provided real business value. It was rewarding, exciting, challenging, and offered absolutely no career progression. So when the Global Reporting Project came along in 1993, it seemed like a smart career move. It was my first glimpse into the "other side," though, of being a cost center and of having to satisfy the greatest common denominator of not one, but 15 different business units and multiple functions. If the yang is like the fire of the business, my move into IT certainly was like walking into the yin of winter. Overnight, I had become a "them."

I went from the hydrocarbons way of minimal requirements analysis for fast delivery of capabilities to an excruciating level of project planning down to the hour. In hydrocarbons, the technology investments were approved by a business team when something sounded reasonable enough. Within information systems, I had to do a full economic analysis for buying a packaged business intelligence solution, calculated by ROI and payback period, when I was frankly guessing at benefits. I was out of my league.

Eventually, I got past my panic attacks. Through the Global Reporting Project, I learned the discipline within information systems that is necessary when building solutions for thousands of users; in hydrocarbons, the users were fewer than 200. I also learned that while I had gained an understanding of the hydrocarbons business unit, my knowledge of business in general was lacking. For the Global Reporting Project, two of the initial subject areas included a product income statement and a business balance sheet. I had no idea what these terms meant, let alone why they were important. So I did what any stubborn person, determined to understand the purpose in all this would do: I quit my career of eight years, left the company that I referred to as my "extended family," and pursued my MBA, albeit with a focus on information systems.

As my own experience illustrates, the career path for a hybrid business-IT person is often unclear. Do you align more with the business or with IT? What is clear is that such hybrid people benefit from indoctrination and training in both disciplines.

The need for hybrid business-IT people is something that business schools throughout the United States increasingly recognize. The importance of this dual skill set is most apparent at the CIO level (see Chapter 6). For example, the Wharton School of Business at the University of Pennsylvania and the IT research firm Gartner have partnered to launch a new executive program, "CIO As Full Business Partner," to educate CIOs in key business issues and ways to become more active members of business management teams.[6] However, it is also important at lower levels and, I would advocate, at any intersecting points in which businesspeople and IT people must communicate directly with one another.

How to Be a Better Partner

Maureen Clarry, the President of CONNECT and an expert in the field of business-IT relationships, defines a partnership as "a relationship in which we are jointly committed to the success of a particular process or goal. The operative word is 'committed.'"[7]

This doesn't mean the business can define their requirements, throw them over the fence, and hope to get a usable business intelligence solution in return. Nor does it mean that the IT personnel can approach the business with a degree of wariness. Partnership starts with a positive attitude. As 1-800 CONTACTS described their business-IT partnership, Jim Hill, the data warehouse manager says, "We are equal partners with the call center. The business comes here and says 'here's what we are trying to accomplish. What do you think?'...If the business feels they are a partner in solution, you get the desired results." Confirming that this idea of partnership must come from both sides and also that it exists with the business users at 1-800 CONTACTS, Dave Walker, vice president of operations, attributes their BI success to this partnership. "The IT people in the data warehouse team understand the call center so well, they could probably take some calls. They are a life saver for so many things. I've never felt an 'us' versus 'them' mentality. The issue is always 'we' not 'they.'"

The first step to building such a partnership is to recognize its importance in successful business intelligence. Business intelligence is a technology that lies at the heart of the intersection between business and technology; without the partnership, your efforts will be met with moderate success at best.

Some specific things that both the business and IT can do to develop a stronger partnership:

Develop an understanding of each other Recognize the different personalities, work approaches, and constraints under which each works. For the business, this may mean recognizing that IT must deliver common solutions and not business-specific solutions. For IT, this may mean greater recognition of why a timely delivery is so critical to the livelihood of the business (see the section on enterprise versus departmental BI in Chapter 11).

Recruit hybrid business-IT people Whether you identify and develop these people internally or hire from the outside, ensuring some hybrid business-IT people are involved in your business intelligence initiative will help foster a greater partnership.

Ban the technobabble! IT people tend to overuse acronyms. As a courtesy to businesspeople, all acronyms should be banned. You wouldn't speak a foreign language in a room otherwise filled with only English-speaking colleagues, so don't revert to technobabble. Chapter 13 contains techniques on how to better frame business intelligence in terms of the business benefits rather than the technical terms. Practice an elevator pitch that describes briefly what business intelligence is all about in business terms.

Team building Work with your human resources department to bring both IT and businesspeople together for team-building exercises, particularly if you use agile development techniques (see Chapter 10). This might include a personality assessment such as the Myers-Briggs Type Indicator so that team members recognize and understand people's unique motivators and styles of working.

Change incentive compensation Most people have a portion of their salary also tied to performance and accomplishment of certain goals. For IT people, it's important that the goals are not only related to cost containment, but also to business enablement.

Consider organizational structures As my own experience demonstrates, reporting lines do affect the business-IT partnership. Consider alternative organizational structures that provide the appropriate partnership and balance for fulfilling career paths, shared resources, knowledge sharing, and expertise as they relate to business intelligence. At Continental Airlines, for example, a strong steering committee and having business users residing within the data warehouse team help foster a partnership. These organizational aspects are discussed further in Chapter 11.

Involve one another   Business units will periodically have staff meetings, an ideal forum for an appointed IT person to gain a greater understanding of the business, and conversely, for a BI representative to provide an update on the business intelligence initiative. IT personnel should study the company's mission statement as well as individual business unit plans.

Have lunch together   Study the corporate cafeteria and you will find the cliques of high school echoed. The IT department sits with themselves, and businesspeople sit with each other—that is, when people even eat lunch together! It is an unfortunate situation that lunchtime, particularly in the United States, is often relegated to a quick sandwich eaten in isolation at one's desk. Lunchtime is an ideal time to build a partnership more casually.

Alignment

While business alignment and business partnership are closely related, they are not the same thing. *Alignment* involves IT and the business working toward a common goal; *partnership* has more to do with commitment and recognition that both stakeholders have an interest in each other's success. The business intelligence initiative must support the company's or business unit's objectives, whether to be a low-cost provider, best in class service, and so on. Ideally, even when BI is delivered for a new subject area for a particular business unit, those capabilities are aligned with the goals of the company overall. In some cases, they aren't. Individual business units may be at odds with another, putting IT resources in the difficult middle position. In this case, IT and that particular business unit may be working as partners, but they are not aligned. Balanced Scorecard experts Robert Kaplan and David Norton describe this alignment "much like the synchronization achieved by a high-performance rowing crew."[8] Partnership is a commitment to achieving this synergy.

When the business and IT are aligned, then both add value to each other, consistent with the concept of the yin-yang. In this way, the business sees IT as a trusted partner to ensure that technology is considered in developing a business's strategic direction, and IT delivers an architecture and set of services consistent with this direction (see Figure 8-1). Alignment should not be construed as an excuse for IT to *react* to all business requests. The CIO of Westchester County, New York, says, "Too often, the phrase 'aligning IT with the business' implies that IT must breathlessly run to catch up with the business as it goes in whatever direction someone else has determined. True alignment means IT and the business units together define the best direction for the organization to go—and IT shouldn't be afraid to take the lead."[9]

Continental's Go Forward Plan, discussed in Chapter 5, is a good example of how IT and the business and functional users were aligned to achieve an amazing turnaround. Then Continental Airlines President Greg Brenneman says, "We have proven that what gets measured and rewarded gets done. The Go Forward Plan has provided us a practical, measurable and flexible way to get all of our co-workers in our huddle and communicate the direction we want to take the Company."[10] Using the generic framework in Figure 8-1, one of the cornerstones of the Go Forward Plan, Fly to Win, spoke to the need for Continental to change its customer mix from one that historically was predominantly leisure travelers who only wanted the cheapest ticket to a mix of more business travelers who valued a higher level of service and were more loyal.[11] To achieve this, all the employees had to be working in the same direction, aligned with the Go Forward Plan. The airline picked 15 key performance measures to track progress in achieving the Go Forward Plan

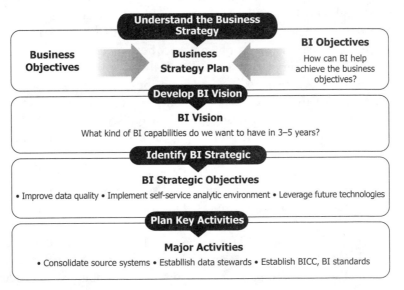

Figure 8-1   Aligning business intelligence with the business

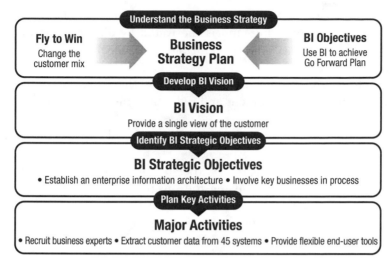

Figure 8-2   Continental's BI alignment to the strategic plan

and how the airline was performing versus its competitors.[12] Figure 8-2 shows how Continental's business intelligence initiatives were aligned with the company's strategic plan.

While alignment is an important ingredient for successful business intelligence, the business intelligence architecture and solution need to be flexible enough to change when the business strategy changes. In this way, Mike Costa, former corporate director of quality process and architecture at Dow Chemical, cautions, "The strategy of the company can change overnight. Business intelligence should be able to react quickly."[13] The same technology and architecture Dow established in 1994, when it first began the Global Reporting Project, continues to be used today. The aspects that have changed the most are the applications (reports, cubes, business views) and the organization.

Best Practices for Successful Business Intelligence

The business IT partnership is one of the most important aspects in succeeding with business intelligence. To foster this partnership and to ensure greater alignment:

- Recognize the importance of the business-IT partnership in successful business intelligence.

- If you feel like the other side seldom understands you, has a radically different way of working, and is motivated by different forces, then congratulate yourself for recognizing some significant differences. They are real!
- Evaluate variable compensation such that the BI team is rewarded not only for cost containment and reduction, but also for the business value added.
- Recruit and develop hybrid business-IT personnel to play a pivotal role in your BI effort.
- Be proactive in developing this partnership by communicating regularly, banning technobabble, studying the business goals, and occasionally having lunch together.
- Align the vision and deliverables for business intelligence with the goals of the company and individual business units that BI serves.

Chapter 9

Relevance

As I contemplate this chapter, the phrase "it's all about me" keeps repeating in my head. I don't know who first coined this phrase. Dr. Phil McGraw (of initial *Oprah* fame) wrote an article by this title for *National Review*. There are 'tween books by this name filled with personality tests. I have heard this phrase shouted by a recent divorcee to another woman who committed the social "error" of being civil to the ex-husband.

> When it comes to business intelligence, you need to be thinking "it's all about me." Or to be politically correct, *Relevance* with a capital *R*.

Webster's dictionary defines relevance as "1. Pertinence to the matter at hand. 2. The capability of an information retrieval system to select and retrieve data suitable for a user's needs." The most successful BI deployments go beyond delivering a massive repository of data with unconstrained, sometimes overwhelming, data access. Instead, they deliver tailored applications *relevant* to the intended user. Some would describe this as personalization, but relevance goes beyond personalization.

In most companies, inside staff such as call center agents don't use business intelligence (as shown in Chapter 4, Figure 4-5, only 28% of inside staff use BI). If you think of BI as synonymous with business query tools for power users only, then inside staff would not need such capabilities. Their information requirements are somewhat predictable. And yet, dozens of times every day they make decisions and take actions, many of which can be supported by *relevant* business intelligence.

Relevance Brings Clearer Vision

At 1-800 CONTACTS, prior to the BI application, call center agents were frustrated with inadequate information access (see the section on frustration in Chapter 5). Agent turnover was high and on exit interviews, agents complained that they were compensated based on things beyond their control. Agents were paid commissions on a number of performance measures, but these measures were only available via a piece of paper posted on the wall the next day—too late, too aggregated, too inaccessible to be actionable. As 1-800 CONTACTS began designing their first BI application, they studied what motivated call center agents and what information could help them do their jobs better. The BI team worked side by side with the agents to the extent that the team could even handle an incoming call. In the initial prototype, the BI application showed agents their daily performance. Call center managers thought this would be a big win for the agents. In debating the dynamics of the call center, senior executives noted that there was a degree of healthy competition among the agents. Executives wanted to tap into their competitive nature to drive better performance. They thought that showing agents what percentile they were performing in would create a kind of horse race among the agents.[1] By increasing the dashboard update to refresh every 15 minutes, it would allow agents to take action that same day.

For example, Figure 9-1 shows multiple performance indicators such as closing ratio, average order size, and productivity (confidential information is intentionally blurred). The top bar within each of these displays shows the individual agent performance. A traffic light indicator next to the bar shows green when the agent is performing well versus the agent's team and the entire call center. The subsequent team and call center bars show just how far ahead or behind the agent is versus his or her peers. Prior to 2006, agents didn't have timely access to this information and not in such a visual way. The very week that the new dashboard went live, there was a measurable lift in sales.

Data about an individual agent's performance is certainly relevant to the agent, but the other piece that gave agents greater control was a customer snapshot. Over the years, the company has amassed a lot of information on how customers behave, such as when they are most likely to need a prescription refill, how often they return, and their lifetime value. When a customer calls 1-800 CONTACTS, the agent now gets a snapshot of this information.

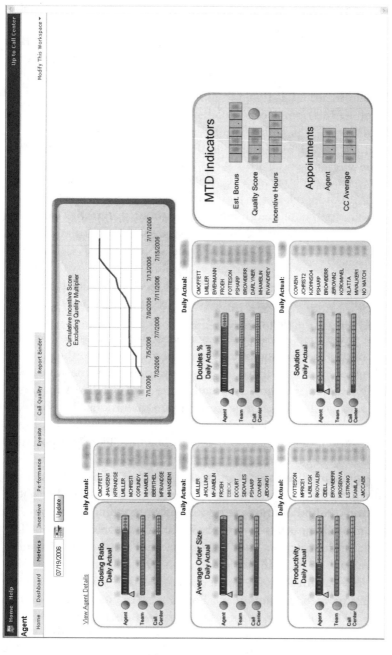

Figure 9-1 1-800 CONTACTS agent key performance indicators (Copyright 1-800 CONTACTS. Reprinted with permission.)

Relevance Improves Patient Care

Emergency Medical Associates described a similar story of relevance. Bio-surveillance is the use of data to try to predict where there may be disease outbreaks or signs of bioterrorist attacks. Some of this data originates in emergency rooms. As patients check into an emergency room, their symptoms and complaints are coded to allow for analysis. In fall 2004, the United States faced a shortage of flu vaccine after one of the main vaccine manufacturers in Britain was forced to suspend manufacturing due to contamination issues at the plant.[2] A few months later, EMA made mainstream news headlines at NBC News with its unique ability to predict a severe flu outbreak in the New York–New Jersey area. While EMA routinely sends such data to a number of reporting authorities including local health officials and the Centers for Disease Control,[3] the ability to analyze the data, predict the outbreak, and graphically show the most affected areas at the hospital level was exceptional. The ability to improve patient care is *relevant* to physicians; that business intelligence tools allow improved care is what makes BI attractive to a group of users who otherwise lag the industry in adoption of information technology.

Another way that doctors use business intelligence to improve patient care is by improving emergency room operations so that staffing levels and patient wait times are optimal. In much the same way 1-800 CONTACTS studied the drivers of call center agents, EMA looked at the factors that most affected emergency room operations. The BI team did not follow the traditional requirements gathering process of going to the doctors and asking "what do you want?" Doctors, like most potential business intelligence users, don't know what they want until they see it and may not know what is even possible with information technology. Jonathan Rothman, director of data management at EMA, had a healthcare background but no experience with emergency room care. So he learned the businesses by interviewing and collaborating with doctors, hospital administrators, and other stakeholders on the dynamics of the emergency room.[4] Rothman kept thinking, "how can we exploit this technology to provide more services at less cost?" Wait time is a key indicator for emergency rooms (ER). For some patients, it's a matter of life and death. For others, it is a matter of patient dissatisfaction. In the United States, ER wait times average 3 hours and 42 minutes.[5] When ER wait times are high, patients walk out and either go to another emergency room or wait to see their regular physician. While this indicator was acknowledged by all the stakeholders as being important, it was not one that was routinely tracked or that could be proven to impact care and finances.[6] Rothman prototyped some reports to demonstrate that when wait times went up, walkouts went up, and care and income went down. The reports evolved into a series of dashboards shown in Figure 9-2.

The top portion of the dashboard provides a scorecard of key performance indicators so users can readily see how many patients have been seen this month versus last, the percentage of patients billed, and the rate that patients left without being seen (LWOB). Visual indicators at the bottom of the dashboard allow decision-makers to focus on certain metrics and to drill down into specific time periods. For example, in Figure 9-2, a barometer in the bottom left shows that the patients left without being seen (LWOB) is at 0.11% for the period. The barometer is color-coded to indicate green (at the bottom) when the metric is within the desired rate, yellow to indicate above the desired rate, and red at the top to indicate an unacceptable rate.

Appropriate staffing levels in emergency rooms are particularly difficult to determine: by definition, emergencies are not scheduled events, and yet, with all the data available, EMA can discern trends to be more proactive. Weekends are peak periods so staffing levels can be adjusted for this. Changing registration procedures and the layout of the emergency room can also bring faster treatment. Simply treating patients faster does not always result in better care and higher patient satisfaction, though. Findings show that optimum staffing level and admittance procedures are important, so another dashboard provides a metric on patient satisfaction displayed next to the number of patients treated per hour. Using some of the same techniques that 1-800 CONTACTS applied, the doctors within a given hospital are allowed to see other doctors' metrics so that a degree of professional competitiveness further contributes to performance. By giving hospital administrators and doctors access to this information, EMA has been able to reduce the ER wait time by 50% in some cases.[7]

Fortunately, my experience with emergency rooms has been rather limited. As EMA shared their story of BI success with me, I couldn't help thinking, "in an emergency, patients have no choice. You go to whichever hospital is nearest." While the reduced ER wait times clearly affect patient satisfaction and care, I was skeptical that there was any connection to ER financials. (Recall from the section on threats in Chapter 5 some of the extreme financial pressures facing hospitals today.) A friend, who just happens to be a somewhat frequent visitor of emergency rooms, enlightened me. Dale has three children, one with asthma and another with unexplained high fevers. Her nearest emergency room is about 20 minutes away. And yet, in an emergency Dale will travel to an

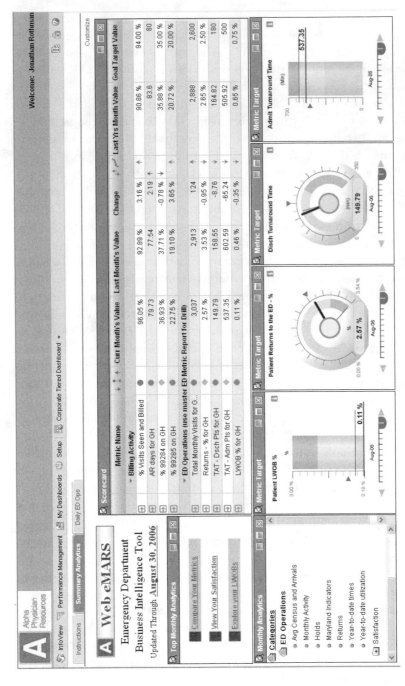

Figure 9-2 WEBeMARS™ Physician Dashboard developed by Emergency Medical Associates (Copyright Emergency Medical Associates. Reprinted with permission.)

EMA-operated emergency room at Saint Barnabas Health Care System, about 45 minutes away. She has visited at least three other area ERs. When once visiting a closer hospital (non-EMA operated), her son was sent home after waiting hours and being told his arm was only bruised. Two days later, when the pain would not subside, Dale took her son to a specialist. Looking at the X-ray herself, Dale could see it was a full break. "I would rather drive further, get seen faster, and have my children better sooner than go to one of these other hospitals." Dale's experiences do not mean that only EMA-operated hospitals provide excellent emergency room care, but they do confirm that my assumptions about emergency rooms were wrong: proximity is not the only deciding factor in which hospital a patient chooses. Instead, for non-life-threatening emergencies, patients will indeed go to the most efficient hospital with the best reputation for quality care.

In many companies, finance and marketing departments often are early adopters of business intelligence. At EMA, business intelligence has wide support at senior levels and across the company. The BI team has been proactive in focusing its BI efforts on the opportunities that most drive the business: information to support physicians and emergency room operations. While BI is still important to the finance department, EMA prioritized finance users as one of the later adopters. Contrast this approach with many BI teams who are more reactive, delivering applications first to those departments who shout the loudest.

Relevance to Continental Gate Agents

Gate agents may not be whom you picture when you think of a typical business intelligence user, and yet, business intelligence is an important tool for gate agents at Continental Airlines. Continental has a policy of filling its business class seats for every flight. When the seats have not been sold, complimentary upgrades are offered to people who have purchased higher-fare tickets and to Continental's most frequent fliers—OnePass Elite members. Filling these seats is a priority for customer satisfaction. If a OnePass Elite member hoping for an upgrade boards the plane and sees the empty business class seats, it creates potential for dissatisfaction.[8]

   Much of the Elite upgrade process is now automated through the airline's web-based check-in, where passengers can check in online 24 hours in advance of their flight. At the time of the check-in, if the business class cabin is not full and predicted to remain that way, a OnePass Elite member is automatically offered an upgrade to business class. Online check-in helps reduce chaos at airport check-in. Customers are given incentives to check in online such as receiving extra frequent flier miles. The challenge is that travel plans can sometimes go awry. So if a business class passenger doesn't show up—say they missed a connecting flight, got stuck in traffic en route to the airport, or had a last-minute change of plans—then a seat is now available for an Elite upgrade. Gate agents may only realize that this seat is available as late as a few minutes prior to departure. Under extreme pressure to ensure an on-time departure, with planes booked to capacity, and 100 other things that demand immediate attention, offering this free upgrade to an unsuspecting passenger may not be high on the list of priorities for the gate agent.

At first blush, it might be easiest to think, "why bother?—giving the free upgrade doesn't even add revenue to the airline!" And yet, it is a customer service differentiator and one of several reasons why Continental has almost no attrition in its OnePass Elite members.[9] For gate agents to provide this service, it has to be incredibly easy both to recognize that the business class seat is empty as well as to identify to which Elite passenger the upgrade should be offered. The final secret to encouraging action on the gate agents' part is once again a combination of co-worker competitiveness and incentives: agents are given quarterly bonuses for having the highest compliance for filling the business class cabin.[10] In this way, business intelligence plays two roles—first in the operational task of identifying which passengers should receive the upgrade and then later in monitoring the key performance indicator of flying with a full business class cabin.

The Role of Incentives

As I pieced together the common threads of each of these three examples, it initially seemed to me that financial incentives were at the heart of relevance. The authors of *Freakonomics* write, "Experts are humans, and humans respond to incentives."[11] The authors provide case after case to show that when misaligned incentives often produce undesirable results. For example, real estate agents may not always sell a house for the highest price (the seller's desired result), but rather, in a way that maximizes their net commission (the real estate agent's incentive).

I began asking interviewees what role incentive compensation played in their use of business intelligence. One responded, quite seriously, "just using business intelligence is its own reward!"(He is one of the enthusiastic users of BI who was previously starved for data and BI tools). He felt that perhaps the relationship between business intelligence and compensation is one of "six degrees of separation," so, somewhat related but not obvious enough to be a motivator. Financial compensation, however, is only one form of incentive, and other forms of incentives in this idea of relevance are

- A desire to win, or to outperform their colleagues
- A desire to do a better job, whether to improve patient care or customer satisfaction
- A sense of happiness or removal of frustration that information they struggled to access and compile before has been made significantly easier to access

There are a number of barriers to BI success, and individual resistance to change is one of them. When this is the case, then incentives—whether financial or other—can play a role in encouraging people to use business intelligence effectively. While I have encountered companies who use specific incentives to encourage BI use, a better approach is to integrate business intelligence into achieving a level of performance that is tied to an existing incentive.

Personalization

Personalizing business intelligence has a role in relevance. Personalization goes beyond simply matching the BI tool with the user segment as discussed in Chapter 12. Personalization involves tailoring the software interface, such as the menus and capabilities, as well as ensuring each individual only sees the data relevant to him or her.

Row-level security is one approach to personalizing the data. With row-level security, each user is granted permission to see certain rows within the database. For example, at 1-800 CONTACTS, a given call center agent can see only his or her individual performance in the dashboard shown earlier in Figure 9-1. Each customer phone call and order record is associated to the agent so that in the dashboard, the information is personalized for that agent. This kind of personalization can be a challenge to implement when data is extracted from multiple systems and aggregated. For example, while it may be straightforward to associate the call and order records, and therefore the detailed rows in a database, with a single call agent, the process is complicated when you want to personalize aggregated information for a call center manager. Somewhere the relationship between call center managers and the particular agents has to be established to provide personalization on this aggregated data. Increasingly within the industry, ERP-vendors are enhancing the transaction systems to ensure personalization implemented in the source systems can later be leveraged in the business intelligence environment. As this is still an emerging capability, many BI administrators are forced to develop their own personalization approaches whether in the physical data warehouse or in the BI tools.

It's important to note that personalization is not synonymous with security. The former emphasizes data restrictions for the purposes of improving relevancy; the latter is about preventing people from seeing information not pertinent to their jobs. Unfortunately, sometimes in the desire to personalize and the need to secure information, access to data in a BI environment can be overly restrictive. Neil Raden, founder of Hired Brains, has written about the issues that unnecessary data restrictions can cause. He argues that when data is restricted based on outdated hierarchical management structures, it may remove valuable context for the information. "In many BI implementations, every user of the system is restricted to the data they are allowed to see. With respect to confidential information, privacy regulations or other mandated restrictions, this seems like a reasonable approach, but in most organizations, the "need to know" restrictions are the result of the pyramid, not logic. The eastern region sales manager is unable to see how the western region sales manager is doing with respect to a certain kind of sale and thus, deprived of potentially valuable insight."[12] It's noteworthy then that the 1-800 CONTACTS dashboard in Figure 9-1 provides context in a way that preserves security requirements: agents can see their performance relative to the team and call center but cannot see details for other agents.

Requirements-Driven BI

A commonly held opinion for successful business intelligence is that it should be requirements driven: the users define their requirements, and the BI team builds a solution according to those specifications. And yet, these stories of relevance show a very different model. The requirements were not explicitly defined by the users at all. They were deduced by the business intelligence experts. These BI experts didn't have a "build it and they will come" mentality, nor did they "build what was asked for"; instead, they studied the activities of these potential users and delivered something that would benefit the individuals.

It is this model of development that is most required for extending BI beyond traditional information workers. Knowledge workers may have a better idea of what data and tools they need to do their jobs so a traditional requirements-driven development model may work for this segment. For others, though, it is up to the BI experts to study people's jobs, daily decisions, and performance incentives, to discover these requirements. In short, relevance is about finding a way to use business intelligence to simplify their work and make it better.

Best Practices for Successful Business Intelligence

When it comes to extending the reach of business intelligence, relevance is a key secret to success. Relevance is business intelligence with an "it's all about me" mindset. To make BI more relevant to all workers in your company:

- Study the drivers of company performance to determine which decisions and people will have the biggest impact. Don't let BI priorities be driven only by those individuals who shout the loudest.
- Look at your current BI deployment rates by roles and understand where there is the biggest room for improvement. (Refer to Figure 4-5, Chapter 4 for current industry averages.)
- Personalize the content of BI applications—whether reports, dashboards, alerts, or scorecards—so that users have information in context and in a way that facilitates insight.
- Don't rely exclusively on the traditional requirements-gathering process of asking people what they want; instead, study the way people work, incentives that influence them, decisions they make, and the information that supports those decisions to derive requirements.

Chapter 10

Agile Development

Agile development is one of those secrets to successful business intelligence that emerged only from a study of common themes in the successful BI case studies. It is not something I surveyed people about. Don't be surprised if you have never heard of agile development: it is not something taught even to newly certified project management professionals.[1]

Waterfall Development Process

Traditional systems development projects follow a waterfall project approach: a set of tasks is completed, and then another set, until several months or years later, you have a working piece of software (see Figure 10-1). The waterfall approach is heavy on defining requirements precisely upfront. The thinking goes that if you get your requirements right upfront, then you save development costs later in the process. The waterfall approach is also preferred when a development project is outsourced and a systems provider must build a solution to a specification.

Such a project approach is reasonable for *portions* of a business intelligence solution and as long as the time frames are reasonable, but it is not acceptable for business-facing solutions. With business intelligence, the project is never-ending and the focus is not on finishing, but rather, on delivering a certain set of capabilities within a defined period. Recall from Chapter 1 that one of the ways in which business intelligence is used is to uncover opportunities. Requirements for discovery-style applications, then, are not precisely known. Instead of a fixed report or dashboard, the BI application has to facilitate exploration of a broad set of data. As well, consider in Chapter 9 that in finding out how BI can be most relevant to frontline workers, the requirements-definition process is much more collaborative versus the traditional, somewhat rigid,

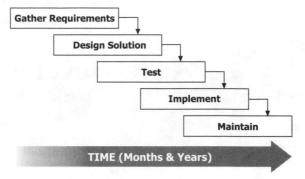

Figure 10-1   Waterfall project methodology

process of "define requirements precisely and build to the specification." These fundamental aspects of business intelligence make the waterfall approach to project management inappropriate to much of the BI initiative. I suspect some of the early failures of data warehouse projects can be attributed to the use of a waterfall approach in which the data warehouse team spent a year or more building out enterprise architecture, later revealing a system not at all useful to the business.

A key secret to making BI a killer application within your company is to provide a business intelligence environment that is flexible enough to adapt to a changing business environment *at the pace* of the business environment—fast and with frequent change.

Within the BI architecture (see Figure 10-2, discussed in Chapter 2), making changes to items on the far left is often more costly to do, requires more time, has a greater risk, and may have less of an immediate value-add to the business. Items farther on the right are less time-consuming to change and therefore more adaptable to changing business requirements. Specific elements are listed in the following table. For each portion of the BI architecture, you may want to adopt a periodic release schedule, but a schedule that balances the need for stability with responsiveness. Items on the far left may only change every few years; in the middle, once a quarter; and items further right, on an as-needed basis (daily, weekly, or monthly). The frequency for change varies due to the cost of change, the degree of difficulty to change, the number of people and related components affected by the change, risk, and the corresponding business value provided by the change. Using the

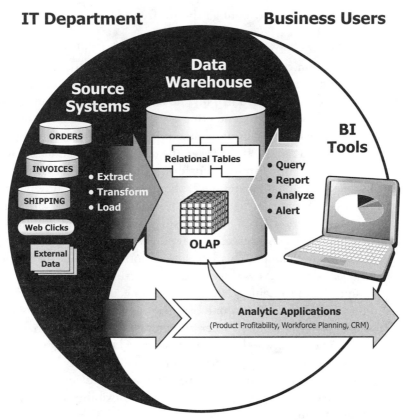

Figure 10-2   Major components in the business intelligence life cycle

Less Frequent Change/ Higher Risk and Cost	Periodic Change	Frequent Change/ Lower Risk and Cost
Hardware	Physical tables	Business views
Software	Custom-coded applications	Reports
Source systems	ETL processes	Dashboards
	Code files and hierarchy definitions	Calculation of key performance indicators within the business view, scorecard, or dashboard
	OLAP database structure	

car analogy again, you may change the oil frequently, the tires periodically, and the actual car every five years.

As an example, getting various stakeholders and individual lines of business to agree on consistent business definitions is difficult and time-consuming. Important metrics such as "customer churn" or "product profitability" can be calculated in a myriad of ways. Once everyone agrees on a definition, however, implementing a consistent calculation of such business metrics within a business view or scorecard is something that can be implemented rapidly. If, however, the definition or calculation logic has been hard-coded into extract, transform, load (ETL) processes or into physical tables in the data warehouse, then consolidating and changing these business rules can mean a major overhaul to multiple programs. Sometimes developers will hard-code business definitions into individual reports: stakeholders can't agree, so a report is the "easiest" and fastest place to define an element. This has some short-term value until there is a new business rule. Now those hundreds of instances of "customer churn" or "product profitability" have to be changed in hundreds of individual reports, as opposed to in one business view. Such business-facing capabilities demand flexibility. Other components, such as the hardware for the BI server or data warehouse, may only need to be changed when a company wants to update the infrastructure or add capacity.

For every BI element, consider carefully where to place the capability and what promotes the most reusability and flexibility while balancing the trade-offs in risk, cost, and business benefit.

Agile Development Techniques

The concept of agile software development emerged from an informal gathering of software engineers in 2001.[2] The group published a manifesto, some of whose principles aptly apply to business intelligence.

Upon first reading the Agile Manifesto, I had to chuckle at "Welcome changing requirements..." In truth, changing requirements is typically something IT people dread because it means rework, which leads to a project deliverable that is over budget and late. However, with agile development, BI developers do not work from a precise list of requirements, in stark contrast to the waterfall approach. Instead, they work from a broad requirement, with specific capabilities that are identified and narrowed down through a prototyping process. This prototyping process may involve sample screens mocked up within an Excel spreadsheet, or reports and dashboards built within a BI tool. When using

A Subset of Principles from the Agile Manifesto

- Our highest priority is to satisfy the customer through early and continuous delivery of valuable software.
- Welcome changing requirements, even late in development. Agile processes harness change for the customer's competitive advantage.
- Business people and developers must work together daily throughout the project.
- The most efficient and effective method of conveying information to and within a development team is face-to-face conversation.
- The sponsors, developers, and users should be able to maintain a constant pace indefinitely.
- Continuous attention to technical excellence and good design enhances agility.
- Simplicity—the art of maximizing the amount of work not done— is essential.
- The best architectures, requirements, and designs emerge from self-organizing teams.

commercial software, building a report or dashboard takes a matter of hours, not days and weeks of custom-coded solutions. Discarding a prototype after a collaborative session is more expeditious than asking the business users to list precisely their requirements, having someone build a solution to those requirements, and then discovering that the requirements have changed or that there was a misinterpretation.

A project plan for a BI solution using agile development techniques is illustrated in Figure 10-3. A specific task is iterated and recycled until the project team is satisfied with the capabilities, within a defined time frame and in adherence to the resource constraints (time and people) agreed upon in the planning stage. Time frames are usually measured in weeks (as opposed to months and years in waterfall-style projects).

For this iterative process to be successful, the business users and the IT developers must work closely together in a collaborative fashion. Some BI project teams will establish "war rooms" to facilitate collaboration in which business users and IT developers routinely meet to review prototypes and hash out requirements. In addition to logistical issues such as war rooms, in order for such collaborative development to be successful, the business and IT must have a strong partnership as described in Chapter 8.

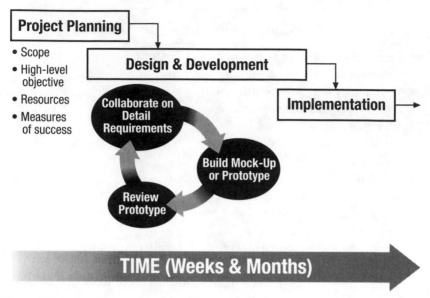

Figure 10-3   Iterative approach to delivering BI capabilities

The State of Agile Software Development

There is no research available on the use of agile development techniques specific to business intelligence. Industry literature suggests
that some of the barriers to adoption are concerns about higher costs
and inability for the business and IT to partner together. Scott Ambler,
an author of several books on agile software development, conducted
a broad survey in March 2007.[3] Some key findings in support of agile
software development include:

- 44% of survey respondents (781 responses) indicated a 90% success
  rate at agile projects and another 33% reported success rates between
  75 and 90%.
- Co-located agile projects are more successful on average than non-
  co-located, which in turn are more successful than projects involving
  off-shoring.
- 83% of agile teams used iteration lengths between 1 and 4 weeks.
  [Author's note: As shown in the earlier table, the ideal length for an
  iteration will depend on the item being produced or modified.]
- Smaller teams had higher success rates than larger teams.

How Well Are BI Projects Managed?

Agile development processes may require stronger project management skills than a waterfall approach. Collaborative design sessions that are characteristic of agile development can too easily slip into never-ending tweaks to the system. Without a detailed requirement document, it's harder for project personnel to declare a particular item is out of scope.

Having a BI program well-managed was averaged very important by survey respondents, and 25% rated it as essential to a successful business intelligence deployment. It seems that data warehouse failures, wasted investments, and late projects were reported more often in the mid-1990s, when the concepts of data warehousing and business intelligence were still new. Nonetheless, the stigma of project failures still seems to linger and is perhaps exaggerated. Research by Professor Hugh Watson of the Terry College of Business at the University of Georgia shows that the majority of data warehouse projects are on-time and on budget.[4] However, as the following chart shows, a sizable portion of data warehouse projects, 44% on average, are late.

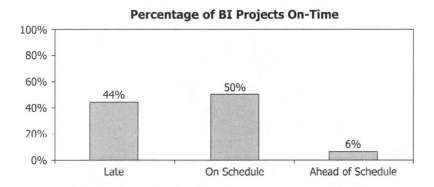

The degree to which data warehouse projects are over budget is also sizable at 37%.

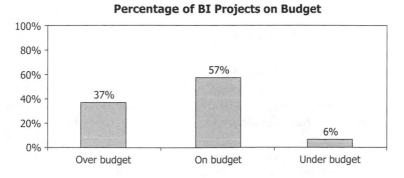

The study did not account for the business intelligence front-end portion, and there is no commentary on the severity of the lateness and budget overrun. While the percentage of on-time and on-budget projects are in the majority, Professor Watson's findings show room for improvement in the management of BI projects.

There are three key variables in managing a BI project effectively:

- **Scope**   For example, the subject areas and data accessible for analysis, the underlying infrastructure, the BI tool capabilities, and the quality
- **Resources**   The amount of money and number of people you have available to invest in the project
- **Time**   The deadline for delivering a set of capabilities

Like a three-legged stool, when any one of these variables changes, it affects the other variables.

So when the business asks for more data than originally agreed upon in the scope, either:

- You need more *resources* to deliver the changed scope on-time.

or

- The resources will stay fixed and the project *timeline* must be renegotiated.

Quality is part of the project scope, and this is an aspect that can sabotage the timeliness of any project, no matter how well-planned. When the severity of data quality problems are not known, allowing appropriate time to handle such issues is guesswork. In an ideal world, data would be 100% accurate, software would be bug-free, and functionality would be as expected. That's not reality. One of the most challenging aspects to project management, then, is delivering a solution whose quality is good enough, within the agreed time constraints and available resources.

To manage a BI project effectively, repeat the project managers' mantra, frequently, and to any one who requests a change: *there's scope, time, and resources. Scope, time, and resources. Scope, time, and resources.* If there is a budget cut, plan to cut the scope. If new capabilities are requested, communicate the corresponding increase in resources and time.

Sharper BI at 1-800 CONTACTS

1-800 CONTACTS implemented agile software development methodology two years ago.[5] Prior to this, users had to define their requirements in advance and formally submit them to the IT group. Now the BI team meets with various businesspeople on a weekly basis to plan the week's iterations. Dave Walker, the vice president of operations at 1-800 CONTACTS, describes the dynamics of agile development as one of the reasons for their success. "We are virtually one team. The IT people in the data warehouse team understand the call center so well, they could probably take some calls. There is partnership, high trust, and it's collaborative. It's not 'make a list, send it over.' It's very iterative. It takes lot of time and effort on both sides, but the end product is well worth it."

The team still works within a high-level roadmap with yearly deliverables, and Data Warehouse Manager Jim Hill says these weekly planning sessions could not work without that roadmap. Disagreements about prioritizations and resource allocation are resolved by a finance director who reports to the executive sponsor.

In many respects, the BI technology itself allows for agile development because the business users themselves may be building the solution. If users are building or customizing their own reports and dashboards, they most likely are not working from a documented list of requirements or at most, from needs and thoughts jotted in an e-mail request. Chris Coon, a senior analyst at 1-800 CONTACTS, says the Microsoft Analysis cube allows for exploration. "Before the data warehouse and these cubes, we always had to go to the IT group who produced something static. It always took a long time. It didn't facilitate a rapid response to change in sales volume or other business event." Now Coon estimates 80% of his requirements can be fulfilled by the

OLAP database, allowing him to explore sales by new customers, by repeat customers, or by different products.

Best Practices for Successful Business Intelligence

Project managers should recognize that because of the ways in which business intelligence is used, solutions must be flexible and modifiable in response to changing business requirements. Given the lack of understanding of what is possible with BI and that users often don't know what they want until they see it, agile development techniques are preferable to traditional waterfall development process.

- Be prepared to change the business-facing parts of BI on a more rapid basis than the behind-the-scenes infrastructure.
- Use collaborative development and rapid prototyping.
- Repeat the project manager's mantra: there is scope, resources, and time. When you change one aspect, expect it to affect the others.
- Understand how quality and the desire for perfection can sabotage a project's timeline. Manage expectations about quality early-on and agree upon acceptable quality levels.

Chapter 11

Organizing for Success

Given the myriad ways that business intelligence reaches across an entire organization, attention to organizational issues can accelerate BI success; failure to address organizational issues hinders success. In each of the successful BI case studies, how the BI team was organized and evolved played a pivotal role in ensuring greater success.

Enterprise vs. Departmental BI

If your company is new to business intelligence, it may be difficult to pursue an enterprise solution. Some of the best ideas may incubate within individual departments or business units, and this may be the ideal place to test the BI waters. However, even if you begin with BI at the department level, keep your view on the enterprise.

> "We started small to avoid enterprise data governance issues and be able to get the foundation right. We are ready to grow from a solid foundation."
>
> —Database administrator from a state agency who describes their BI deployment as very successful

Some of the same challenges in establishing a strong business-IT partnership also affect whether business intelligence is approached as an enterprise solution or as a departmental initiative. When a particular business unit is under time pressure to perform better, to identify an opportunity, and so on, that business unit may not have the luxury of waiting on decisions and solutions from a central organization. The consequences of underperforming at a departmental or business unit level can be severe. If a business unit does not perform:

- The business unit may be sold off, or if it involves a new product launch, a new way of doing business, or a new location, the unit may be shut down.
- Job lay-offs may follow the underperformance.
- The service function may be outsourced.

When business intelligence is deployed departmentally or at the business unit level and is pivotal in ensuring the success of that department or business unit, then the BI team is usually at liberty to do whatever it takes to be successful. The goals, requirements, and constraints for one business unit are often at odds with the goals of the enterprise:

Departmental BI	Enterprise BI
Focus on the individual business unit needs	Focus on the needs of the company and all business units and departments
Use whatever technology works	Adherence to corporate standards
Short-term success	Long-term viability
Dedicated resources	Shared resources

Asking people and business units to consider the greater good of the company when their jobs and livelihoods are at risk seems a preposterous proposition. And yet, for greater company success, business intelligence must be treated as a strategic asset managed at the enterprise level. Treating BI as a departmental resource seems a best practice only when:

- That department is a self-contained business unit.
- The business unit does not derive any added value from synergies with other business units in the company.
- The department or business unit does not leverage shared services (whether IT-related, accounting, human resources, purchasing, and so on).
- Employee compensation at the business unit level is not tied to any total company performance objectives.

Rarely, then, is treating BI as a departmental resource a best practice.

In looking at how BI is typically delivered, according to survey respondents, it is fairly mixed with 51% describing their BI deployment as enterprisewide and 49% as departmental. However, as Figure 11-1 shows, the percentage that describes their deployments as very successful is almost double for enterprisewide deployments (31%) as for departmental (16%). Conversely, the percentage of those who describe their project for departmental BI as a failure (11%) is double that for enterprise solutions (5%).

As discussed in Chapter 4, one measure of BI success is the percentage of employees who routinely use business intelligence. Here, too, enterprisewide deployments report a higher rate of users at 28% of employees versus departmental at 22% of employees.

Surprising to me is that the size of the company did not have much relationship to whether BI was treated as a departmental or enterprise solution. Roughly the same percentage of small companies (less than 100 employees or less than $100 million in annual revenues) delivered BI departmentally as did large companies (greater than 5,000 employees or greater than $1 billion in revenues). Likewise, the age of the BI deployment did not reveal any major split in whether BI was approached departmentally or enterprisewide. I would have expected that newer projects (less than one year) would have been more departmental in nature and older deployments (greater than three years) would grow to an enterprise focus. However, the split in approach remained fairly constant across survey respondents.

Departmental vs. Enterprisewide BI

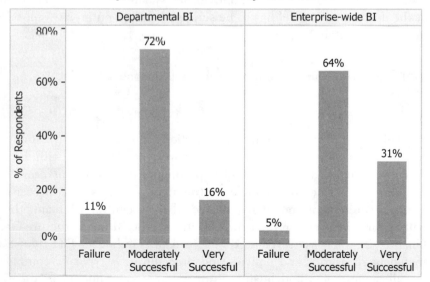

Figure 11-1   Enterprisewide deployments have a higher percentage of very successful deployments than departmental solutions

Departmental BI may allow for a faster solution, tailored to the specific needs of a business or department, but enterprisewide BI allows for greater success that is sustainable.

Departmental BI may show success faster because the BI team is dealing with less diverse requirements, requiring less buy-in, and with less consideration to an enterprise-class infrastructure. As discussed in Chapter 5, the Dow SUCCESS solution was built so quickly because only one business unit was involved, and they had a dedicated programmer. With only one programmer, there was not even a project plan! Meanwhile, the Global Reporting Project was trying to understand, prioritize, and meld requirements from 15 different business units, with developers spread around the world. Despite these differences, there is no excuse for a BI project, enterprise or otherwise, to take years. Use the agile development techniques described in Chapter 10 to deliver enterprise capabilities in time frames that mirror those of departmental solutions, ideally every 90 days.

All too often when BI success is shown in an isolated department, other departments subsequently demand similar capabilities, and IT is forced to try to replicate that departmental success for the enterprise. Often, this success can't be replicated. The software, processes, and approach break under the strains of increased demand, more diverse requirements, limited funding, and so on. Whatever was initially built at the departmental level has to be scrapped and an enterprise solution built from scratch.

"The customer can have any color he wants so long as it's black."

—Henry Ford[3]

This is not to say that enterprise solutions should neglect the unique requirements of a business unit or department. The goal with BI is to deliver what is common to all departments in a way that provides economies of scale. If ever a department or business unit perceives critical requirements are being neglected by a central BI team, they will be forced to develop their own solutions. The BI infrastructure (see Chapter 2), such as server hardware, a data warehouse, ETL tools, a metadata repository, and policies and procedures, is typically common for all departments and business units. Some components of the BI front-end (see Chapter 3), in particular the business views, dashboards,

BI & Tragedy of the Commons

The tragedy of the commons "involves a conflict over resources between individual interests and the common good."[1] This concept has been used to describe a number of social and economic problems where individuals pursue their own gain at the expense of the group. Herders, for example, who have to share pasture for sheep, will continue to add sheep to the property when the products from the sheep (wool production) exceed the cost in degrading the common pasture. Global warming problems have been explained by the tragedy of the commons in that individual countries and people don't inherently want to cut emissions or drive smaller cars, not wanting to trade national or personal sacrifices for the greater good of the world.

The tragedy of the commons was first introduced to me in business school. In truth, I was a skeptic, thinking people, countries, businesses are not *that* self-interested. I believed that if the negative impact on the common good were better understood, we'd behave differently. Yet several professors did "tests" to illustrate how often the tragedy plays out. One professor would offer an individual an A or the group one less assignment if the group acted in unison. The individuals always won out. Another professor resorted to cold, hard cash as the common resource. Everyone contributed a couple of dollars that either a few individuals would win or we could all get back our small contribution, if as a class we made decisions that benefited the entire class. A few made out like bandits, while the more naïve of us were left mouths agape at how greedily some behaved.

It seems to me that a similar tragedy exists with business intelligence. According to industry research, 42% of companies buy business intelligence tools at a departmental level.[2] Funds for technology investments are limited and so are the resources and expertise to deploy them. It would make sense to build an enterprise solution once, rather than build multiple islands of solutions that end up costing the company more. Yet when the department buying the BI tool derives all the benefit (whether in time to implement BI capabilities or in software that meets a high portion of their requirements), their BI success is sometimes at the expense of other departments who would also benefit from business intelligence. Individual departments are forced to fight for their own solutions, rather than working together to share resources, data, and expertise. The more important question, then, is not whether BI is deployed only departmentally but rather *why?*

"There are many levels of BI initiatives in a company as large as the one in which I work. There are rogue initiatives started by people with a need that can not convince the official corporate program to undertake since the corporate program has bigger projects in mind. These rogue programs can be much more effective since the people with the need are designing the system. Some of the data I need for my business is owned by another department, and I can not get my hands on it because they are too busy with other projects to work on my request. However, they refuse to allow me access to the database because they own it."

—Business user in customer service in the computer industry

and reports, will be specific to each individual department. The decision on which components should be tailored for a particular business unit or department should be based on whether the differentiation adds business value. Sometimes, that business value might be in time-to-market.

Table 11-1 lists items and responsibilities that are either best centralized at an enterprise level or optimized at a business unit or departmental level. In comparing this table to the BI life cycle (see Figure 2-3 in Chapter 2), the farther left on the BI life cycle, the greater the likelihood it can be treated as an enterprise resource; the farther right on the diagram, the more likely it will be optimized by or for a business unit or department.

Centralized or Enterprise Resources	Optimized by/for Department or Business Unit
▪ Technical infrastructure (servers, backup servers) ▪ Data warehouse infrastructure (ETL processes, modeling, cleansing) ▪ Software standards, acquisition, deployment ▪ Policies and procedures ▪ Best practices and quality assurance ▪ Project management services ▪ Training services ▪ Companywide business views and reports ▪ User ID definition and authentication (ideally integrated with HR records)	▪ Business views ▪ Reports ▪ Dashboards ▪ Definition of roles for role-based security ▪ Analytic applications

Table 11-1   Enterprise BI

As an example, fraud detection is a type of analytic application used by a number of banks. Within a bank, there may be a credit card business unit, a mortgage unit, and a consumer checking account unit. Fraud detection capabilities may be most important to the credit card unit and will be of less importance to the mortgage unit. Here, then, the credit card business unit may decide to buy its own fraud detection solution. This solution may or may not run on hardware supported at the enterprise level (the left-hand column of Table 11-1); ideally it would use common technical infrastructure, just as ideally it would use a common approach to setting up development, test, and production environments (policies and procedures), a consistent set of user IDs for authentication, and so on.

One of the items in the right-hand column in Table 11-1 that seems to generate the most debate is the responsibility for the business views (see the section on a business view of the data in Chapter 3). In companies with enterprisewide BI deployments, these business views are jointly developed with the business units and departments. In some cases, though, responsibility for building the business views gravitates to the individual departments. A central organization continues to quality assure the business view, ensuring adherence to naming conventions, SQL optimization, and other best practices. The ability to do this and whether it's in the best interest of the company and the business unit will depend greatly on:

- Availability of technical resources within the business unit or department
- Responsiveness of the central BI group
- Business or domain expertise of the central BI group
- Degree to which a business unit–specific business view must be reused by other departments and business units

All of these best practices, however, are only possible when other aspects of the company and the business intelligence initiative are working well. If, for example, the business and IT are not working in partnership, then the business has to pursue solutions on their own. When personal agendas, politics, or analysis-paralysis prevail, then an enterprisewide approach to business intelligence also becomes less viable.

The BI Steering Committee

The BI steering committee includes senior representatives from the various businesses and functions who set priorities on both the data and functional capabilities of the BI portfolio. The BI program manager is also an active member of the steering committee. Other IT directors that have integration points with BI, such as the enterprise resource planning (ERP) owner, should also be on the steering committee. Steering committee members will meet on a regular basis, as often as weekly, to resolve conflicting priorities, identify new opportunities, and resolve issues escalated from the project team. The steering committee is an important forum for the BI project leader to understand the business context for BI, ensure business alignment, and to keep business leaders abreast of new project developments.

For example, at Continental Airlines, the Data Warehouse Steering Committee is comprised of 30 people, most of whom are at the director level and higher.[4] This steering committee sets the priorities for the data warehouse and identifies ways for the BI team to be more involved with the individual business units.

While the steering committee at Continental Airlines is quite large and commensurate with the size of the corporation, sometimes working with such large committees can make progress more difficult. I found in working with a biotechnology client that they too had a large steering committee but one whose effectiveness I would question. In many respects, it was necessary to include all functions and business units to ensure buy-in to the BI initiative. However, cultural and political issues that existed outside the BI steering committee impacted the dynamics of the committee. Trying to schedule face-to-face meetings with larger groups became a logistical nightmare. When key committee members failed to participate in such meetings, they would later second-guess priorities and decisions agreed upon by those present. In this regard, the ideal size of the committee balances the trade-offs of being able to perform with the needs of ensuring buy-in and alignment with the business.

At 1-800 CONTACTS, an IT Steering Committee initially determined the priorities of the overall data warehouse activities. With the infrastructure established, the BI team meets with the director of treasury, financial planning and analysis on a weekly basis to coordinate and prioritize activities. The BI team meets with the executive sponsor, the CFO, only on an as-needed basis, such as to review major milestones or prototypes.[5]

Business Intelligence Competency Centers (BICC)

Gartner Research defines a BICC as a "cross-functional team with specific tasks, roles, responsibilities, and processes for supporting and promoting the effective use of BI across the organization."[6] BICCs may also be referred to as "BI Centers of Excellence." While the terminology for BICCs is relatively new, the concept is not, and some of the successful BI case studies have had BICCs (but refer to them with different terminology) for more than a decade.

The desire to implement a BICC will be influenced by the degree to which your company uses a shared services model. If you are trying to transform your BI focus from a departmental resource to an enterprise solution, a BICC is an effective organizational model that will facilitate this. A major difference between a BICC and a BI project is that a BICC is a permanent organization, whereas a BI project has a clear scope, set of deliverables, and time line. A BI project may be partially or fully staffed by BICC personnel. When there are no available BICC resources to staff a new project, then the BICC may act as an advisor and quality assurer to the BI project. The BICC can either be a virtual team or a dedicated team with permanent resources and a formal budget. Figure 11-2 shows an organizational model for the BICC, steering committee, and executive sponsor.

Some of the roles within the BICC may be dedicated resources or they may be shared with other groups. For example, the BICC may have a dedicated database administrator who creates the physical tables, optimizes indexes, and so on. Alternatively, a DBA (database administrator) from a central IT department may allocate a percentage of his or her time to the BICC. Similarly, the business subject matter experts may be part-time resources that the business allocates to their BI efforts, or they may be full-time BICC staff. For example, Continental Airlines has four business-oriented people as part of its 15-person data warehouse team

Figure 11-2   BI organizational model

(Continental does not call their team a BICC but it acts as a BICC).[7] The data warehouse manager recognized early in the process that they needed business subject matter experts to do analysis, testing, and second-level support, so she hired people from the business units. As more data sources and capabilities were added, these people transitioned into a permanent role on the data warehouse team, expanded their expertise, and applied the same skills to other subject areas. When to staff a person as a full-time member of the BICC will depend on how much of a full-time resource you need, career progression, and funding.

BICC Guiding Principles

Develop a vision for BI and establish guiding principles that all the stakeholders, steering committee members, project teams, and BICC can refer to. Use the following list as inspiration for developing your own principles:

- Business intelligence is a strategic asset that provides a competitive differentiator.
- The business will establish the priorities, and IT will deliver according to those priorities.
- Issues that cannot be resolved by the project team will be escalated to the steering committee.
- We will strive to focus on the business value of business intelligence and not get sidetracked by technology for technology's sake.
- We will borrow great ideas from people who have gone before us, garnering the best ideas from departmental innovations (otherwise known as, no "not invented here" attitude).
- Data errors will be corrected at the source.
- Success will be measured according to perceived business impact, number of active users, and return on investment. These successes will be communicated and actively promoted.
- Services that can be shared and that provide economies of scale will be centralized, including hardware, software, policies and procedures, data acquisition, cleansing, and modeling. Customize those items in which there is a major difference in requirements and fulfilling those requirements adds value to the business.
- The BICC will promote a buy versus build mentality.
- Technology adoption will fall into the leading edge, not bleeding edge category.

Funding for a BICC can be a point of contention. For example, a large aerospace manufacturer began moving to a BICC model in 2004. Today there are 34 employees in the BICC but there is only budget for 11 resources. The remaining staff get billed to specific BI projects. The leader of the BICC describes, "it's an ongoing process of trying to strike the right balance of teaching people to fish versus doing the projects for them. Our goal is to help our IT counterparts within the businesses to succeed."[8]

Organizationally, support for training often comes from the BICC. The BICC may develop common training materials and select a vendor to deliver the training. Business subject matter experts may facilitate the data-specific training. In larger organizations, training may be coordinated via the human resources department.

BI Shake-Up at Corporate Express

At Corporate Express, reorganizing the BI team was one of the secrets to achieving BI success.[9] Like many companies, IT was initially responsible for authoring reports and designing decision support systems (DSSs). Up until three years ago, 31 DSS experts were scattered around the United States. Each developed his or her own reports, using whichever tool they were most familiar with. All of them used the data warehouse as the data source, but differences in how data was extracted, resaved, and recalculated in different spreadsheets, thousands of Microsoft Access databases, and multiple BI tools, led to multiple versions of the truth.

When business leaders met, the first point of discussion was the numbers, not the business. Why were the numbers different? Whose numbers were right? Executives were fed up and appointed a director of business analysis to address the problem. Part of the solution involved selecting a new BI tool. Another aspect was reorganizing the DSS experts. As part of this reorganization, the regional DSS expert positions were eliminated and a central business analysis group established.

Explains Matt Schwartz, director of business analysis, "I inherited seven years of frustration. If you mentioned BI or reporting, you got a dirty look. Thirty-one people around the U.S. were developing the same reports. There were some job protection issues. It was ripe for consolidation and automation."

The 31 regional DSS roles were eliminated and replaced by 4 centralized experts. In another organizational twist, it was decided that the business analysis group should reside within finance, not within IT. While companies may have a team of reporting experts within the finance group, they normally focus on financial reporting only, and not merchandising, inventory, and so on. At Corporate Express, the business analysis team serves all the functional areas. IT meanwhile kept responsibility for the data warehouse, but the business analysis team led the charge to select a new BI tool (MicroStrategy—see Chapter 12), build the business views, and build the reports.

Eliminating people's jobs, changing reporting lines, and shifting power and responsibilities is a difficult process, one that is nearly impossible without the executive level sponsorship that Schwartz has (see Chapter 6). While the CFO is the formal sponsor and the person to whom Schwartz reports, the CEO and VPs of the major business units supported the organizational changes. Walter Scott, vice president of marketing, was one of the early beneficiaries of the reorganized business analysis team and new tool. Scott says, "Matt fought through organizational issues and stayed focused on the vision. People thought he was crazy for a while! But the changes have led to outstanding success for Corporate Express. It has helped pull together cross-functional teams in ways we couldn't before."

The Best People

Organizing the BI team in a way that enables agile development (see Chapter 10) and stronger business alignment (Chapter 8) is important for a successful BI initiative. It's also important to ensure that that team is comprised of the best people. Robert VanHees, CFO, Corporate Express, recognizes the business analysis team as one of the key ingredients to their BI success. "Like most functions, success comes from the people you hire, putting the right team in place with strong development capabilities. You need more than a great BI tool. You have to invest in hiring and retaining top talent."

This may sound obvious. With the best people, a clear vision, and empowerment, you can accomplish anything, not just successful business intelligence! It's not that anyone sets out to hire mediocre people, right? In reality, though, attracting and keeping the best people is no small task. The job market for BI experts is extremely tight; employee turnover can be high, and sometimes the best people simply go to the highest bidder. Keeping the business analysis team excited and fired up is a priority at Corporate Express. Like many companies, they invest heavily in training, but also, they apply for industry awards so that experts are recognized and proud of their accomplishments. "There has to be a pride of ownership. I want them excited about coming to work and working for me," explains Schwartz. He also credits the success of the BI team to its diversity. The diversity comes from gender, different nationalities, business versus IT expertise, and expertise in different technologies. "There is a power in getting a mix of people together. You can have the best tool in the world, but if you don't have the best team, you won't succeed."

Having a successful BI initiative and a culture that fosters information sharing and fact-based decisions can further help companies attract the best people. Eric Bachenheimer, director of client account management at Emergency Medical Associates (EMA), joined EMA in 2004 and was previously an administrator at a New York hospital. Bachenheimer describes his initial reaction to EMA's BI application: "When interviewing here three years ago, I saw a report and drooled! My hospital was struggling with this stuff. So I wanted to work for a company that is leading edge."

Professor Rosabeth Kanter of the Harvard Business School, describes three mechanisms companies can use to ensure greater commitment in a tight labor market: meaning, membership, and mastery.[10]

- **Meaning**   Ensuring the work has meaning to the company and to the world at large. This is one reason why it's important for technical experts to understand the business value of what they are building and that success stories are actively promoted (see Chapter 13).
- **Membership**   Demonstrate concern for the individual and ensure they feel they are an integral part of the team. One way companies can foster a greater sense of membership is to celebrate major BI milestones, whether it's by giving out silver dollars or throwing a party.
- **Mastery**   The ability for employees to enjoy challenging work, gain new skills, and contribute to the future. This last dimension of ensuring commitment can be a challenge with BI when an overemphasis on the latest technology can distract from the business focus of the BI project. New expertise, though, can come from working with different business units and ensuring a clear career path.

> Attracting the best people and keeping the BI team motivated is only possible when the importance of BI is recognized by senior management. When it's not, the best BI people will leave.

BI Team Leaders as Level 5 Leaders

Some of the organizational concepts covered in this chapter become increasingly important with larger companies and more complex deployments. The BI director plays a pivotal role in evangelizing BI to business leaders, ensuring positive team morale, and a steady flow of deliverables. (Note: The precise title for this person will vary company to company. I am referring to data warehouse managers, directors of business analysis, data managers, and so on, collectively as "BI director.") In small to mid-size businesses, the BI director is even more important because this may be the whole team or the director may have only a couple of full-time resources. Data modelers, report designers, and so on, may all be outsourced or supplemented with interim consulting services.

As I interviewed sponsors, users, and BI directors from multiple companies, people often attributed their BI success to the BI director, particularly in the smaller firms. What I found most interesting is the way these smaller companies described their BI directors; it was not an autocratic leadership style that led them to adopt business intelligence, nor do these directors want too much credit for their contribution. Instead, there is a degree of humility about the role they have played in their company's BI success. I started to think of these BI directors as what author Jim Collins describes as level 5 leaders in *Good to Great*.

Collins describes a level 5 leader as "an individual who blends extreme personal humility with intense professional will...Level 5 leaders channel their ego needs away from themselves and into the larger goal of building a great company. It's not that level 5 leaders have no ego or self-interest. Indeed they are incredibly ambitious—but their ambition is first and foremost for the institution, not for themselves."[11] In the case of level 5 BI leaders, the ambition is for the success of the BI project and the vision for how it can add value to the company.

At one point, I was concerned my admiration for Collins's work was skewing my perception, that this phenomenon was perhaps not as big a driver of success as I was making it. But then I spoke to Dave Walker, the vice president of operations at 1-800 CONTACTS, who declared that one of the three key reasons for their BI success rests with their data warehouse manager, Jim Hill.[12] "Before Jim joined the company, everything was just queries. You might take cookies with you to the IT group depending on how badly you needed something. Jim established a discipline and vision." I challenged Walker, arguing that anyone can come in and establish a greater sense of discipline. Walker was insistent that not all leaders are like Jim Hill. "He has an air of approachability, an air of competency, but he's very humble. He just wants to dig in and has an amazing service attitude. Jim will take our ideas and amplify them. He interjects energy into all these projects and is so engaging in meetings. His attitude has trickled down to his team." Walker then concluded, "He really is one of those leaders in that book...that book..." I waited, not wanting to put words in his mouth. Finally, I asked, "you don't mean a level 5 leader in *Good to Great*, do you?" He did! So there you have it:

> The most successful BI deployments, particularly in small to mid-sized companies, have BI directors who exhibit the characteristics of level 5 leaders, those who blend personal humility with professional will to focus not on their personal gain, but rather, on ensuring the success of the BI efforts for the value of the company.

Best Practices for Successful Business Intelligence

Organizational issues can hinder or accelerate successful business intelligence. To accelerate success:

- Use departmental BI initiatives for inspiration and innovations when your company first embarks on business intelligence. Even in the early stages, keep a view on the future and consider how the departmental initiative will evolve into an enterprise effort. Recognize the reasons that departments want to do their own BI projects and address them; remove the arguments against an enterprise solution, the prime one being the time it takes to deliver capabilities.
- Establish a BI Steering Committee comprised of senior executives from all major business units and functions who use business intelligence.
- Share resources and best practices in a central way that provides economies of scale. Establish a Business Intelligence Competency Center, whether virtual or physical.
- Don't underestimate the job protection issues and personal agendas you will encounter in changing organizational structures.
- Hire, motivate, and retain the best people.
- In small and mid-sized companies, look for BI directors who exemplify the characteristics of level 5 leaders.

Chapter 12

The Right BI Tool
for the Right User

It was 1994. The Dow BI tool selection process was contentious from the start. One of the main justifications for the Global Reporting Project was to reduce the cost of multiple, regional homegrown systems. We had a "buy not build" strategy and agreed to be "leading edge, not bleeding edge." And yet, everything about BI tools in the early 1990s was bleeding edge.

Within the Global Reporting Project, we formed a BI tool selection team that was charged with gathering and ranking requirements, conducting proof of concepts, and recommending standards. Technical experts and end users were jointly involved in the process, a best practice by today's standards but a somewhat novel approach then. We consulted leading analysts firms, one of whom suggested that we take a "throwaway" mentality, as whatever we selected would be superseded within two years by solutions from Microsoft. Having gotten burned by the IBM OS/2 demise beneath Microsoft Windows, we did not want to underestimate Microsoft's force in the BI market. (At the time, Microsoft BI or Analysis Services and Reporting Services did not exist.)

We attended software industry conferences, such as CeBIT in Germany and Business Intelligence Forum in England (TDWI—The Data Warehousing Institute—also did not yet exist), searching for solutions. Many of the leading products today were not available then or were in 1.0 releases. A solution installed in Dow Elanco (a subsidiary of Dow Chemical in Indiana, now Dow AgroSciences) caught our attention. That was another guiding principle—no "not invented here" syndrome allowed. We would borrow great ideas from any region or subsidiary who had come before us. Dow Elanco had BusinessObjects installed for a couple hundred users. At the time, Business Objects was a privately held company that few had heard of and was viewed as a risky investment.

We gave preference to solutions from vendors with whom we had relationships, which included Oracle, our database standard, and SAP, our ERP standard. After a few months of research, demos, and proto-types, we ultimately recommended two standards: BusinessObjects for query and reporting to answer "what" was going on in the business and Cognos PowerPlay for OLAP to discover "why" performance appeared a certain way. We had intended BusinessObjects to be for power users and Cognos PowerPlay for managers who were accustomed to guided screens and drill-downs of the decision support systems.

As soon as we published our recommendations, they met with resis-tance on all sides. The commercial users declared Cognos PowerPlay was too hard for them. They wanted a custom solution like SUCCESS (see Chapter 5). The finance users wanted to know what our transi-tion plans were for their thousands of FOCEXECs (files created with Information Builders Focus, a fourth-generation programming language or 4GL that was then the primary method for creating ad hoc reports). Our explanation that these FOCEXEC reports would have to be rewrit-ten anyway as the regional systems were being phased out didn't help our cause. Further inciting dissatisfaction, the Global Reporting Project manager said we only had time and resources to deploy one of the two tools recommended. PowerPlay's MOLAP architecture (see Chapter 3) made IT balk: IT could not guarantee data integrity if data had to be replicated into a proprietary storage mechanism.

It seemed the only adequate buy-in we got was from the database and ERP standard leaders.

> As with politics, BI selections require consensus building along the way. No matter how sound your recommendations or that they may be in the best interests of the company, if you fail to build consensus with a *wider* constituency along the way, your recommendations will be rejected out of fear, uncertainty, job protection, and other random reasons. In hindsight, this was our biggest mistake.

As the marketing users were not satisfied with the Global Reporting Project's decision to support only one tool, they did what 42%[1] of departments continue to do today: they went out and bought their own BI solution and proceeded to deploy Cognos PowerPlay on their own. Germany and the Polurethane's business unit followed a similar path and continued to develop a custom solution with SUCCESS. This departmental initiative was highly successful until the lead programmer left Dow.

In 1996, just two years after our initial recommendations, when the arguments about which BI tool or tools to use would not subside, we embarked on yet another BI tool selection. The prediction that Microsoft would have a dominating solution had not yet come true, but one prediction had: Oracle had just acquired OLAP vendor and product IRI Express. Yes! We really could have a single standard with both the RDBMS and BI tool coming from the same vendor. We never got beyond the prototype. Ultimately, this second selection team reinforced the initial recommendation: the company needed multiple tools based on different user requirements and use cases. What was initially a backroom deployment of Cognos PowerPlay became an officially supported solution from the Global Reporting Project, in addition to BusinessObjects.

The Dow Chemical Company today continues to have both BusinessObjects and Cognos as its global BI standards. There are now over 12,000 users who access 90 BusinessObjects universes and 2500 Cognos PowerPlay cubes.[2] While these two vendors are fierce competitors with competing solutions, in 1994 when Dow began its BI initiative, the product differences and user audiences they served were more distinct. Dow's BI tool strategy continues to be based on aligning the tool capabilities with the corresponding user requirements and use cases. SAS JMP has also been added to Dow's portfolio to provide users with visual predictive analysis capabilities. Although Dow's BI tool decisions took place more than a decade ago, the challenges they faced then still hold true for many organizations. Market leadership and tool capabilities are in a constant state of flux. Where Dow has excelled is in ensuring the business value these tools provide remains the first priority.

The Importance of BI Tools

BI front-end tools seem to get the lion's share of attention from business users. Customers today continue to tell me they can confidently embark on data integration selections within the confines of IT, but undergoing a BI tool selection jointly with business users invokes never-ending contention. (See Chapter 2 for an explanation of technical components and Chapter 3 for BI front-end tools.) Providing users with a BI tool that facilitates access, decision-making, and action is essential to successful business intelligence. Fail to do this and your data warehouse is a wasteland of bits and bytes. Contrary to widely held opinion, business users do not care *only* about BI front-end tools. In fact, on average, both IT personnel and business users alike agree that the information architecture and underlying data quality is the most important technical aspect in successful BI (see Figure 7-2 in Chapter 7).

Business users do, however, give a slightly higher rating to the importance of BI tools than either system reliability or available subject areas. It's not clear from the survey results if this suggests that business users are willing to tolerate a degree of unreliability in exchange for better tools or if this suggests users assume reliability is a given and that their data is available. Based on case study insights, it seems to be the latter.

Given the importance of the BI front-end, the tool selection in terms of both the modules and the vendor is a decision that cannot be made in isolation by either the business or IT. The business users must embrace the tool, and IT must be able to support it. If you have any doubt about the relative importance of the BI front-end tools, consider this: the BI tool and its adaptability are cited equally as the cause for failure and for success.

> "We let the user group select the tool, and the process was only facilitated by IT. When it came time to sign, it was the user selection team that signed the agreement, not IT. TOTAL BUY-IN resulted."
>
> —Karen Larson, senior director, IT, Lawson Products Inc.

The Role of BI Standardization

With the plethora of BI tools now on the market and the degree to which individual departments and business units buy BI solutions, multiple front-end tools have only added to data chaos and multiple versions of the truth. A single, consistent data element in a data warehouse, say, revenue, can get further transformed, manipulated, massaged, and displayed in spreadsheets, report-based calculations, OLAP databases, dashboards, and so on. Revenue in one instance may be calculated on gross invoice amount; in another it could include adjustments for returns and discounts; and in another it may include bad debts. While lower cost of ownership is the main criterion for BI standardization, the ability to deliver a single version of truth is the second-highest-ranked criterion.[3] A single version of the truth requires consistent representation in BI tools, in addition to a common data architecture.

BI standardization should not be confused with a "one size fits all" approach. A business analyst who is a power user does not have the same functionality requirements as a frontline worker who may only need a visual gadget of a smaller amount of information.

Historically, companies had to buy multiple BI front-end tools from multiple vendors because no single vendor offered the full spectrum of tools described in Chapter 3. Increasingly, vendors do offer a spectrum of tools in a complete suite or toolset. These integrated suites provide IT the benefit of having one business view to maintain, on a common set of servers, with common security. It offers users the benefit of seamlessly navigating from a dashboard, through to a report, to a business query. That's the theory! Some products and vendors are already there; for others, it's only a vision but one that is closer to reality than ever before.

When you think of BI standardization, also recognize that companies and vendors may advocate standardizing beyond just the front-end components to include the back-end components such as the ETL tool, data quality tool, and data warehouse platform (as shown in Figure 12-1 and discussed in Chapters 2 and 3). How much you pursue this broader standardization effort depends largely on where you are in your BI deployment, in which vendors you have already made investments, and if your company pursues a "best-of-breed" strategy versus single-vendor solution.

At this time, I more often see a multivendor approach across the entire BI life cycle but increasing standardization within the BI front-end tools. In other words, companies may buy multiple modules within a BI suite that is comprised of business query, reporting, analysis, and Microsoft Office integration but will buy from a different vendor for ETL, the data warehouse platform, or the source systems. If you have multiple tools in any single component, such as multiple business query tools, rationalizing some of this duplication should be your first standardization priority.

According to a survey I coauthored for TDWI, most companies have multiple BI components from different BI vendors, with an average of 3.2 components from different BI vendors. When you read of seemingly outrageous numbers of companies having as many as 13 BI tools, such numbers often reflect an overcount, as they are talking about the number of individual components. If you consider all the components described in Chapter 3, then you have potentially eight tools right there.

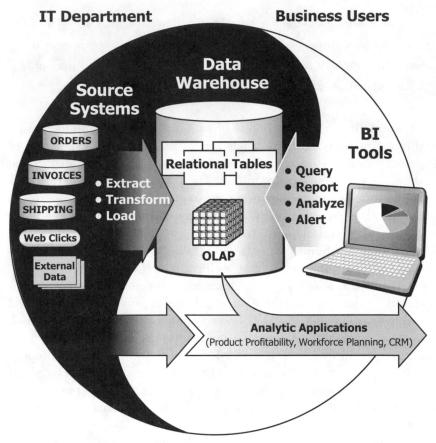

Figure 12-1   Major components in the business intelligence life cycle

The question is, how many of those eight modules can you buy from a single BI vendor?

Table 12-1 shows roughly an equal percentage of companies using multiple BI front-end modules from a *single* vendor versus multiple modules from *multiple* vendors. A minority of survey respondents deploy

BI Tool Approach	Percentage Survey Respondents
Mostly custom BI front-ends	17%
Multiple vendors	41%
Primarily from a single vendor	42%

Table 12-1   Most Companies Use Purchased BI Products with an Equal Split in Buying Approach

custom front-ends as their primary tool approach. These percentages do not change significantly according to the length of the deployment, even though vendors and analysts have been increasingly advocating BI standardization in the last few years as the modules have become more integrated. The percentage of companies with newer deployments (less than three years) who have multiple modules mostly from a single vendor is only 5% higher than newer deployments that use multiple components from multiple vendors. The successful BI case studies reflect a similar pattern to the survey results (see later Table 12-2); some of the case study companies have standardized on a single BI vendor and some have partnered with multiple BI vendors.

While I would have expected the recent push for BI standardization from new deployments to be higher, the total percentage of 42% is still relatively high. Just two years ago, only 24% of the TDWI respondents said they had standardized on a BI platform. In the Successful BI survey, of the 41% who currently use multiple BI tools from multiple vendors, 57% are actively trying to reduce the number of modules from different BI vendors.

While it is clearly harder to switch standardization strategies and vendors mid-deployment, the survey results indicate the BI tool approach plays a role in successful business intelligence. As shown in Figure 12-2, 50% of the respondents who describe their deployment as very successful have BI tools from a single vendor, a higher percentage than the average. Contrast this with those who classify their deployment as a failure, where the percentage standardizing is much lower. The failed deployments also have a higher rate of primarily custom applications.

> Failed BI deployments have a higher rate of primarily custom applications. The operative word here is *primarily*. Custom applications can complement a purchased BI solution but they should not be the primary or exclusive way of delivering business intelligence.

Table 12-2 shows the BI front-end tools and vendors deployed at the successful BI case study companies. While several companies have solutions from multiple BI vendors, none reported overlapping functionality. This is a significant difference versus the industry. Another interesting aspect was that three out of four of the companies changed their preferred BI tool during the course of their BI deployment and attribute greater BI

Successful BI Company	Primary Vendors for BI Front-End Tools	Switch to Different BI Vendor?
1-800 CONTACTS	Microsoft	No, new to BI
Continental Airlines	Hyperion, SPSS, custom applications	No
Corporate Express	MicroStrategy, SPSS	Yes
The Dow Chemical Company	Business Objects, Cognos, SAS	No
Emergency Medical Associates	Business Objects	Yes
FlightStats	JasperSoft	Yes, licensing costs
Norway Post	Hyperion, SAS	No

Table 12-2 Tool Approach at Successful BI Case Studies

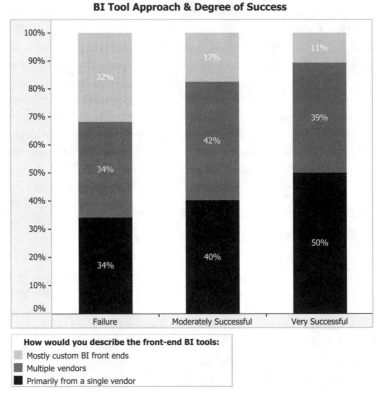

Figure 12-2 Successful BI companies more often buy multiple BI modules from a single vendor.

success to that change. The reasons for the change varied, including licensing costs, vendor complacency, and need for a more flexible solution.

The Right Tool for the Right User

A common misconception about BI standardization is the assumption that all users must use the same tool. It would be a mistake to pursue this strategy. Instead, successful BI companies use the *right tool for the right user*. For a senior executive, the right tool might be a dashboard. For a power user, it might be a business query tool. For a call center agent, it might be a custom application or a BI gadget embedded in an operational application.

Use the marketing concept of customer segmentation to identify and understand the various user groups within your company. A simple starting point of classifying your users is recognizing that there are two main groups: information consumers and information producers. However, to match the BI tool with the appropriate user group, you need to refine these two user segments. Figure 12-3 shows how different user segments require different tool capabilities.

Segmentation is a way of looking at one large user base—for example, all employees in a company—and dividing it into smaller groups. Each segment, or smaller group, has similar characteristics, needs, and desired benefits. Segmentation provides a way of better understanding your users and why their requirements are different. Following are

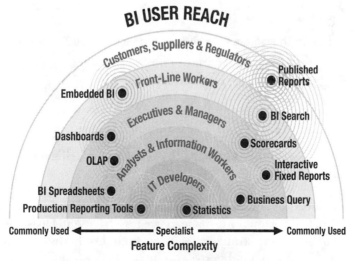

Figure 12-3   Different users require different tool capabilities.

some characteristics that will help you segment potential business intelligence users. Use the self-assessment worksheet in following table to develop your own user segments.

Business Unit, Department, or Function	Executives	Managers	Inside Staff	Field Staff	Customers	Suppliers
Percentage or number of users per segment						
Frequency & nature of decision-making						
Predictability of information requirements						
Analytic job content						
Need for detailed data (vs. aggregated)						
Need for multiple data sources and subject areas						
Data literacy						
Familiarity with source system						
Technical literacy						
Spreadsheet expertise						
Web knowledge						
Use of SmartPhones						
Degree of travel						

H = High, M = Medium, L = Low

> Understand the extent to which each segment currently uses business intelligence and the percentage that you believe *should* use business intelligence, assuming the interface and information is optimized for that user segment.

Frequency and Nature of Fact-Based Decisions

The types of decisions supported by business intelligence can be classified into:

- **Strategic decisions** of longer-term consequences with broader implications. Such decisions are made on a less frequent basis, perhaps yearly or longer. Some strategic decisions include whether to acquire a particular company, launch a new product, change suppliers, or enter a new market.

- **Tactical** decisions are made on a more frequent basis, weekly or monthly. They may include planning for a plant outage, increasing capacity, changing distribution routes, and optimizing pricing policies. To date, many of the business intelligence initiatives have focused on tactical decision makers.

- **Operational** decisions are more detailed in nature, and in isolation, affect a smaller number of people than strategic decisions. Can an order be sourced from a particular warehouse? Should a loan application be approved or denied? A larger number of people make many more operational decisions on a daily basis. Brenda Jansen, director of information systems at Energizer Holdings, refers to this group of users as the "difference makers" because of the big impact these thousands of individual decisions have in aggregate.[4] As an industry, the use of business intelligence to optimize operational decisions is still in its early stages.

In *Smart Enough Systems,* authors Neil Raden and James Taylor use the chart in Figure 12-4 to describe the relationship between the value of the decisions made and the frequency of those decisions.[5] Figure 12-4 clearly shows that any individual operational decision taken in isolation does not have a major impact on a company's performance

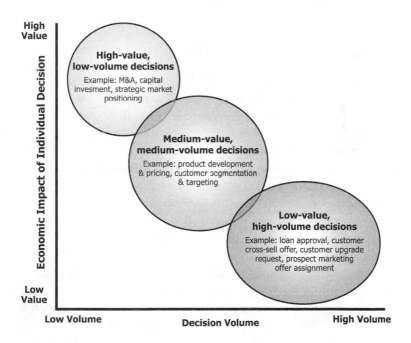

Figure 12-4 The value and volume of different kinds of decisions (Source: Smart Enough Systems. Reprinted with permission)

in aggregate. Yet as the case study companies demonstrate and as the *Smart Enough Systems* authors advocate, these "difference makers" have a profound impact when viewed in total. As 1-800 CONTACTS explained in Chapter 9, they saw an immediate lift in sales when they enabled the call center dashboard. Prior to the call center dashboard, it might have been all too easy to assume that the decisions of a single call center agent didn't have such a big impact. They do!

Predictability of Information Requirements

The degree to which information requirements are predictable is somewhat related to the type of decision (strategic, tactical, operational) but also to the application. When business intelligence is used for management and control purposes, information needs may be static. The BI application (whether an individual report, dashboard, or widget) should provide an overview as to the health, efficiency, or progress of the business. When something is trending in a negative direction, then the information requirements will change and become more exploratory. Information needs for operational BI users also may be relatively predictable. When the requirements are predictable, modules such as dashboards, standard reports, or custom-built applications are ideal.

Job Level

A user's job level will affect the breadth of data the user wants to access and the level of detail. Executive-level jobs may need a broad set of data but without a lot of detail. *Access* to information may be critical but *analyzing* the data is a minor aspect of these jobs, making this segment of users ideal candidates for dashboards with key performance indicators. Mid-level jobs may still need a broad set of data but with more detail. The combination of broad data requirements and more detailed data may make it hard to deliver only dashboards. Such workers may need access to multiple dashboards, standard reports, OLAP data sources with slice-and-dice ability, and so on. At the other end of the spectrum, office staff such as accounts payable clerks or customer service representatives may want to see only very detailed data. As their information requirements are narrow, these users may need only a few standard reports with interactive prompts or a custom application, perhaps integrated within an operational application.

Job Function

You also can segment users according to job function. For example, supply chain users will all have similar information needs, which will be different from the information needs of users in the finance department. Functional requirements also may vary by function: consider how many spreadsheet power users there are in any finance department. This group of users then may not care about dashboards as much as they care about spreadsheet integration. Marketing personnel will have different information requirements, and with respect to functionality, they may ask for things such as predictive analysis or Microsoft PowerPoint integration that other groups have not requested.

Degree of Analytic Job Content

Some jobs require a significant amount of data analysis. The analytic component also may relate to either the job level or the job function, or sometimes to both. For example, financial analysts may be fairly senior in a business; these jobs have a high analytic component. These are the number crunchers who will work intensely with business intelligence tools. They understand the different data nuances and even the potential data sources. It's easy to assume that these people are your only users, since they may have solutions implemented first, complain loudest when something is wrong, live and die by access to information, and control the information flow to secondary users. According to the Successful BI survey, this user segment currently shows the highest BI usage rate. Remember, though, that not everyone can spend all day collecting, manipulating, and exploring data. Some users need access to standard reports and dashboards simply to know what is going on at a glance. They may only log into a BI tool for ten minutes a day (or week) just to make sure the business is running smoothly. When the information indicates a problem area, it may not be their job to sift through the data to identify the underlying cause. Instead, they may call the business or financial analyst to figure out why there is a problem.

In BI, we seem to have a tendency to want all end users to become experts. It's a profound difference to *empower* a user—to provide them with easy tools to access and explore information when they need to— and an altogether different scenario to assume accessing and analyzing data is their primary job.

Users whose job content requires a fair bit of data analysis often demand more features and functions. Do not let their demands fool you into thinking all your users need these advanced capabilities. As you segment your users, recognize these differences in analytic abilities and job requirements.

Level of Data Literacy

Data literacy and computer literacy are two entirely different things. I may be computer literate, but if you ask me to decipher the meaning of baseball statistics, I'm clueless (RBIs maybe, but ERA and SO, forget it!); I don't know the data! So too with corporate data. Source system users and users whose jobs have a high analytic content may understand the data well and have a high level of data literacy. Certain users may understand the finer points of "revenue" (is it invoiced amount, net of returns, and so on?). Other users may not understand these nuances. In this regard, how you deploy particular BI modules will influence your success. If you give users with low data literacy access to a business query tool and they create incorrect queries because they didn't understand the different ways revenue could be calculated, the BI tool will be perceived as delivering bad data.

ERP or Source System Use

Some of your users may also enter data into the transaction or ERP system. Regardless of whether your company uses a BI tool directly against the transaction system or an ERP-populated data warehouse, these users will be more familiar with the precise meanings of individual data elements. At the same time, dimensional groupings and hierarchies that don't exist in the source system may be a completely new concept. These users may need additional explanation as to why there is a data warehouse, a BI platform, and how the data has been transformed.

Technical Literacy

Potential BI users who have worked with personal computers and the Internet since their inception will greet business intelligence differently than those who did not. Users who primarily surf the Web but who are not proficient with spreadsheets and other Windows-based programs fall somewhere in the middle. As discussed in Chapter 1, the changing workforce demographics mean that technical literacy today is much higher than in the early 1990s, when business intelligence as an industry first emerged. Information sharing is much more prevalent, yet boundaries still exist, and less tech-savvy employees may greet BI with a degree of trepidation. Recognize that such users still may need information to do their jobs, yet they may not see the BI application as their primary resource. These users may request scheduled, printed reports or, in the absence of such automation, may rely on gut-feel decision-making.

> Even if you have previously tried to engage tech-wary users and were met with a lackluster response, try again. Technical and information literacy is evolutionary. BI tools have gotten significantly easier to use with more interface options to suit diverse user requirements, even for users with less affinity for information technology.

Level of Spreadsheet Usage

Spreadsheet users deserve their own segment and, thus, sometimes their own BI interface. These users are spreadsheet enthusiasts and think everything should be delivered in a spreadsheet. There are a number of reasons why users want all their data delivered via spreadsheets; some reasons are valid, and others less so (for more discussion on this, see BIScorecard.com, "Spreadsheet Integration Criteria"). If spreadsheet usage is high for a particular user segment, then you may deploy spreadsheet-based BI interfaces to this segment. These spreadsheet-based BI interfaces are a far cry from the far too prevalent approach of exporting data into a spreadsheet and the ensuing data chaos. Instead, users work within a spreadsheet and refresh the data live from the BI platform into the spreadsheet, preserving data integrity. For users who are not as savvy with spreadsheets, such an interface is not optimal for that segment.

Amount of Travel

Certain job types require more travel than others. Some users may access BI tools only from their desktop or a corporate browser; users who travel may want access via a SmartPhone such as BlackBerry or a notebook computer. Support for mobile capabilities within the BI tool will be important for this user segment.

Internal vs. External Users

Consider the different needs of employees of the company and suppliers and customers that you may provide information to via an extranet. Internal employees may be allowed to access whatever software module you have licensed, whereas external customers and suppliers often will have more restrictions on content and functionality. External users have different requirements from your internal users. Authentication in large extranets can be one challenge if you will have thousands of potential extranet users.

The Most Successful BI Module

Figure 12-5 shows which front-end modules of a BI deployment survey respondents considered most successful. Within the survey (see question 18 in Appendix A), the list of available options was randomly ordered for each respondent to ensure that the order did not skew the rankings.

Given the recent excitement around dashboards and predictive analytics and some negative industry comments about ad hoc query tools only being good for power users, I investigated if the results were skewed by a larger portion of power users responding to the survey (67%). In filtering the survey results according to BI users who access standard reports (37% of respondents) and users who rely on information from BI authors (23% of respondents), the order of items changed only slightly. Fixed report users ranked standard reports as the most successful part of the BI deployment, followed by ad hoc query tools by a slight margin. That report consumers and even indirect BI users rank ad hoc query tools so highly confirms my belief that their success is not because they answer ad hoc questions per se, but rather, that they give

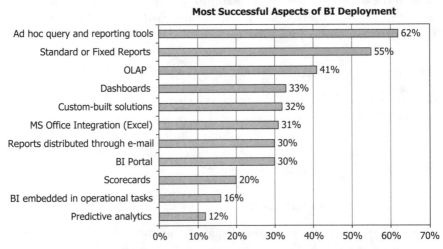

Figure 12-5   Overall, ad hoc query tools are considered the most successful aspect of a BI deployment, followed by standard reports.

the business users an ability to respond more quickly to questions and the changing business environment. What may initially start as an ad hoc report may evolve to a standard report, but one that was authored primarily by business users rather than professional IT report developers. This kind of self-service reporting environment continues to be a key ingredient to BI success not only for the power users, but also for those who benefit from the results of this flexibility.

However, it's important to remember that the ranking of which BI modules have been most successful is according to user perception and not according to a consistent measure of the business contribution any given BI tool module has provided.

A Word about Microsoft Office Integration

Microsoft Excel is sometimes referred to as the leading BI tool, and yet, it ranked in the middle of tool modules, with only 31% of respondents selecting Microsoft Office integration and Excel as the most successful part of the BI deployment. I suspect this is in part because of the chaos that disconnected spreadsheets have wreaked on business intelligence efforts. The problem is not with spreadsheets per se, but rather, with how they are used and not managed. Some of the biggest problems from spreadsheet errors include

- Kodak had to restate earnings because of an incorrect number of 0's being entered into a spreadsheet.[6]
- RedEnvelope, a catalog gift company, shares fell 25% when Cost of Goods Sold was incorrectly reported due to a spreadsheet error.[7]
- A number of companies have reported security breaches when laptops containing unencrypted spreadsheet data were stolen.

Despite these problems, BI users consistently say that a large percentage of ad hoc and standard BI reports are routinely exported to Excel. In a 2006 webinar I did, 67% of poll respondents said that more than half their reports are routinely exported to Excel. This percentage has remained fairly consistent in conferences polled in Orlando, Florida (November 2006), and Rome, Italy (June 2007).

Of the successful BI case studies, Excel is widely used, but for routine reports, spreadsheets are used in a managed way in which data is updated from the BI platform rather than manually exported. The ability to integrate with Excel in this managed way has been an area of continuous improvement for many BI vendors.

Microsoft Office and BI integration have recently extended beyond spreadsheets to include PowerPoint and Word. Corporate Express, for example, has given its field sellers access to MicroStrategy Office, which allows reports to be delivered and refreshed directly from within PowerPoint. Field sellers can then access these PowerPoint files in a disconnected environment while visiting customers.

Best Practices for Successful Business Intelligence

For business users, the BI tool is the face of the entire business intelligence architecture. Fail to select an appealing and intuitive BI tool, and your technical architecture will remain unused. Deploy a good BI tool on top of messy data or an unreliable system, and the tool will be blamed for underlying difficulties. To ensure the BI tool facilitates rather than impedes your success:

- Standardize on a BI platform to provide users with seamless navigation between BI modules. Supplement the BI platform with niche products and custom applications on a limited basis, only where the BI platform is lacking in capabilities.
- Be prepared to change BI platforms as you undergo mergers and acquisitions, requirements changes, or you gain a greater understanding of which capabilities and vendors meet your company's needs.
- Do not constantly change products and vendors only for technology's sake, as BI vendors innovate at different rates, and vendors may leapfrog each other in capabilities for any individual module. *Do* switch vendors if your BI tool is largely shelfware and if the lack of capabilities or right interface have been a deterrent to greater BI success.
- Segment your users to understand their unique requirements, and deploy the correct BI module for that group of users.

Chapter 13

Other Secrets to Success

The preceding chapters highlight the nine most important technical and organizational aspects that catapult companies to greater BI success. Aspects in this chapter are not as significant but they are common themes that warrant attention: company culture, promoting the BI application, training, and the use of graphical display.

The Role of Culture

Business intelligence is not just about technology; it is about the people who actively pursue new opportunities, who seek to make the best decisions for the company, and about the processes that enable increased efficiencies. A company can have a perfect business intelligence architecture, and yet, if they don't have a culture that supports business intelligence, that perfect architecture is a waste. It will only be leveraged in isolated pockets and will have less of an impact.

Culture is one of those intangible forces that nonetheless profoundly affects how people view and value business intelligence. As part of the Successful BI Survey, I asked respondents how much they agreed or disagreed that the following statements describe their company culture:

- Access to data is overly controlled, and executives fear workers know too much.
- Decisions are made from gut feel and not fact-based analysis.
- We are innovative and always looking for ways to do things better.
- We are a lean company that operates efficiently.
- We use computers and information technology to achieve competitive advantage.

I grouped these statements into characteristics that are considered enablers of BI and barriers to BI. Neutral responses were filtered out.

183

One of the biggest cultural differentiators between successful BI companies and those who describe their deployments as failures was the degree to which decisions are made based on facts versus gut feel (see Figure 13-1). In successful BI companies, 73% of respondents agreed or strongly agreed that decisions were predominantly made based on facts, and only 27% disagreed (described as gut-feel companies in Figure 13-1). Contrast this with survey respondents who describe their BI deployments as failures, in which a staggering 80% can be described as having gut-feel decision making and only 20% as having fact based. In those who describe their deployments as only moderately successful, the split in decision-making styles is roughly even between fact-based (49%) and gut-feel (51%).

Management expert Jim Collins in his book *Good to Great* identifies one of the key characteristics of companies with sustained competitive advantage as the ability to "confront the brutal facts...You absolutely cannot make a series of good decisions without first confronting the brutal facts. The good-to-great companies operated in accordance with this principle, and the comparison companies generally did not."[1] Even at Corporate Express, CFO Robert VanHees says that one of the challenges to consistent BI adoption has been in getting people to think about fact-based decision making.[2]

However, the benefits of gut-feel decision making should not be dismissed entirely. Sometimes experience and numerous facts may

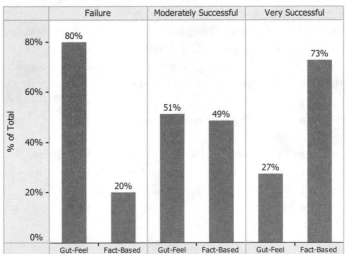

Fact-Based vs. Gut-Feel Decision Making

Figure 13-1 Decision making in successful BI companies is more fact-based (based on 377 non-neutral responses).

get synthesized into what is our "gut" feel. For doctors in emergency rooms, gut-feel decision making may be all that time allows for. As Jonathan Rothman, director of data management at Emergency Medical Associates, says, "Doctors often have to rely more on experience than fact-based decision making. They get so used to making big decisions based on so little information. In the emergency room, you may not have time to run a lot of tests, and you have to make fast decisions. So for other things like the efficiency of the emergency room, we have to teach them the importance of getting the complete picture."[3]

The problem is when biases and inaccurate data also get filtered into the gut. In this case, the gut-feel decision making should be supported with objective data, or errors in decision making may occur.

Take the case of a small plastics packaging business. One of their most important national customers was consolidating suppliers, and the plastics packaging company was about to lose one of their best longtime customers. Or so they thought. At the threat of losing this customer, the company began looking for ways to retain the customer. With a new purchasing manager in place at the customer, it seemed a longstanding relationship was not an influencing factor in the decision to change suppliers. It was price and price alone. While this customer accounted for a significant portion of the supplier's revenue, when the supplier analyzed the profit margin for this customer, they found little to none. This customer was certainly keeping the supplier busy, but they were not helping them improve profitability. The supplier only realized this when they began studying the data to understand the impact of this customer loss. Based on the facts, the plastics company decided to let this customer go without a battle and without further cutting their prices.

Even when company culture encourages fact-based decision making, recognize that facts can still be misinterpreted, misrepresented, or buried. Experts in decision making describe one of the common errors in decision making as the "confirming evidence trap."[4] The confirming evidence trap causes decision makers to seek information that supports a decision they have already made (by gut or intuition or personal agenda) and to ignore facts that may contradict that decision. In the case of the plastics packaging company, the analysis of the customer profitability was specifically performed by someone who did not have a personal or long-term relationship with the customer. During the analysis, there were lively debates about how much fixed and overhead cost should really be allocated to the customer; any underallocation would make retaining the customer seemingly more attractive.

> Business intelligence tools can only present the facts. Removing biases and other errors in decision making are dynamics of company culture that affect how well business intelligence is used.

Sometimes the facts are available but they are so buried that information is not actionable. In his article "The Formula," Malcolm Gladwell recounts all the warning signs of a pending catastrophic failure at Enron.[5] Some may argue that the "confirming evidence trap" was somewhat in play at Enron. Banks with sizable investments in the company would not want to see their money so at risk. Employees with sizable pensions and stock investments would also not want to contemplate the extent of the risk. A bigger problem, though, is that the facts were so convoluted and poorly presented that the poor financial health of the company was not readily discernible.

> Knowledge workers and BI experts must continually evaluate the reports, dashboards, alerts, and other mechanisms for disseminating factual information to ensure the design facilitates insight.

For example, Continental Airlines offers a concierge service to its BusinessFirst international passengers. In the past, the concierges worked with 11 different reports to understand passenger requirements.[6] By redesigning the reports, the BI team could give the concierges more information, but in one report, allowing the concierges to more readily see the most important information.

Fostering Fact-Based Decision Making

Decision-making experts say that being forewarned about decision-making traps is the most important first step to improving decision making. "At every stage of the decision-making process, misperceptions, biases, and other tricks of the mind can influence the choices we make...the best protection against all psychological traps...is awareness."[7] Beyond that, encouraging fact-based decision making is taking root in management literature and in business schools around the world. The number of MBA programs that offer business intelligence and statistical analysis courses increases each year. Some BI vendors such as Teradata, SAS, and Hyperion have been proactive in introducing analytical concepts in universities.

Keep in mind that the chicken-and-egg syndrome will play out here too. Fact-based decision making may be absent when data access is a problem. You have to first deliver BI capabilities in order for people to make routine decisions based on facts.

Other Cultural Enablers

Some of the other cultural aspects that enable successful business intelligence will come as little surprise (see Figure 13-2):

- A higher percentage (93%) of successful BI companies use information technology to achieve competitive advantage than those who are failing (44%).

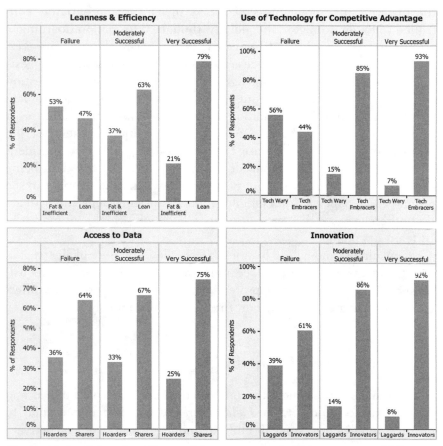

Figure 13-2 Cultural enablers to BI are consistently higher at successful BI companies.

- Besides fact-based decision making, the second biggest cultural difference between those who are very successful with BI and those who are only moderately successful was in whether the survey respondent saw their company as being a lean, efficiently operated one. The survey showed that 79% of successful BI companies see themselves as lean, whereas only 63% of moderately successful BI companies see themselves as lean, and 47% of the failures describe themselves as lean.

One cultural surprise to me was the degree and consistency of data hoarding. Among the failures and very successful BI companies alike, there was not a major difference in whether respondents felt access to data at their company was overly controlled or that executives fear workers know too much (see Figure 13-2, Access to Data chart). The majority of respondents disagreed with this statement; in other words, the majority of respondents said access to data is appropriately controlled (69% on average). Anecdotally, though, information hoarding is often cited as a barrier to BI success. While not in the majority, 31% of survey respondents said access to data is overly controlled, suggesting a sizable problem. In hindsight, I also think this survey question could have been framed without attributing the source of the problem to executive control. Information hoarding has also been cited as a problem among power users and other information workers for job protection issues. At Corporate Express, Walter Scott, vice president of marketing, explains, "Some departments don't like the data being exposed. The attitude is 'get out of my sandbox.' If other people can see pricing discrepancies, for example, then the pricing department fears that others may see they are not doing a good job, which can make the BI team unpopular."

Consultants and hybrid business/IT people were more likely to agree with the assessment that data access is overly controlled than were businesspeople and corporate IT professionals. There were no major differences in these averages based on the size of the company.

Promoting Your BI Capabilities

With business intelligence, there is often the attitude of "build it and they will come." And yet, the *Field of Dreams* notion does not apply to business intelligence: you can build it, and users won't come. There are a number of reasons users won't automatically use the business intelligence application:

- Resistance to change
- Predominance of gut-feel decision making
- Lack of relevance (see Chapter 9)

You never want "lack of awareness" to be one of the reasons, though, and to avoid this pitfall, you must proactively promote your company's BI capabilities.

Users will go through an evolution as you promote your business intelligence solution (see Figure 13-3). During the funding and development stages of the project, you want to build *awareness* about what is coming and how it affects people. You want everyone—not just power users or initial users—to have heard of business intelligence. As you get closer to delivering capability for a particular group of users, you want to increase *knowledge* about business intelligence so that people will understand when and how to use business intelligence. The third phase of promotion is to increase *usage,* in which people within all levels of

Figure 13-3   The phases of promoting business intelligence

the organization are *aware* of business intelligence, *know* when to use it, and *use* it as an invaluable tool to achieve business goals. Use a variety of media to achieve these different promotional stages. Different user segments (see Chapter 12) will be at different stages simultaneously.

When to Promote

There is a comfort in waiting to promote your BI capabilities only when you are finished with the first phase of your project. If you wait until then, however, you are starting too late and it will take you longer to achieve any measurable benefits. Users must be aware of business intelligence long before they sign up for a training class. Clearly, you need to manage user expectations and not promise more functionality than you can deliver. In early promotions, emphasize the high-level benefits, implementation waves, and broad time frames. Battered IT departments who have been criticized for being late in the past may truly cringe at this approach, preferring to keep a low profile until everything is done. However, to break down barriers and slowly build demand and excitement, you must promote early, well before you are ready for deployment.

Focus on Benefits

As you do so, focus as much as possible on the *benefits* your implementation will deliver, not the technical *features* of the deployment. Consider some of the products you buy as a consumer. Particularly with business intelligence, a number of technical features will have little meaning to users. Restating the features in terms of the benefits is one of the hardest language barriers for the project team to overcome. Table 13-1 highlights some features that are better described to users in terms of the benefits they provide.

Feature	Benefit
Aggregate or summary tables	Fast queries.
Disconnected access	Ability to work with reports while traveling or at a customer site.
Ad hoc queries	Explore the root cause of a problem, without waiting for an IT report developer.
Exception-based reporting	Proactively manage the business when indicators fall below a certain threshold; fix a problem before it is out of control.

Table 13-1   Emphasize Benefits, Not Features

In a few instances, the feature and related benefit will be clear; but these instances are in the minority. For example, "24/7" (as in 24 hours a day, 7 days a week) is a feature of when the BI application may be available. As this phrase is repeated in so many contexts, users will immediately recognize the benefit as being access on demand, no matter the time of day, world time zone, or day of the week.

A fun team-building exercise is to have the BI project team practice their elevator speech for real business users. The elevator speech is a one-minute description of what the BI project team is developing, stated in terms of business benefits users can readily understand. It is a big departure from the technobabble that may be more familiar. It's also a useful way to ensure the team stays focused on the business value of BI, rather than the cool technology!

Before—Technobabble	After—Business Benefits
"We're building a 10-terabyte data warehouse on a Netezza appliance. It's all in 3rd normal form and we've custom-coded the ETL process."	"We're implementing software that allows you to explore information to reduce inventory holding costs and to deliver product faster to customers."

Key Messages   When you promote your BI solution, develop key messages or taglines that emphasize these benefits. The tagline you develop depends on the current situation and goals you have for deploying or enhancing your BI capabilities. For example, if users currently have to wait months to receive a custom report, a key message may be "information now." If one of the business goals is to retain customers, a BI tagline may be "helping you know our customers." In developing your BI taglines, look for inspiration from some of the most successful promotional campaigns, as shown in Table 13-2.

Product	Benefit	Tagline
Dunkin' Donuts	Their coffee and snacks give you energy.	"America runs on Dunkin'"™
MasterCard	Using MasterCard makes you happy.	"There are some things money can't buy, for everything else, there's MasterCard."
Milk, sponsored by the California Milk Processor Board	Drinking milk gives you strong bones and makes you healthier.	"Got Milk?"®

Table 13-2   Famous Taglines

FlightStats, for example, initially used the tagline "FlightStats transforms information into travel intelligence." As summer 2007 became one of the worst on record for on-time performance and flight cancellations, they creatively promoted a new tagline: "When the travel gets tough, the tough fly smarter." Emergency Medical Associates uses "the premier on demand reporting and analytics tool for your Emergency Department" as its tagline for their BI solution. A New Jersey school district uses the tagline "data drives instruction."

Naming Your BI Solution

In promoting your BI solution, you may refer to it by using the BI vendor tool name or with a unique name. The benefit of including the vendor-provided name is that you can leverage some of the vendor's marketing efforts. The downside is if the vendor changes product names (frequent in an industry where mergers and acquisition abound), then you may have to change your internal product name as well. If you are suffering from a stalled implementation or if there were negative impressions early in the implementation, change the name! Corporate Express, for example, actively moved away from a vendor-specific name to Apollo. As part of the renewed BI effort, the project team held a contest to see who could think of the most appropriate name. To encourage creativity and participation, the person submitting the winning name won an iPod. Apollo, the Greek god of truth, was selected over other entries such as Moose and Infobahn.[8] When you develop your own BI product name, be sure to consider the acronym created. If it is a global deployment, take into account the cultural impact of acronyms. Table 13-3 lists the BI product names used at Successful BI Case Studies.

Following are some other clever product names:

- **WISDOM**   Web Intelligence Supporting Decisions, from Owens & Minor. WISDOM Gold is an enhanced extranet version.
- **OASIS**   Online Analysis Sales Information System.
- **Honeycomb**   Used by Burt's Bees to brand information accessed via BusinessObjects XI. A tagline displayed in the BI portal, "A Bee's Eye View," also conveys the message that this information helps the "worker bees" in the company.
- **YODA**   Your On-line Data Access.

Promotional Media

In promoting your BI application, you must repeat your message often and use a variety of media. Remember, the goal with promotion is to move

Successful BI Company	BI Product Name
1-800 CONTACTS	Call Center Incentives (CCI) & Executive Dashboard
Continental Airlines	Enterprise Data Warehouse (EDW), plus BI tool vendor names, plus specific application names
Corporate Express	Apollo
The Dow Chemical Company	Shared Data Network (SDN), plus BI tool vendor names, plus specific applications such as TPM (Transactional Pocket Margin)
Emergency Medical Associates	WEBeMARS™ (Emergency Medicine Analysis & Reporting Services)
Conducive Technology (FlightStats)	FlightStats

Table 13-3   BI Product Names at Successful BI Case Study Companies

people from *awareness* of business intelligence to *usage*. It will take a number of repetitions, with different messages and media, to get there.

- **Road shows**   When companies first start developing a business intelligence solution, many have corresponding information sessions about what is coming, when phase 1 will be available, and who will be trained first. The most successful "road shows" include business success stories and user testimonials on how business intelligence has had a measurable impact.
- **Video clips and podcasts**   Some companies have created web videos and podcasts to explain their BI program and the benefits it delivers. Emergency Medical Associates, for example, has a web video on their home page describing the BI application. Podcasts are a newer medium that allow people to listen to short sound-bites and interviews over the Internet or via an iPod. Any of these media can be used in conjunction with a road show, and they are particularly useful if the executive sponsor states their vision for BI or if a business user gives a testimonial as to how BI has helped them. While a video or podcast may be difficult to produce at first, it helps reduce travel costs and logistic issues in always getting the right people together.

The Business Intelligence Network has been an innovator in the use of podcasts. You can access a number of customer testimonials and experiences with business intelligence from their website (www.b-eye-network.com/podcast/archive).

- **Company newsletters** Existing corporate newsletters are an excellent medium for high-level messages to a broad audience. Given the readership of company newsletters, the primary purpose of these articles should be to build awareness, not necessarily usage. These articles should include information about the business goals and project milestones. It is not an ideal medium for explaining detailed functionality.
- **Industry journals** Companies have a misconception that participation in user conferences and articles in industry journals help only the careers of the project staff and not necessarily the company. In fact, successful BI companies have said that the external media attention has helped motivate, attract, and retain top talent. Emergency Medical Associates also credits client wins to industry exposure. There are a number of ways to get your project into an industry journal. You can author an article. You can volunteer to be interviewed by one of your BI vendors for a press release. Your company's public relations department can issue a press release either to technical journals such as *Computer World, DM Review, Intelligent Enterprise, Business Intelligence Network, Information Age,* and *CIO Insight,* or, if it has more of a business slant, to industry journals. Finally, consider submitting an application for industry awards. In addition to taking time to reflect on your accomplishments, award winners enjoy additional exposure and speaking opportunities.
- **Brown-bag lunches** A brown-bag lunch is a casual information-sharing session in which participants bring a bagged lunch (coffee or breakfast works too) and discuss effective usage of business intelligence. Vendors may also participate in these sessions. A facilitator may start the lunch with a success story, tip, or project update. These provide a useful follow-up to training and another opportunity to raise awareness about best practices, success stories, and benefits.
- **Internal user conferences** Just as BI vendors host periodic user conferences, do the same in your own company. Kick off the meeting with a review of the benefits, project milestones, and a key success story. Then ask users to share tips and techniques on both the how-to of BI tools and how it has helped them achieve business goals.
- **T-shirt days** Many project teams give away T-shirts, sunglasses, mouse pads, and other promotional items to reward staff for their accomplishments. As both a motivational technique and a promotion opportunity, get the entire team to wear their giveaway on milestone dates. This works particularly well if the T-shirt is brightly colored. Seeing 50 yellow T-shirts in the company cafeteria will generate

interest and curiosity about what's new. One of Dow Chemical's early giveaways was silver dollars. Using the theme of the captain in *Moby Dick,* the project manager gave each team member a silver dollar for every 100 users trained. The goal was to ensure team members stayed focused on the user requirements and did not get distracted by what was then a new technology. (I still have my silver dollars.) An automotive company printed tips on mouse pads to promote usage and reduce help desk calls.

- **Portal**   The company portal or BI portal is useful for promoting to existing users and keeping them informed; however, it is a poor medium for new or potential users who may not see these messages. You can best reach these potential users through staff meetings and company newsletters.

- **Routine staff meetings**   Most departments and business units have regularly scheduled staff meetings. Ask for five minutes on the agenda each quarter to give an update on new deliverables, problem resolution, and how other departments are benefiting from business intelligence. A real sign of success is when the department invites you and requests 30 minutes!

Training

A common theme with the successful BI case studies was the attention to training and that the training focused on the data and not only on the BI tools. Conversely, survey respondents who described their BI project as failing or only moderately successful cited lack of attention to training as an impediment to greater success.

> "Training and adoption has been longer and harder than expected."
>
> —IT director, state agency

Some of the promotional media such as internal user groups, newsletters, and brown-bag lunches are useful supplements to initial training mechanisms. Training should also be tailored to meet the needs of the various user segments (see Chapter 12). For example, executives may need only an introductory walkthrough (via web or phone), whereas knowledge workers who will become power users may need multiday classroom training.

At Emergency Medical Associates, this is where ease of use and web-based BI are also important. Explains Eric Bachenheimer, director of client account management, "You don't have to be a techy or a programmer to use WEBeMARS. It's self-serve and only takes a few clicks to call up a report. Nobody has to take a three-week training class. It uses a skill set they already have." In training hospital administrators to use WEBeMARS, EMA uses a combination of presentation and interactive demonstration that only lasts two hours.[9]

Following are some additional things to consider in developing a training approach:

- **Data vs. the tool** A BI tool delivers no value without the underlying data users' wish to analyze. If you train users only on the BI tool with only sample databases, users may not be able to apply these skills against their own data. Generic software training is recommended only for IT professionals and power users. As you extend the reach of BI, a greater emphasis must be given to the specific data, business insights, and desired actions.

> Brown-bag lunches are a good way to supplement classroom training on the tool with ongoing discussions about the data.

- **Internal vs. third-party** BI tool vendors and their training partners will train end users on the software. Some will customize the training material to include your specific business views, reports, dashboards, and data in the screen shots. You also may be able to buy the training material from vendors and incorporate your own screen shots.
- **Training method** While classroom-style training is the most traditional, it can pose a logistical challenge when users are at different sites, have busy schedules, and access different data sources. Some users may do quite well to read a book and then supplement that with webinars, on their own schedule and at their own pace.

> Regardless of the formal training method, for a successful implementation you must supplement scheduled training classes with other means to share tips, techniques, and uses.

Training will receive a reasonable amount of consideration early in the BI process, but it seems to fall by the wayside as BI usage expands and new capabilities are delivered. One of the successful BI case studies expressed concern. "Early on, we were committed to training, but then as the demands grew to build more capabilities, the BI team has gotten pulled into more development and less training." In this regard, recognize that training is an ongoing service and requirement that needs to be separated from the development team. The development team may still deliver initial training as part of a new capability, but at some point, consideration must be given to delivering ongoing training.

A Picture Is Worth a Thousand Numbers

Many of the successful BI case studies make much better use of visualizations than other companies I have worked with. This conclusion is not based on any statistical data; it's simply an observation. When I asked to see sample screen shots of how the case study companies were using business intelligence, rarely did I get a dense page of numbers. Instead, I would see reports and dashboards with charts, trend lines, arrow indicators, and greater use of conditional formatting (green to communicate good performance and red to indicate a problem). Visualization expert Edward Tufte suggests that a tabular display of numbers is better when 20 numbers or fewer are involved. And yet, I look at the reams and reams of reports with thousands of numbers. In truth, sometimes you do need a precise number—you want the part number, the customer phone number, the charge on your credit card bill. But when you are trying to uncover patterns, anomalies, and opportunities, a dense page of numbers is useless. All too often, it seems report developers first try to re-create a report as it existed in a legacy system (that may lack graphing capabilities). This approach may be a necessary first step to build confidence in the data coming from the BI solution, but it should not be the last. Instead, BI experts should better leverage the visualization capabilities within BI tools to more effectively communicate the data. All too often, longtime business query users will declare, "I never even knew the BI tool could create graphs!" Instead, data is either left as a dense page of numbers or routinely pulled into spreadsheets for graphing. This suggests that the problem lies in both inadequate training and lack of awareness on how best to communicate data.

Best Practices for Successful Business Intelligence

You've built a perfectly architected BI solution, and followed the other best practices in each of the preceding chapters, garnering executive support and fostering a strong business-IT partnership. And yet, you may still encounter only moderate success unless you take into account the subtle—yet profound—effect of company culture. To harvest the full value of your BI efforts:

- Recognize the role that company culture plays in facilitating successful BI (or as a barrier to greater success). Work with senior executives to foster a fact-based decision-making environment and one that encourages appropriate access to data.
- Promote business intelligence uses and success stories on an ongoing basis, using a variety of media.
- Deliver training that is tailored to user segments on an ongoing basis. Supplement formal classroom training with periodic web-based updates, internal user conferences, and brown-bag lunches. Train users on both the tool and the data they are accessing with their preferred tool.
- Leverage visualization capabilities in BI tools to more effectively present the data and communicate trends and exceptions.

Chapter 14

The Future of
Business Intelligence

The future of business intelligence centers on making BI relevant for everyone, not only for information workers and internal employees, but also beyond corporate boundaries, to extend the reach of BI to customers and suppliers. As the Successful BI case studies have demonstrated, when best practices are applied, BI usage can explode beyond the paltry 25% of employees today to a much more prevalent business tool. It will take cultural shifts, new ways of thinking, and continued technical innovation. Business intelligence has the power to change people's way of working, to enable businesses to compete more effectively and efficiently, and to help nonprofits stretch their dollars further. All of this is possible based on insights available at the click of a mouse, push of a button, or touch of a screen.

As discussed throughout this book, much of the key to successful business intelligence has to do with the people, processes, and culture. Don't rely on technical innovation alone to solve the biggest barriers to BI success, but by all means, do get excited about the innovations that will make BI easier and more prevalent. BI as a technology has changed dramatically since its inception in the early 1990s. This chapter focuses on the most recent technical innovations with examples of how customers are taking advantage of them. In the final section, I leave you with some words of wisdom to inspire you to think about how business intelligence can become your company's next killer application.

Emerging Technologies

As part of the Successful BI Survey, respondents were asked to choose items from a list of emerging technologies that they believe will help their companies achieve greater success. Figure 14-1 shows which items

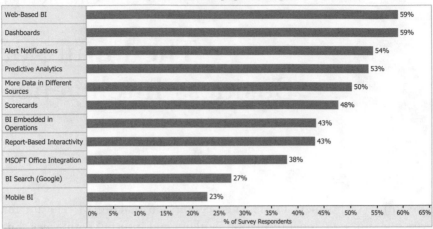

Importance of Emerging Technologies

Technology	%
Web-Based BI	59%
Dashboards	59%
Alert Notifications	54%
Predictive Analytics	53%
More Data in Different Sources	50%
Scorecards	48%
BI Embedded in Operations	43%
Report-Based Interactivity	43%
MSOFT Office Integration	38%
BI Search (Google)	27%
Mobile BI	23%

% of Survey Respondents

Figure 14-1 The majority of survey respondents believe web-based BI, dashboards, alerting, and predictive analytics will allow greater success. (Results based on 513 responses.)

are considered most important in helping companies achieve greater success. Web-based business intelligence and dashboards were rated the highest, with predictive analytics and alerting also at the top. Surprising to me, Microsoft Office Integration, BI Search, and Mobile BI were selected by only a small percentage of survey respondents.

The view according to business users, however, is slightly different, as shown in Figure 14-2. Business users account for only 10% of the survey respondents. Those who describe themselves as hybrid business-IT personnel account for 23% of respondents. I have specifically excluded IT personnel and hybrids from Figure 14-2, to show the gap in perceived importance of certain technologies. When viewing responses only for business users, the importance of Microsoft Office integration moves to the top of the list, while alerting moves down.

Some of these differences can be explained by gaps in understanding of the feature benefits, but also by a respondent's point of view. For example, IT professionals have been burned in the past by the thousands of disconnected spreadsheets and the ensuing data chaos. As Microsoft Office integration with BI has improved dramatically in 2007, IT professionals may not realize that spreadsheet-based analysis can now be "safely" enabled and can be something to be embraced for knowledge workers familiar not just with Microsoft Excel, but also with Word, Outlook, and PowerPoint. In a similar fashion, if you are a BlackBerry user, you may rate Mobile BI high. While web-based business intelligence may have been introduced in the late 1990s, these solutions only

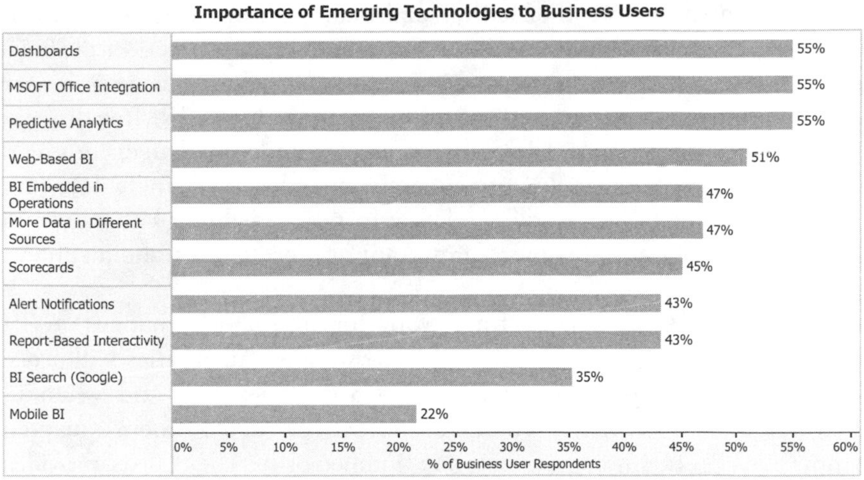

Importance of Emerging Technologies to Business Users

Dashboards	55%
MSOFT Office Integration	55%
Predictive Analytics	55%
Web-Based BI	51%
BI Embedded in Operations	47%
More Data in Different Sources	47%
Scorecards	45%
Alert Notifications	43%
Report-Based Interactivity	43%
BI Search (Google)	35%
Mobile BI	22%

% of Business User Respondents

Figure 14-2   For business users, Microsoft Office integration with BI moves up in importance. (Results based on 51 responses.)

reached the rich functionality of their desktop predecessors in the 2005 time frame. A number of companies are not yet on the latest releases, though, and still use client/server BI deployments. Depending upon where a survey respondent is in their web-based BI deployment will influence how this capability was rated.

At The Data Warehousing Institute's (TDWI) Executive Summit in February 2007, I participated in a panel on the role of emerging technologies in extending the reach and impact of business intelligence. Attendance was restricted to BI directors and executive sponsors who influence their company's BI strategy. Attendees could vote on a limited number of items that they thought would have the biggest impact in the next few years. The most highly ranked item: performance management and predictive analytics. The things that got few to no votes were BI search, dashboards, and rich Internet applications, contrary to what I believe will have the biggest impact. As we delved into what these technologies mean, and in some cases, demonstrated them, the perceptions changed significantly. In this way, we sometimes don't know the impact any of these capabilities will have until the technology has become more mature and the industry understands it better. If you think about the way breakthroughs like the iPod and YouTube have revolutionized their markets, when they first were introduced, they were met with a mixture of fascination and confusion, without a clear understanding of where they would lead. Recent BI innovations must go through a similar process of the industry first understanding their potential, accepting or rejecting them, and then either embracing or adopting the innovations in a limited fashion. Another fundamental difference in evaluating impact is whether the impact is measured by the value of one user or decision or aggregated by multiple users and decisions. Recall from Chapter 12 (see Figure 12-4), thousands of individual decisions can have as big, if not bigger, an impact on a company than a single decision. There seems to be a natural tendency to rate capabilities that have a single big impact as being more important or more likely to help achieve greater BI success.

Figure 14-3 provides a framework for evaluating changes in BI technology to determine which new and emerging capabilities will prove most valuable to your company, how mature they are, and when to monitor them or when to embrace and actively deploy them (adapted from TDWI's Technology Evaluation Framework). The X axis provides an indication of how mature the technology is, and the Y axis gives an indication of which technology will make BI pervasive. Recall from the section on BI users as a percentage of employees in Chapter 4 that the average usage of BI within a company is currently at 25%, and even if budget were available and the deployment were wildly successful, survey respondents felt the use rate would extend only to 54% of employees.

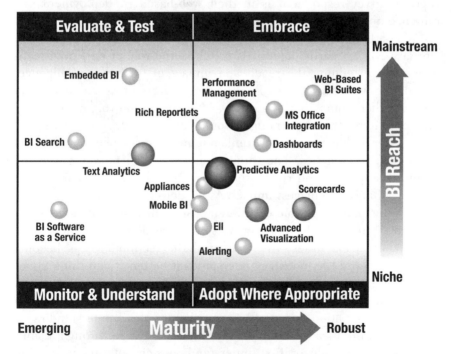

Figure 14-3   BI technology evaluation

The Y axis, then, indicates the degree to which an enabling technology will take BI's reach closer to 100% of employees. Business impact and BI prevalence are not linearly correlated, however. One enabling technology, such as predictive analytics, may yield a big value for a single decision, say, a $4 million savings by better marketing campaign management. Another enabling technology such as BI embedded in operational processes may affect thousands of users, each of whom makes dozens of decisions on a daily basis; the monetary value of these individual decisions may be small when measured in isolation, but enormous when taken in aggregate. The size and shading of the bubbles in Figure 14-3 give an indication of which items have a bigger single value. The bigger the bubble and darker the shading, the bigger the impact on a single decision or person.

For each innovation, consider both the technical maturity and the business impact to decide how to proceed:

- **Embrace** Items in the upper-right quadrant show innovations that are mature and that should be embraced as they will help speed user adoption across multiple user segments.
- **Adopt Where Appropriate** Items in the lower-right quadrant show innovations that are mature but that may serve only specific segments of users. Mobile BI is an example of this; the technology is more mature than BI search, for example, but benefits only those users who have smartphones such as a BlackBerry.
- **Evaluate and Test** Items in the upper-left quadrant are relatively new but will have a profound impact on user adoption. BI Search is a good example of this. The technology is very new and not well under-stood. A number of usability and performance issues still need to be worked out, but the potential impact on user adoption is enormous.
- **Monitor and Understand** Items in the lower-left quadrant are so new that they may be riskier investments. Items here are less proven and have less market adoption.

Figure 14-3 portrays broad industry maturity of these capabilities and the degree to which most vendors offer the capabilities. For clarity, I have selected only certain innovations; it is not meant to be an exhaustive list of all things going on in the industry (for this, check the BIScorecard blog). All items are in the context of business intelligence as a technology. So while performance management is certainly a mature concept and technology, the integration of performance management with business intelligence is still a work in progress, leaving this item positioned slightly behind web-based BI and Microsoft Office integration on the maturity spectrum.

The subsequent sections describe these capabilities that have not otherwise been addressed in Chapters 2 and 3.

Predicting the Future

Data mining, statistical analysis, and predictive analytics are nothing new. These technologies are well established and are used in a number of different applications such as fraud detection, customer scoring, risk analysis, and campaign management. What's changed is how they have become integrated in the BI platform. Traditionally, predictive analytics has been a backroom task performed by a limited few statisticians who would take a snapshot of the data (either from a data warehouse or from a purpose-built extract from the source system), build a model, test a model, finalize it, and then somehow disseminate the results. While the expertise to build such models remains a unique skill set, the industry recognizes that the results of the analysis should be more broadly shared, not as a stand-alone application, but rather, as an integral part of the BI solution. This does not mean that predictive analytics software will become "mainstream," but rather that the results of such analyses can be readily incorporated into everyday reports and decision making. The analysis, then, is what needs to become mainstream.

Predictive analytic tools from different vendors do continue to differ significantly in how they work and in what information is stored in the database versus calculated and presented in a report or incorporated into an operational process.

At Corporate Express, for example, predictive analytics are being used to improve customers' online shopping experience.[1]

Market basket analysis helps retailers understand which products sell together and provide product recommendations. In the past, Corporate Express provided these recommendations by logical product pairings. So if a customer ordered a stapler, the online store would recommend a staple remover as the marketing team had marked this as a complementary product.[2]

In analyzing the data, though, it turned out that what was most often purchased with a stapler was not a staple remover, but rather a ruler, tape dispenser, and a wastepaper basket—items that indicate a purchase for a new employee. With the manually associated product recommendations, there was no significant impact on sales. Leveraging MicroStrategy and SPSS, Corporate Express tested a new market basket option. The model analyzes past shopping carts and produces recommendations to ensure the greatest lift. As a result, the average order size for market basket pairings doubled (versus those orders with no pairings), and the market basket application is expected to generate an incremental gross profit of more than $2 million in 2007.

Dow Chemical also has begun extending the reach of predictive analytics with SAS's JMP product (pronounced "jump"), a solution that combines visual analysis with statistics. As discussed in Chapter 12, Dow uses BusinessObjects and Cognos PowerPlay as enterprise reporting and analysis standards. Through these tools and the data in the data warehouse, Dow began looking at the high cost of railroad shipments: $400 million annually across North America.[3]

A team of statistical experts studied the variables that most affected these costs and pulled data from the data warehouse and external data sources into SAS JMP. By benchmarking current payments versus industry norms, the analysis showed Dow was overpaying by 20%, or $80 million. In entering new contracts, the purchasing department now uses the software to predict appropriate rates, enabling them to negotiate more aggressively.

For both Corporate Express and Dow Chemical, the move to predictive analytics has been evolutionary. The underlying information architecture and a culture of fact-based decision making had to first reach a level of maturity and data quality before predictive analytics could be embraced. While both companies have been doing statistical analysis for decades, the degree to which predictive analytics has now been incorporated into daily processes (online store at Corporate Express and purchasing negotiations at Dow Chemical) reflects the degree to which predictive analytics has shifted from the backroom to the front line, with the most casual of users deriving value from such analytics.

BI Search & Text Analytics

BI Search offers a number of promising benefits to business intelligence:

- Simple user interface.
- A more complete set of information to support decision making, with the integration of structured (quantitative) and unstructured content (textual). Structured data refers to the numerical values typically captured in the operational systems and subsequently stored in a data warehouse. Unstructured content refers to information stored in textual comment fields, documents, annual reports, websites, and so on.

- Users can find what they need through search, rather than through navigating a long list of reports.

Text analytics is closely related to search in that unstructured information or text can be transformed into quantitative data. For example, it allows for searching of information in a comment field to see how many times a customer praised a particular product. Text analytics is the numerical analysis of textual information.

Despite all the improvements in data warehousing and BI front-end tools, users continue to feel overwhelmed with reports yet undersatisfied with meaningful information. They don't know what's available or where. Similar reports are created over and over because users don't know which reports already exist or how, for example, the report "Product Sales" differs from "Product Sales YTD." Some of the most valuable information is hidden in textual data.

A BI Search interface promises to change the way users access information. Picture a Google interface to BI. Without any training in a BI tool, users can enter a phrase such as "Recent sales for customer A" and then be presented with either a list of predefined reports or, in some cases, a newly generated query. The added benefit is that in addition to displaying reports coming from the BI server, the search engine will also list textual information that may be relevant—a customer letter, sales call notes, headline news. When search capabilities are combined with text analytics, a report may include numerical data that scans the comment field to indicate number of complaints with number of positive comments. Never before has such unstructured data been so nicely accessible with structured or quantitative data.

If the integration of search and BI is successful, it is yet another innovation that will make BI accessible and usable by every employee in an organization. According to Tony Byrne, founder/president of CMS Watch, a technology evaluation firm focusing on enterprise search and content management systems, search as a technology has existed for more than 50 years.[4] *Consumer* search (Google and Yahoo, for example) as a technology emerged with the Internet in the mid-1990s. In many respects, the success of consumer search has helped spur hype around *enterprise* search, in which companies deploy search technology internally to search myriad document repositories. Text analytics has existed for 25 years but with usage in limited sectors, particularly, the government. The convergence of search with business intelligence first emerged in 2006. Google is not the only enterprise search solution that BI vendors support but it is one that has the most consumer recognition and thus has helped business users to understand the possibilities. To illustrate the point, note that BI search was selected by only 27% of the Successful BI Survey respondents as a capability that would help foster greater success (see earlier Figure 14-1). Yet in discussing these technologies with individual executives who don't currently use business intelligence, a Google-like interface to BI generated the most enthusiasm.

The incorporation of text analytics with traditional business intelligence is still in its infancy. I place both BI search and text analytics close to the Monitor and Understand quadrant but in the Evaluate and Test quadrant in Figure 14-3. Again, both technologies independent of BI have existed for decades; it is that convergence with BI that is new. While the convergence is still relatively immature, the promise it brings for BI to reach more users and in the value of incorporating textual data is enormous.

The number of customers taking advantage of the BI Search and text analytics integration is only a handful. BlueCross BlueShield (BCBS) of Tennessee (TN) is an early adopter of these capabilities.[5] BCBS of TN is a not-for-profit provider of health insurance. In 2006, it paid $17 billion in benefits for its 2 million commercial members.[6] Managing claims and negotiating rates with providers is critical in ensuring BCBS can meet its obligations to the members it insures. While the insurer has had a mature business intelligence deployment for ten years,[7] Frank Brooks, the senior manager of data resource management and chief data architect, recognized that there was value in bringing the text data stored in comment fields from call center notes together with information in the data warehouse.[8] Given how new the technology is, Brooks asked their BI vendor, Cognos, along with IBM (who produces the search solution OmniFind) and SAS (who offers text analytics solution Text Miner) to work together to develop several prototypes and show the business users the concept of bringing BI, enterprise search, and text analytics together. With this capability, a business user can enter the key word "diabetes" in the OmniFind search box and be presented with a ranked list of things such as:

- Cognos reports and OLAP cubes that show claims paid for diabetic treatments
- Call center notes that involve diabetes
- New research on improving care for diabetes patients

The business was enthusiastic. There has been a high degree of collaboration between BCBS of TN and its information technology partners to understand the new capabilities, develop the right infrastructure, and optimize the indexes to provide the best search performance.

Consistent with the evaluation framework in Figure 14-3, understanding new technologies requires a significant amount of evaluation and testing. BCBS of TN evaluated the capabilities for more than a year before developing plans for implementing in production.

Advanced Visualization

All leading BI tools have basic visualization capabilities: you can take tabular data and turn it into a bar chart, trend line, and so on. They also support some kind of conditional formatting of data: display positive numbers in green, display negative numbers in red, and enlarge those with the worst variances. *Advanced* visualization goes beyond a simple chart such as a bar or line chart to include things as:

- Spark lines, a highly condensed trend line the size of a word.
- Bullet graphs, a construct by Stephen Few that includes a target indicator within the bar chart. See Figure 3-3, Chapter 3.
- Small multiples, which are series of small, similar graphics or charts.[9] As they use the same scale and are positioned side-by-side, they facilitate visual discovery by letting users make comparisons at a glance.
- Heat maps that display two variables as different intensifying colors.
- Decomposition trees, a visualization that displays each drill-down akin to an ever-expanding organization chart.
- Geographic maps that display things such as sales figures in a map form, using color to highlight sales performance. By mousing over a particular country, region, or state, you can see the individual data values.

Advanced visualization software and capabilities also help you apply best practices in data visualization, even for basic visualizations. As an example, many reports today are designed as a dense page of numbers. The dense page of numbers may not help facilitate insight, but they are what users are accustomed to. With visualization software, a dense set of numbers can quickly be converted to a more meaningful display. Figure 14-4 shows several charts created in Tableau Software. By displaying multiple graphs side-by-side, as "small multiples," you can more easily see which product category—technology in this case—is the top-selling product

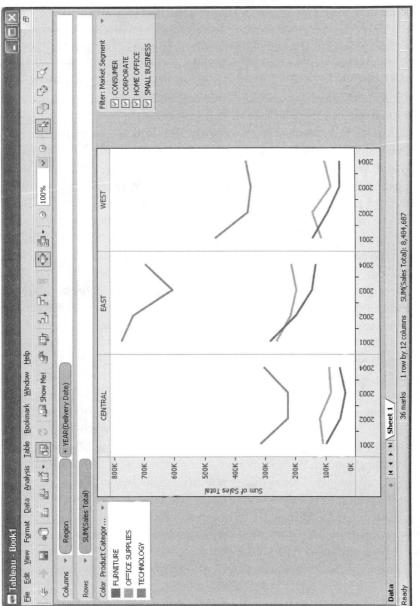

Figure 14-4 Advanced visualization with Tableau Software

category for all regions. The dimensions (time and region) and scale within each graph are the same, allowing for a rapid comparison. Sales seem to have dipped in 2003, particularly in the eastern region. By toggling the quick filters (shown on the right in Figure 14-4), it's possible to focus on the individual customer segments to see that technology sales to corporations are on a steady decline, whereas consumer and small business segments show strength.

Creating this kind of display with standard BI software is theoretically possible, but one that would take many, many more steps. As well, if I am uncertain as to the best way to display the information, advanced visualization software can make suggestions. The capability to create easily such advanced visualizations is generally not available in BI suites. Users must rely on specialty products. In a theme similar to predictive analytics and search, visualization software has existed for years; the change is in its convergence with business intelligence such that advanced visualizations are appearing in dashboards and reports. In this regard, the emphasis for BI tools is changing from a focus of simply "getting to the data" to "what insights can I discover from the data and how can the most information be displayed in the smallest space."

Rich Reportlets

Report-based interactivity is a ho-hum term that warrants a better name. "Active reports," "on-report formatting," and "navigable reports" are similar terms that also don't fully capture the value of this capability. I suspect poor terminology and lack of awareness also explains why survey respondents ranked this capability on the low end of importance for emerging technologies (see Figure 14-1). So after much thought and brainstorming with some colleagues, I will refer to this capability as "rich reportlets." The difference in power and appeal with rich reportlets versus, say, green-bar paper reports and much of what is currently deployed over the Web, is comparable to the difference between a black Ford Model T and a red Mercedes sports coupe.

Rich reportlets are powered by Web 2.0 technologies to create rich Internet applications (RIA). When BI suites were first re-architected for the Web, report consumers could only view a static page. Given how static a display this was, more sophisticated users would export the data to Excel for analysis. Less sophisticated users would submit requests to IT or to the BI team to modify the report design. The Web in this case is only a delivery vehicle for data; it does not facilitate user adoption and insight. With rich reportlets, someone accesses a report over the Web but in a much more interactive and appealing way. At a simple click, data can be re-sorted, filtered, or graphed, without having to launch a complicated report editor. With the use of either Adobe Flex or Macromedia Flash, these reports come to life in ways that make business intelligence fun. I have seen, for example, a bubble chart that displays bubbles dancing across the screen as the time axis marches onward. Such animation makes BI appealing as well as insightful as users see the trend in action. In this regard, the term "report" doesn't do justice to the capability that is more akin to a mini application.

This type of interactivity affects all BI users, whether casual or power users. The appeal makes BI more engaging, and while some technologists may scoff at the importance of this, when other barriers to adoption exist, appeal matters. A lot! The ability to interact with the data in a simple and intuitive way facilitates greater insight at the hands of the decision maker. The report consumer is not forced to delay this insight until a power user can modify the report. Lastly, the cost of ownership is lowered because a single reportlet can be "tweaked" to that decision maker's needs, without IT having to maintain thousands of individualized reports.

The Future Beyond Technology

Technical innovation is only one aspect that will help increase BI's prevalence. In discussing future plans with many of the case study companies, much of their concern was not about technology, but rather, in finding new ways to use BI to address common business problems. For the more large-scale deployments, some expressed concern about managing the risk of making any kind of major change to such a business critical, complex application. With success, of course, comes greater demands on the systems and the people. Ensuring an effective way of prioritizing competing requests warrants constant attention. One business leader expressed frustration at his department's inability to make wise investments, while witnessing other departments, working in more unison and getting more value from business intelligence. Yet he remains optimistic that his business will get there and that BI will be the first thing people look at, even before email. "To have one screen I can get to with a single click, that shows sales, margin, price, opportunities in graphical form, with drill down—that would be magic!" His comments remind me that the technology is sometimes the easy part; getting the organization aligned is harder. Even the most successful BI companies, then, continue to have their battles.

Words of Wisdom

I hope this book will inspire you to ensure business intelligence has a profound impact on your organization. I'd like to see the techniques and insights shared by the most successful BI companies and the innovations from leading and niche vendors help move the industry beyond the current average of 25% usage rate within companies and 24% success rate to much higher rates. Business intelligence is all encompassing in its ability to improve an organization's efficiency, competitiveness, and opportunities. Through the process of writing and researching this book, these business intelligence visionaries have assured me that this way of thinking is not just analyst-speak or vendor hype; it can be a reality. Following are some words of wisdom that I hope will inspire and guide you as you strive to make business intelligence a wild success in your company.

"Slicing and dicing the data has to be easier—easier than picking up a piece of paper. Even then, there is an education that needs to happen—getting people to *think* business intelligence."

—Dr. Ray Iannaconne, vice president of operations,
Emergency Medical Associates

"Senior management needs to take a leap of faith. It may take years, lots of time and money before you get value, but you have to ultimately know where you are going with this."

—Mike Gorman, senior director of customer relations,
Continental Airlines

"The data is compelling. The business model is a challenge. We haven't proven the market wants this system. We get the feeling they do, but how to package it will be a challenge."

—Jeff Kennedy, CEO, FlightStats

"Implementing an integrated reporting system for the company was a significant undertaking, but the result, Dow's Shared Data Network, is now a fundamental building block to managing Dow on a global basis. It's a very significant capability to manage our strategy."

—Dave Kepler, CIO, The Dow Chemical Company

"Strong management and a cultural change have most contributed to our success. The CEO got Norway Post to be more business oriented, and the CFO drove the management system. In adopting this cultural change to one of accountability, sometimes we had to change the people."

—*Dag Vidar Olsen, Norway Post,*
Manager Business Intelligence Competency Center

"I need to continue to push for BI to have a greater influence in the organization in order to maximize the returns on our BI investment. I see BI providing new insights into the business and serving as an enabler to profitable growth in the future."

—*Robert VanHees, CFO, Corporate Express*

"Our business intelligence initiative has been a terrific success in the way we can optimize our team and the greater sense of control of the business. We are always tweaking things. Before, too many decisions were based on assumptions, generality, anecdotal, off the gut. It's made us more agile as a company."

—*Dave Walker, vice president of operations, 1-800 CONTACTS*

Appendix A

This Successful BI Survey

This Successful BI survey ran for six weeks from April 2007 until mid-May 2007. The full survey is included here. Questions that involved ranking of items used a survey feature to randomize the order of the displayed options so that results were not skewed by the order of the possible selections. The survey was promoted through multiple media outlets and elicited 513 qualified responses.

Successful Business Intelligence

The purpose of this survey is to understand why and how some companies are more successful with business intelligence than others. The results of the survey will be published in an upcoming book *Successful Business Intelligence: Secrets to Making BI A Killer App* (published by McGraw Hill, due November 2007). As a way of thanking you for your input, survey respondents will be entered into a random drawing to win a pair of Bose QuietComfort® 2 Acoustic Noise Cancelling® headphones and 10 others will receive a free copy of the book. I will also email you a key survey finding, ahead of the book's release.

For the purpose of this survey, the definition of Business Intelligence (BI) is a set of technologies and processes that allow users to access, analyze, and explore data for decision making. These technologies include both the backend data warehouse systems and the front-end user tools.

The survey contains 30 questions and should take 10 minutes to complete. I thank you in advance for your invaluable insights!

Sincerely,

Cindi Howson
Founder, BIScorecard®

1. How do you currently use business intelligence?

❏ I rely on information from analysts who use BI tools directly
❏ I access pre-built reports and analyses
❏ I create my own reports and analyses
❏ I don't use BI at all
❏ Other (please specify)

If you selected other please specify:

_____

2. How successful do you consider your current business intelligence deployment?

○ Very Successful
○ Moderately Successful
○ Mostly a failure

3. How much has BI contributed to your company's performance?

○ Significantly
○ Somewhat
○ Not at all

4. How do you define the success or failure for your BI deployment? (select all that apply)

❏ Return on investment
❏ User perception that it is mission critical
❏ Support of key stake holders
❏ Number of defined users
❏ Percentage of active users
❏ Cost savings
❏ Improved business performance
❏ Better access to data

Additional comments:

_____

5. **For how many years has your BI deployment been available? Enter 0 if not yet in production.**

---

6. **How would you characterize your BI deployment?**

   ○ Independent business unit or departmental implementations

   ○ Enterprise-wide BI deployment, based on corporate IT standards

7. **How would you describe the front-end BI tools:**

   ○ We use multiple modules (query, reporting, OLAP) primarily from a **single** vendor

   ○ We use multiple modules (query, reporting, OLAP) from **multiple** vendors

   ○ We mostly **custom develop** our own BI front ends

8. **If you use multiple modules from multiple BI vendors, are you trying to standardize on a single BI vendor?**

   ○ Yes, we are trying to reduce the number of different modules from different vendors

   ○ No, we are not actively reducing the number of different modules from different vendors

9. **How does your company view BI (data warehousing, query, reporting, analysis, dashboards) and performance management (budgeting, planning, financial consolidation, and strategic scorecards)?**

   ○ Separate initiatives

   ○ Closely related but separate projects and people address those needs

   ○ One initiative with solutions provided via the same group

   Additional comments:

   ---

10. **When you think of the total number of employees in your company, what *percentage* of your company's total employees have access to a BI tool?**

_____

11. **If your BI deployment were wildly successful and you had available budget, what percent of company employees *should* have access to a BI tool?**

_____

12. **When considering employees that *currently have access* to a BI tool versus *should have access* to a BI tool, how would you break this down by job type? For example, you might say 80% of your analysts currently have access, but 100% should have access to a BI tool. Please use the drop-down menus to select a percentage in increments of 10.**

	Current %	Should %
Executives		
Managers		
Business and financial analysts		
Inside staff (accountants, customer service reps, shop floor)		
Field staff (sales agents, drivers, technicians)		
Customers		
Suppliers		

13. **Is your CIO or IT Manager an active member of the corporate business team or operating committee?**

    ○ Yes

    ○ No

    ○ Not Sure

14. Do you have executive level sponsorship for your BI initiative?

- O Yes
- O No

15. Who is the primary sponsor of your BI initiative?

- O Chief Operating Officer (COO)
- O Chief Executive Officer (CEO)
- O Chief Information Officer (CIO) or IT Manager
- O Chief Financial Officer (CFO)
- O Marketing VP
- O Other Line of business leader

16. How much do you attribute these cultural/ organization items to the success of your BI project?

	Essential	Very Important	Important	Not Very Important	No impact
IT and business partnership	O	O	O	O	O
Company culture fosters fact-based decision making	O	O	O	O	O
Executive support	O	O	O	O	O
BI program has been well-managed	O	O	O	O	O
Effective BI Steering Committee	O	O	O	O	O
Stakeholders evangelize the effective use of BI	O	O	O	O	O
Establishment of a BI center of excellence or competency center	O	O	O	O	O
BI projects are appropriately funded	O	O	O	O	O

	Essential	Very Important	Important	Not Very Important	No impact
BI projects are aligned with company or business unit goals	O	O	O	O	O
Quality and expertise of external consultants	O	O	O	O	O
Quality and expertise of internal BI staff	O	O	O	O	O

17. How much do these technical items affect the success of your BI deployment?

	Essential	Very Important	Important	Not Very Important	No Impact
Availability of relevant subject areas	O	O	O	O	O
Data Quality - clean data	O	O	O	O	O
Appropriate and effective BI tools	O	O	O	O	O
Incorporation of BI into operational processes	O	O	O	O	O
Reliability of the BI system	O	O	O	O	O
Fast query response time	O	O	O	O	O
BI system is continuously improved (data and tools)	O	O	O	O	O
Data warehouse updates are near realtime	O	O	O	O	O

18. What aspects of your BI deployment have been most successful?

❑ Standard, fixed reports

❑ Ad hoc query and reporting tools

❑ OLAP (multidimensional analysis with drill down and drill across)

- ❏ MS Office integration (Excel, PowerPoint)
- ❏ Dashboards
- ❏ Predictive analytics
- ❏ Custom-built solutions
- ❏ BI Portal
- ❏ Reports distributed through e-mail
- ❏ Scorecards
- ❏ BI embedded in operational tasks
- ❏ Other (please specify)

If you selected other please specify:

_____

19. How would you describe your company culture?

	Strongly Agree	Agree	Neutral	Disagree	Strongly Disagree
Access to data is overly controlled, and executives fear workers know too much.	O	O	O	O	O
Decisions are made from gut feel and not fact-based analysis.	O	O	O	O	O
We are innovative and always looking for ways to do things better.	O	O	O	O	O
We are a lean company that operates efficiently.	O	O	O	O	O
We use computers and information technology to achieve competitive advantage.	O	O	O	O	O

20. Which emerging technologies do you think will help you achieve greater success? (select all that apply)

- ❏ Web-based BI tools
- ❏ Dashboards

- ❑ Scorecards
- ❑ Search-enabled BI (Google interface to BI)
- ❑ Microsoft Office-enabled BI (Excel/PowerPoint integrated with BI)
- ❑ Greater interactivity within fixed reports (filter, rank, drill)
- ❑ Predictive analytics
- ❑ Getting to more data in different sources
- ❑ Alert notification for problems and exceptions – proactive monitoring
- ❑ Integration with mobile devices such as Blackberries
- ❑ BI embedded in operational tasks

21. What are your future plans for making BI more valuable to your company?

_____

_____

_____

22. Any other insights or comments you wish to provide on why your BI initiative is succeeding or failing?

_____

_____

_____

23. What best decribes your role?

- ○ Corporate IT professional
- ○ Business user
- ○ Hybrid business / IT person
- ○ Independent consultant or systems integrator
- ○ Vendor (sales, service, support, or development)
- ○ Academic

24. Which best describes your *business unit* or *functional unit*

O Finance

O Sales

O Marketing

O Customer Service

O Corporate IT

O Operations

O Manufacturing

O Human Resources

O Supply Chain/Logistics/Shipping

O Purchasing

O Other (please specify)

If you selected other please specify:

_____

25. What are the annual *revenues* of your organization?

O Less than $100 million

O $100 million to $ billion

O $1 billion +

O Don't know

26. What is the number of employees in your company?

O 1-100

O 101-1000

O 1001-5000

O Greater than 5000

27. Please select an industry from the drop-down list:

28. **Please select your Country location from the drop-down list:**

29. **Please provide your contact details.**

30. **BIScorecard® respects your privacy and information will not be shared with third parties. The survey results will be aggregated and used for an upcoming book. Any comments you provide will remain anonymous, unless you grant specific permission to quote you. May we quote you?**

   ○ Yes, you may quote me
   ○ No, you may not quote me

THANK YOU FOR YOUR PARTICIPATION!

As a way of thanking you for your participation in this survey, your name will be entered in a random drawing to win a BOSE headset or a copy of the book. In order to be entered into this drawing, your survey must be complete and you must provide your contact details. Winners will be notified by email in May 2007.

Sincerely,

Cindi Howson

author, *Successful Business Intelligence: Secrets to Making BI a Killer App*

Recommended Resources

There are dozens of excellent resources on data warehousing and business intelligence. Some are relevant to a specific vendor's solution and some are more conceptual in nature.

Following are a few recommended reads:

Building the Data Warehouse by William Inmon

Business Intelligence: The Savvy Manager's Guide by David Loshin

Business Intelligence Roadmap: The Complete Project Lifecycle for Decision-Support Applications by Larissa Moss and Shaku Atre

Competing on Analytics by Thomas Davenport and Jeanne Harris

Customer Data Integration: Reaching a Single Version of the Truth by Jill Dyche and Evan Levy

Data Modeling Made Simple: A Practical Guide for Business and Information Technology Professionals by Steve Hoberman

Information Dashboard Design: The Effective Visual Communication of Data by Stephen Few

Performance Dashboards by Wayne Eckerson

Smart Enough Systems: How to Deliver Competitive Advantage by Automating Hidden Decisions by James Taylor and Neil Raden

The Data Warehouse Toolkit: The Complete Guide to Dimensional Modeling by Ralph Kimball and Margy Ross

Following are a few Media Resources that focus on business intelligence:

Intelligent Enterprise (www.intelligententerprise.com)

The Business Intelligence Network (B-eye-network.com)

The Data Warehousing Institute (www.tdwi.org)

Notes

Chapter 1

1. Davenport, Thomas and Harris, Jeanne, *Competing on Analytics*, HBS: 2007, page 45.
2. Collins, Jim, *Good to Great: Why Some Companies Make the Leap... and Others Don't*. HarperCollins: 2001, page 79.
3. Walt Disney World presentation, Business Objects User Conference, 2005.
4. Computerworld Technology Briefing, "The Business Value of Analytics."
5. Continental Airlines, interview notes, April 2005.
6. Information Builders press release, March 19, 2007.
7. Thomas, Kim, "Humberside Police Updates Criminal Intelligence Databases," Computing, March 15, 2007.
8. Opportunity International website and Hyperion user conference, April 2005.
9. Vesset, Wilhilde, McDonough, "Worldwide Business Analytics Software 2006-2010 Forecast and 2005 Vendor Shares," IDC, July 2006.
10. Age Positive Team, Department for Work and Pensions, UK, News, July 28, 2006.
11. "Shifting Workforce Demographics and Delayed Retirement," Microsoft, October 18, 2006.
12. Horrigan, John, "A Typology of Information and Communication Technology Users," Pew Internet & American Life Project, May 7, 2007.
13. Adapted from timeline developed by Wayne Eckerson, TDWI, for course "Evaluating BI Toolsets," co-taught with Cindi Howson, May 2003.
14. Vesset, McDonough, "The Next Wave of Business Analytics," *DM Review*, March 2007.
15. Mearian, Lucas, "A zettabyte by 2010: Corporate Data grows fiftyfold in three years," *Computerworld*, March 6, 2007.
16. McGee, M. InformationWeek, "Managers Have Too Much Information, Do Too Little Sharing." January 8, 2007.

Chapter 2

1. Loshin, David, "Master Data and Master Data Management: An Introduction," DataFlux Whitepaper.
2. Watson, Hugh, "Which Data Warehouse Architecture Is Most Successful," Business Intelligence Journal, Q1 2006.
3. TDWI, What Works, November 2006, "Enhancing the Customer Experience and Improving Retention Using Powerful Data Warehousing Appliances."

Chapter 3

1. Groff, James and Weinberg, Paul, SQL: The Complete Reference: McGraw-Hill/Osborne: 2002, p 4.
2. Few, Stephen, Information Dashboard Design, O'Reilly: 2006, p 34.
3. Schiff, Craig, "Fact vs. Fiction in Performance Management," Business Intelligence Network, May 16, 2007.
4. Morris, Henry, "Trends in Analytic Applications," DM Review, April 2001.

Chapter 4

1. Atre, Shaku, "The Top 10 Critical Challenges for Business Intelligence Success," Computerworld, June 30, 2003.
2. Howson, "Seven Pillars of BI Success," Intelligent Enterprise, September 1, 2006.
3. Norway Post Annual Reports and Tonneson, Jan, Hyperion User Conference presentation, April 2006.
4. Norway Post, interview notes, May 2007.
5. Morris, Henry, et al., "The Financial Impact of Business Analytics, an IDC ROI Study," December 2002.
6. Wixom, et al., "Continental Airlines Flies High with Real-time Business Intelligence," p 23.
7. Continental Airlines, interview notes, April 2007.
8. Ibid.
9. Ibid.
10. Eckerson & Howson, "Enterprise Business Intelligence," TDWI Report Series, August 2005.
11. Klein, Allen, Up Words for Down Days, Gramercy Books: 1998.
12. The Dow Chemical Company, interview notes, May 2007.
13. Corporate Express, interview notes, May 2007.

14. OfficeMax press release, "One of Nation's Largest Commercial Banks Chooses OfficeMax to Boost Efficiencies, Make Employees' Jobs Easier," September 1, 2005.
15. Corporate Express, interview notes, May 2007.

Chapter 5

1. WorldofQuotes.com.
2. Computerworld Honors Program 2005.
3. Richardson, Karen, "Keeping accounting close to home," *The Wall Street Journal,* October 29, 2006.
4. FlightStats, interview notes, April 2007.
5. DOT, Bureau of Transportation Statistics website. (http://usgovinfo .about.com/gi/dynamic/offsite.htm?site=http://www.dot.gov/airconsumer).
6. FlightStats, interview notes, April 2007.
7. FlightStats website (www.flightstats.com).
8. "On-Time Performance: Flight Delays at a Glance," Bureau of Transportation Statistics, May 2007, (http://www.transtats.bts.gov/ HomeDrillChart.asp).
9. JetBlue website, "An Apology From David Neeleman," February 2007, (http://www.jetblue.com/about/ourcompany/apology/index.html).
10. Emergency Medical Associates, interview notes, April 2007.
11. EMA, website video.
12. Tullo, Alex, "Dow Will Cut Workforce by 8%," *Chemical & Engineering News,* May 7, 2001.
13. The Dow Chemical Company, interview notes, May 2007.
14. Ibid.
15. Brenneman, Gregg, "Right Away and All at Once: How We Saved Continental," *Harvard Business Review,* 2000.
16. Continental Airlines, interview notes, May 10, 2007.
17. 1-800 CONTACTS website, company profile.
18. 1-800 CONTACTS, interview notes, May 2007.
19. Corporate Express, interview notes, May 2007.
20. Brenneman, Gregg, "Right Away and All at Once: How We Saved Continental," *Harvard Business Review,* 2000.
21. The Forums Institute for Public Policy, "An Overview of Charity Care in NJ—Past, Present and Future," September 29, 2004.
22. New Jersey Hospital Association, "What Will Happen To My Hospital?" 2007.
23. Joint Commission website (www.jointcommission.org).
24. EMA website.

Chapter 6

1. Burson-Marsteller, "A Missing Competency: Boardroom IT Deficit. Helping Your Board Get 'IT,'" 2005.
2. Gillooly, Brian, "CIO: Time to Step Up," *Information Week,* June 4, 2007.
3. Lutchen, Mark, *Managing IT as a Business*, Wiley: 2004, p 33.
4. Corporate Express, interview notes, May–June 2007.

Chapter 7

1. English, Larry, "Do We Need a Clean Information Quality Act?," *Business Intelligence Network*, May 9, 2007.
2. English, Larry, "Plain English about Information Quality: Information Quality Tipping Point," *DM Review,* January 2007.
3. Gartner press release, "Dirty Data is a Business Problem, Not an IT Problem," March 2, 2007.
4. Russom, Philip, "Taking Data Quality to the Enterprise through Data Governance," March 2006.
5. Costa, Mike, board of directors, Central Michigan University Research Corporation, interview notes, May 2007.
6. Harry, Mikel, Schroeder, Richard, *Six Sigma: The Breakthrough Management Strategy Revolutionizing the World's Top Corporations*, Doubleday: 2000.
7. Ibid, p 14.
8. Department of Transportation, "Airline On-Time Performance Slips, Cancellations and Mishandled Bags Up in June," August 6, 2007.
9. Norway Post, interview notes, May 2007.
10. Norway Post presentation, Hyperion user conference, April 2006.
11. Ariyachandra, Thilini and Watson, Hugh, "Which Data Warehouse Architecture is Most Successful," *Business Intelligence Journal,* First Quarter 2006.
12. Linstedt, Dan, "Inmon vs. Kimball: Data Warehousing: Our Great Debate Wraps Up," *Business Intelligence Network*, May 3, 2005.
13. Whyte, Jim, Corporate Data Architect, The Dow Chemical Company, "Dow's Master Data Management Business Processes," Chemical Industry SAP User Group, April 2006.
14. ARC Advisory Group, "Master Data Management World Wide Outlook," November 2006.
15. White, Colin, "Building the Real-time Enterprise," *TDWI Report Series*, November 2003.
16. 1-800 CONTACTS, interview notes, May 2007.

17. Hackathorn, Richard, "The BI Watch: Real-Time to Real-Value," *DM Review,* January 2004.
18. FlightStats, interview notes, April 2007.

Chapter 8

1. Wikipedia
2. 168 Feng Shui Advisors, Yin and Yang Theory (web site)
3. Martin, Charles, Ph.D., *Looking at Type and Careers,* Center for Applications of Psychological Type, 1995.
4. Ibid, page 19.
5. Ibid, pages 42 and 50.
6. Wharton School, "The Wharton School and Gartner Launch CIO Academy to Prepare the Chief Information Officer to Partner with the CEO," press release, July 19, 2007.
7. Clarry, Maureen, "Building Partnerships in Siloed Envoronments," Business Intelligence Network, July 10, 2007.
8. Kaplan, Robert, and Norton, David, *Alignment,* Harvard Business School Press: 2006, p 3.
9. Dr. Jacknis, Dr. Norman, "Beyond Typical Business Intelligence," *Network Computing,* November 9, 2006.
10. Continental Airlines 2000 Annual Report, page 7.
11. Brenneman, Greg, "Right Away and All at Once: How We Saved Continental," *Harvard Business Review,* 2000.
12. Ibid, p 6.
13. Dow Chemical, interview notes, May 2007.

Chapter 9

1. 1-800 CONTACTS, interview notes, July 2006.
2. Frankel, Glenn, "Britain: U.S. Told Of Vaccine Shortage," *Washington Post,* October 9, 2004.
3. Whiting, Rick, "BI Tracks Disease Outbreaks," *Intelligent Enterprise,* November 2005.
4. Emergency Medical Associates, interview notes, April 2007.
5. Costello, Tom, "Hospitals work to improve ER wait times," *NBC News,* November 20, 2006.
6. Emergency Medical Associates, interview notes, April 2007.
7. Robb, Drew, "EMA: Measuring the Emergency Room's Pulse," *Computerworld,* September 18, 2006.

8. Continental Airlines, interview notes, April 2007.
9. Continental Airlines, interview notes, April 2007.
10. Watson et al., "Continental Airlines Flies High with Real-time Business Intelligence," p 9.
11. Levitt, Steven and Dubner, Stephen, *Freakonomics: A Rogue Economist Explores the Hidden Side of Everything,* HarperCollins Publishers: 2005, p 7.
12. Raden, Neil, "Toppling the BI Pyramid," *DM Review,* January 2007.

Chapter 10

1. Heldman, Kim, *Project Management Professional Study Guide,* Sybex: 2002 and confirmed by a PMP certified in 2006.
2. http://www.agilemanifesto.org/history.html.
3. http://www.ambysoft.com/surveys/agileMarch2007.html.
4. Watson, Hugh, "Are Data Warehouses Prone to Failure?," *TDWI Journal,* Fall 2005, 454 respondents.
5. Interview notes, 1-800 CONTACTS, May 2007.

Chapter 11

1. Wikipedia.
2. Wayne Eckerson & Cindi Howson, "Enterprise Business Intelligence," *TDWI Report Series,* August 2005.
3. http://www.modelt.org/tquotes.html.
4. Watson, Hugh, et al., "Continental Airlines Flies High with Real-Time Business Intelligence," p 22.
5. 1-800 CONTACTS, interview notes and e-mails, April 2007 and September 2007.
6. Miller et al., *Business Intelligence Competency Centers,* Wiley: 2006.
7. Continental Airlines, interview notes, April 2007.
8. Customer presentation, Cognos Analyst Summit, September 2007.
9. Corporate Express, interview notes, May 2007.
10. Kanter, Rosabeth, *e-volve! Succeeding in the Digital Culture of Tomorrow,* Harvard Business School Press: 2001, p 205.
11. Collins, Jim, *Good To Great, p 21*
12. 1-800 CONTACTS, interview notes, April 2007.

Chapter 12

1. Eckerson & Howson, "Enterprise BI," *TDWI,* July 2006.
2. Wayne Eckerson & Cindi Howson, "Enterprise Business Intelligence," *TDWI Report Series,* August 2005.

3. Eckerson & Howson, "Enterprise BI," *TDWI*, July 2006.
4. Microsoft User Conference, May 2007.
5. Taylor, James and Raden, Neil, *Smart Enough Systems,* Prentice Hall: 2007, p 15.
6. Jim Jelter, "Kodak restates, adds $9 million to loss," *MarketWatch*, Nov 9, 2005.
7. RedEnvelope Cuts Outlook, Shares Fall, CFO Eric Wong Resigns Amid Budget Errors, NEW YORK (AP), March 29, 2005.

Chapter 13

1. Collins, Jim, *Good to Great,* Harper collins, 2001, p 70.
2. Corporate Express, interview notes, June 2007.
3. Emergency Medical Associates, interview notes, April 2007.
4. Hammond et al., "The Hidden Traps in Decision Making," *Harvard Business Review,* 1998.

Chapter 14

1. Corporate Express, interview notes, May 2007.
2. Corporate Express TDWI award application, provided by Corporate Express.
3. Beyers, Tim, "As manufacturing goes global, use of BI makes for smart business," *Manufacturing Business Technology,* June 2007.
4. Byrne, Tony, CMSWatch, interview notes, August 2007.
5. BlueCross BlueShield of Tennessee, interview notes, April 4, 2007.
6. BlueCross BlueShield BCBS of Tennessee, 2006 Annual Report.
7. Morris, Henry, "Bridging the Structured/Unstructured Data Gap at BCBS of TN," *IDC Opinion,* December 2006.
8. BlueCross BlueShield of Tennessee, interview notes, April 4, 2007.
9. Tufte, Edward, *Envisioning Information,* Graphics Press: 1990, p 67.

Index